The Survey of Academic Library Cataloging Practices, 2013 Edition

ISBN: 978-1-57440-234-6
Library of Congress Control Number: 2013937156
© 2013 Primary Research Group, Inc.

Questionnaire development assistance for this report was provided by Michael A. Cerbo II. Mr. Cerbo II is the Bibliographic Access and Resource Management Librarian at the University of Rhode Island. His responsibilities include cataloging and managing electronic resources. He holds a Masters Degree in Political Science from the University of Rhode Island and a Masters of Science in Library Science from Clarion University.

TABLE OF CONTENTS

LIST OF TABLES

THE QUESTIONNAIRE

1. Please provide the following contact information.
   Name:
   Organization:
   Country:
   Email Address:
   Phone Number:

2. Which term best describes your college?
   (a) Community College
   (b) 4-Year Degree Granting College
   (c) MA or PHD Granting College
   (d) Level 1 or Level 2 Carnegie Class Research University

3. What was the full-time equivalent (FTE) attendance for all divisions of the college in the past year?

4. Is your college is public or private?
   (a) Public
   (b) Private

5. What is the full price for annual tuition at your institution?

6. With the new Resources Description and Access (RDA) cataloging rules that will be formally adopted by the Library of Congress and other national libraries, what has your library done to prepare for this transition?

7. How will RDA impact the cataloger's role in future library decisions?
   (a) Strongly enhance
   (b) Enhance
   (c) Not really enhance
   (d) Detract

8. Has there been an increase in funds for your training in RDA and its effects on the library catalog
   (a) Yes
   (b) No

9. What are your initial first impressions of RDA?

10. Who will be responsible for training staff and copy catalogers this new method of cataloging (RDA)?

11. Has the library marketed theses new cataloging rules (RDA) outside the library?
(a) Yes
(b) No

12. How does your Integrated Library System (ILS) handle these new RDA records?

13. As a cataloger, how does the future of cataloging look to you?
(a) Good
(b) Stable
(c) Weak
(d) Poor

14. Has the library spent more on cataloging over the past five years?
(a) Significantly more
(b) Somewhat more
(c) About the same
(d) Somewhat less
(e) Significantly less

15. If there has been a shift in resources at the library away from cataloging, to which library needs have these resources been reallocated?

16. How would you characterize the future of consortia's in cataloging? Do you believe that central consortia cataloging will be the future of cataloging?

17. What outreach projects can library catalogers take part in to increase awareness of what they do?

18. How much staff time in the past year did your cataloging staff expend in viewing webinars, videos, online tutorials, conferences, formal classroom training and other aids for cataloging education?

19. What should library administrators understand about cataloging that they do not seem to understand?

20. To what extent has technology usurped the need for catalogers and the library catalog?

21. How do other librarians view catalogers?
(a) Essential
(b) Needed
(c) Somewhat needed
(d) Not needed

22. At your institution, what basic responsibilities and job requirements are listed in a cataloger's job description?

23. If your institution has a metadata librarian/cataloger, what basic responsibilities and job requirements are listed in the job description?

24. List briefly the cataloging and authority tasks, concepts, and cataloging tools used to train catalogers.

25. Which of the following cataloging functions are routinely performed by library paraprofessional support staff and which are performed by professional librarians? Indicate which group, or both, perform the following functions.
    (a) Original cataloging
    (b) Copy cataloging
    (c) Name authority cooperative work (NACO)
    (d) Subject authority cooperative work (SACO)
    (e) Master bibliographic record enhancement in OCLC
    (f) Participation in PCC, CONSER and BIBCO 1 bibliographic record work
    (g) Master bibliographic record enrichment (adding Call Numbers, Subjects, Tables of Contents) in OCLC
    (i) Subject analysis and subject heading application
    (j) Classification
    (k) Master bibliographic record upgrades in OCLC
    (l) Establishment of local series, uniform title headings and authority records
    (m) Establishment of local name, corporate body and conference headings and authority records
    (n) Establishment of local subject and geographic headings and authority records

26. How many positions in cataloging library support staff has your organization gained or lost in the past five years?

27. How many positions for professional librarians in cataloging functions has your organization gained or lost in the past five years?

28. Does your cataloging division participate in library school student mentoring or internships, or recruiting existing staff and student workers into the cataloging profession?
    (a) Yes
    (b) No

29. How many of each of the following do you believe will be retiring from your institution within the next five years?
    Professional Librarians Performing Mostly Cataloging Functions:
    Library Paraprofessional Support Staff Performing Mostly Cataloging Functions:

30. Do catalogers at your institution have salaries comparable to public service librarians?
    (a) Yes
    (b) No
    (c) Unsure

31. Which phrase best describes the trend in pay rates for catalogers at your institution over the past four years?
     (a) Generous annual increases averaging more than 5%
     (b) Increases averaging between 2.5% and 5%
     (c) Increases but less than 2.5%
     (d) Pay has remained flat with no increases or decreases
     (e) Pay has been declining

32. Does your cataloging division have cataloging quotas? Please explain why or why not.

33. Does your technical services area track turn-around time from Acquisitions receipt to Cataloging to shelf-ready distribution?
     (a) Yes
     (b) No
     (c) Don't know
     (d) Other (please specify)

34. How would you rate the use of the following quality indicators in cataloging work?

Cataloger or Staff Work Product Quotas
     (a) Very useful
     (b) Somewhat useful
     (c) Not useful
     (d) Misleading
     (e) Detracts from quality

Turnaround Time from Receipt in Cataloging to Ready for Shelf
     (a) Very useful
     (b) Somewhat useful
     (c) Not useful
     (d) Misleading
     (e) Detracts from quality

Error Rates per Bibliographic Record
     (a) Very useful
     (b) Somewhat useful
     (c) Not useful
     (d) Misleading
     (e) Detracts from quality

Completeness of Bibliographic Record
     (a) Very useful
     (b) Somewhat useful
     (c) Not useful
     (d) Misleading
     (e) Detracts from quality

Error Rates per Authority Record
   (a) Very useful
   (b) Somewhat useful
   (c) Not useful
   (d) Misleading
   (e) Detracts from quality

Error Rates per Holdings Record
   (a) Very useful
   (b) Somewhat useful
   (c) Not useful
   (d) Misleading
   (e) Detracts from quality

Error Rates per Physical Processing
   (a) Very useful
   (b) Somewhat useful
   (c) Not useful
   (d) Misleading
   (e) Detracts from quality

Patron or Staff Complaints
   (a) Very useful
   (b) Somewhat useful
   (c) Not useful
   (d) Misleading
   (e) Detracts from quality

Patron or Staff Commendation
   (a) Very useful
   (b) Somewhat useful
   (c) Not useful
   (d) Misleading
   (e) Detracts from quality

Support or Accomplishment of Departmental or Library Goal
   (a) Very useful
   (b) Somewhat useful
   (c) Not useful
   (d) Misleading
   (e) Detracts from quality

35. How does your cataloging department define quality?

36. What difficulties has your area faced in improving and upgrading staff use of hardware and software technology?

37. Briefly list and explain what you consider the most useful new technologies (hardware, software, etc.) in cataloging and metadata today, such as wikis, blogs, harvesting software, DSpace for institutional repositories, any OCLC or vendor products or services, etc.

38. What functions or value-added services, if any, does your division outsource to any degree? Select all that apply.
    (a) Authority control: obtaining new and updated authority records
    (b) Authority control: updating headings in bibliographic records
    (c) Bibliographic records: obtaining new bibliographic records
    (d) Item records and inventory
    (e) Physical processing, barcoding
    (f) Table of contents notes added
    (g) Book reviews added
    (h) Book jackets added
    (i) Not applicable (no outsourcing done)

39. What types of library resources are outsourced? Select all that apply
    (a) Continuing resources (print)
    (b) E-journals
    (c) E-books
    (d) AV formats
    (e) Foreign language resources for which the cataloging agency has no expertise
    (f) Other digital formats
    (g) Materials in cataloging backlogs
    (h) All materials are outsourced
    (i) Not applicable (no outsourcing done)

40. If you have outsourced library resources, please briefly explain why you outsourced certain types of library resources.

41. What are the criteria you use, if any, to analyze and determine the best sources of high quality records for outsourced materials?

42. What quality control methods do you use, if any, to assure vendor supplied records are accurate and complete? Select all that apply.
    (a) Use MarcEdit or other MARC editor to preview records and globally edit to local standards prior to loading
    (b) Use local integrated system to review loaded records and globally edit to local standards.
    (c) Review all vendor records whenever possible. Spot check vendor records whenever complete review isn't possible
    (d) Always spot check all vendor records
    (e) No or minimal review performed
    (f) Other (please specify)

43. What are your opinions and thoughts regarding cataloging education in present and future ALA-accredited library and information schools?

44. Please categorize the preparedness of your recent library hires in the following cataloging and metadata competencies, philosophies, principles and practices.

Classification Systems
    (a) Not at all prepared
    (b) Minimally prepared
    (c) Prepared
    (d) Well prepared

Subject/Genre Thesauri Systems
    (a) Not at all prepared
    (b) Minimally prepared
    (c) Prepared
    (d) Well prepared

Classification and Subject/Genre Analysis Principles, Rules and Tools
    (a) Not at all prepared
    (b) Minimally prepared
    (c) Prepared
    (d) Well prepared

Java and PERL Script Applications
    (a) Not at all prepared
    (b) Minimally prepared
    (c) Prepared
    (d) Well prepared

Cataloging Rules and Tools (Including Descriptive Cataloging)
    (a) Not at all prepared
    (b) Minimally prepared
    (c) Prepared
    (d) Well prepared

Information Technology and Social Behavior in the Organizational Context
    (a) Not at all prepared
    (b) Minimally prepared
    (c) Prepared
    (d) Well prepared

Metadata Standards for Digital Resources (Dublin Core, MODS, VRA, Open Archives Initiative, etc.)
    (a) Not at all prepared
    (b) Minimally prepared

(c) Prepared

(d) Well prepared

Abstracting and Indexing

    (a) Not at all prepared

    (b) Minimally prepared

    (c) Prepared

    (d) Well prepared

Electronic Delivery of Services

    (a) Not at all prepared

    (b) Minimally prepared

    (c) Prepared

    (d) Well prepared

Technical Services in Libraries

    (a) Not at all prepared

    (b) Minimally prepared

    (c) Prepared

    (d) Well prepared

Web and Local Network System Administration and Management

    (a) Not at all prepared

    (b) Minimally prepared

    (c) Prepared

    (d) Well prepared

Cataloging Formats: Books

    (a) Not at all prepared

    (b) Minimally prepared

    (c) Prepared

    (d) Well prepared

Cataloging Formats: Non-Books, Digital Resources

    (a) Not at all prepared

    (b) Minimally prepared

    (c) Prepared

    (d) Well prepared

Cataloging Formats: Continuing and Integrating Resources

    (a) Not at all prepared

    (b) Minimally prepared

    (c) Prepared

    (d) Well prepared

Cataloging Special Materials: Law

(a) Not at all prepared
(b) Minimally prepared
(c) Prepared
(d) Well prepared

Cataloging Special Materials: Music
(a) Not at all prepared
(b) Minimally prepared
(c) Prepared
(d) Well prepared

Cataloging Special Materials: Archives and Rare Materials
(a) Not at all prepared
(b) Minimally prepared
(c) Prepared
(d) Well prepared

XML and/or XSLT
(a) Not at all prepared
(b) Minimally prepared
(c) Prepared
(d) Well prepared

Economics and Metrics of Information
(a) Not at all prepared
(b) Minimally prepared
(c) Prepared
(d) Well prepared

Discovery Tools and Applications
(a) Not at all prepared
(b) Minimally prepared
(c) Prepared
(d) Well prepared

Authority Control
(a) Not at all prepared
(b) Minimally prepared
(c) Prepared
(d) Well prepared

Web Usability, User Research, and Human Interface Design
(a) Not at all prepared
(b) Minimally prepared
(c) Prepared
(d) Well prepared

International MARC Bibliographic, Authority and Holdings Standards
  (a) Not at all prepared
  (b) Minimally prepared
  (c) Prepared
  (d) Well prepared

Data Modeling, Warehousing and Mining
  (a) Not at all prepared
  (b) Minimally prepared
  (c) Prepared
  (d) Well prepared

Information Systems Analysis
  (a) Not at all prepared
  (b) Minimally prepared
  (c) Prepared
  (d) Well prepared

Programming Languages and Applications
  (a) Not at all prepared
  (b) Minimally prepared
  (c) Prepared
  (d) Well prepared

Relational Database Design
  (a) Not at all prepared
  (b) Minimally prepared
  (c) Prepared
  (d) Well prepared

OCLC Systems and Services
  (a) Not at all prepared
  (b) Minimally prepared
  (c) Prepared
  (d) Well prepared

Digital Libraries and Collections
  (a) Not at all prepared
  (b) Minimally prepared
  (c) Prepared
  (d) Well prepared

Practicum: Experiential Learning
  (a) Not at all prepared
  (b) Minimally prepared

(c) Prepared
(d) Well prepared

Information Storage, Retrieval, Architecture
(a) Not at all prepared
(b) Minimally prepared
(c) Prepared
(d) Well prepared

Social Networking and Information
(a) Not at all prepared
(b) Minimally prepared
(c) Prepared
(d) Well prepared

Electronic Publishing and Scholarly Communication
(a) Not at all prepared
(b) Minimally prepared
(c) Prepared
(d) Well prepared

Principles of Historical and Contemporary Bibliographic Control
(a) Not at all prepared
(b) Minimally prepared
(c) Prepared
(d) Well prepared

SURVEY PARTICIPANTS

Ambrose University College
Arizona State University
Arkansas Tech University
Australian National University
Bard Graduate Center
California College of the Arts
California State University, Fresno
Calvin College and Calvin Theological Seminary
Chan Shun Centennial Library
Chicago State University
City University of Seattle
Clemson University
Colorado School of Mines
DePaul University
East Carolina University
East Los Angeles College
Eastern Kentucky University
Eastern Michigan University
Finlandia University
Florida Southern College
Fond du Lac Tribal and Community College
Furman University
Georgia Perimeter College
Gogebic Community College
Johnson & Wales University
Kent State University
Lake Forest College
Lebanese American University
Lincoln University (PA)
Maranatha Baptist Bible College
Massachusetts Institute of Technology
Messiah College
Minneapolis College of Art and Design
Missouri State University
Murray State University
Niagara University
Northwestern State University of Louisiana
Oakland University
Pennsylvania State University
Philadelphia University
Randolph-Macon College
Regent University
Sacred Heart University

Saginaw Valley State University
Saint Anselm College
Saint Mary's College, Notre Dame IN
Siena Heights University
Simpson College
Southeastern Louisiana University
St. Charles Community College
St. Cloud State University
Sul Ross State University
Texas A&M University
Texas A&M University-Central Texas
Texas State University
University at Albany, SUNY
University of Alaska Anchorage
University of Hawaii at Manoa
University of Miami
University of Minnesota, Morris
University of Montana
University of New Hampshire
University of North Alabama
University of North Florida
University of North Texas
University of Northern Iowa
University of Puerto Rico
University of Saskatchewan
University of South Carolina
University of the West Indies
University of Utah
University of West Alabama
Utah State University
Valdosta State University
Vanderbilt University
Western Illinois University
Western Kentucky University
Western Michigan University
Wright State University
Xavier University of Louisiana

CHARACTERISTICS OF THE SAMPLE

Sample by Country

	United States	Other
Entire Sample	93.83%	6.17%

Sample by Type of College

	Community College	4-Year Degree Granting College	MA or PHD Granting College	Research University
Entire Sample	6.17%	46.91%	28.40%	18.52%

Sample by Public or Private Status

	Public	Private
Entire Sample	64.20%	35.80%

Sample by Total Student Enrollment

	Less than 10,000	10,000 to 20,000	More than 20,000
Entire Sample	38.27%	40.74%	20.99%

Sample by Annual Tuition

	Less than $8,000	$8,000 to $18,000	More than $18,000
Entire Sample	32.10%	35.80%	32.10%

SUMMARY OF MAIN FINDINGS

RESOURCES DESCRIPTION AND ACCESS

Impact of RDA on Future Library Decisions

The majority of survey participants (60.49 percent) say the new Resources Description and Access cataloging rules will "not really enhance" the cataloger's role in future library decisions. Just 2.47 percent say it will "strongly enhance" the cataloger's role here, and 6.17 percent say it will "detract" in this manner. The remaining 29.63 percent then (1.23 percent did not answer the question) say the cataloger's role will be "enhanced," including 60 percent of community colleges and 47.06 percent of those schools with more than 20,000 enrolled students. 20 percent of research universities believe the RDA will "detract" from the cataloger's role in future library decisions, by far the highest percentage among all types of colleges, and 79.31 percent of libraries at private schools in the sample say the RDA will "not really enhance" the role of the cataloger. 50 percent of public schools rated the impact the RDA will have on the cataloger's role in future library decisions the same way.

Increase in Funds for RDA Training

92.59 percent of all survey participants say there has not been an increase in funds for RDA training. Broken out by type of college, it is the research universities that have most seen an increase in funds for such trainings, as 13.33 percent of them have, compared to just 4.35 percent of MA- and PhD-granting colleges and 0 percent of community colleges. The split is fairly even between public schools (7.69 percent say they have seen an increase) and private schools (6.9 percent), but broken out by annual tuition there arises a great discrepancy: whereas 15.38 percent of schools with an annual tuition of less than $8,000 have seen an increase in funds here, this percentage is not higher than 3.85 percent for any other breakout in this category.

Marketing the RDA Outside the Library

Just 7.41 percent of libraries in the sample have marketed the new RDA cataloging rules outside the library, none of which are private schools. Community colleges have been the most active here, as 40 percent have done such marketing, while the next closest percentage in this category belongs to the MA- and PhD-granting colleges at 8.7 percent. As total student enrollment increases, so too does the likelihood of marketing the RDA outside the library: 3.23 percent of those with less than 10,000 students do so, but this figures jumps to 9.09 percent for the next enrollment range (10,000 to 20,000 students) and then 11.76 percent for those with more than 20,000 students. 15.38 percent of participants with an annual tuition of less than $8,000 market these rules outside the library, or twice the percent of those with an annual tuition of more than $18,000 (7.69 percent).

THE FUTURE OF CATALOGING

Outlook on Cataloging

20.99 percent of survey participants say the future of cataloging looks "good," while another 43.21 percent categorize it as "stable." A third of participants predict it to be "weak," and the remaining 2.47 percent think the future of cataloging is "poor." Between 20 and 21.75 percent of all four types of colleges in the sample find the future of cataloging to be "good." There is a bit more of a difference here between public schools (23.08 percent say it is "good") and private schools (17.24 percent say the same). 29.41 percent of those schools with more than 20,000 students say this future is "good," compared to 19.35 percent of those with less than 10,000 students. More than half (55.17 percent) of participants with an annual tuition between $8,000 and $18,000 say this future looks "stable." The next highest percentage in this category belongs to those schools with an annual tuition of more than $18,000 (38.46 percent).

Spending on Cataloging

Nearly half (48.15 percent) of all survey participants say the library has spent "about the same" on cataloging over the past five years, while 38.27 percent estimate that they have spent "somewhat less" in this regard. Just 3.7 percent of participants say they have spent either "somewhat more" or "significantly more," all of which are public schools with annual tuitions less than $8,000. An anomaly occurs when the data is broken out by total student enrollment, as 52.94 percent of schools with more than 20,000 students say they have spent "somewhat less" on cataloging over the past five years, while no other category posted a percentage higher than 38.5 percent here.

Staff Time Spent on Cataloging Education

The survey participants spent a mean of 49.09 hours of staff time in the past year in viewing webinars, videos, online tutorials, conferences, formal classroom training, and on other aids for cataloging education. The median here was 30 hours, and the range was from 0 to 320. Community colleges (mean of 35) and MA-/PhD-granting colleges (mean of 32.03) allocated considerably less staff time to these activities than 4-year colleges (58.69) and research universities (54.25). While at least one of every other type of college reported spending zero time on this in the past year, no research university spent less than 13 hours to this end. Broken out by public and private schools, the former dedicated less time (mean of 43.55) than the latter (mean of 59.9). Schools with the largest enrollments (more than 20,000 students) posted a mean of 73.05, well beyond the mean of 46.34 for those schools with less than 10,000 students.

Librarians' Views on Catalogers

The majority of survey participants (65.44 percent) say librarians consider catalogers to be either "needed" or "essential." A sizable amount (30.86 percent) say they are just "somewhat needed," although just 3.7 percent of the sample believe catalogers to be "not needed." Catalogers are perhaps most appreciated by research universities, where 26.67 percent find them to be "essential" and 53.33 percent think of them as "needed." Community colleges, too, espouse a similar line of thinking: 20 percent see them as "essential," 60 percent as "needed." However, it is worth noting that 20 percent of community colleges also believe catalogers to be "not needed," by far the highest percentage in this category. Broken out between public and private schools, the splits were nearly even, as just one answer differs by more than 3 percent (5.77 percent of public schools answered "not needed," whereas no private schools answered in this manner). Based on total student enrollment, the smallest schools (those with less than 10,000 students) were the most positive here, with 32.26 percent viewing catalogers as "essential," while the next closest percentage in this category belonged to those schools with more than 20,000 students at 23.53 percent.

PERSONNEL ISSUES

CATALOGING FUNCTIONS AS PERFORMED BY PARAPROFESSIONAL SUPPORT STAFF, PROFESSIONAL LIBRARIANS, OR BOTH

We asked our survey participants which of an array of cataloging functions are routinely performed by library paraprofessional support staff, professional librarians, or by both.

Original Cataloging

Nearly three-quarters (74.07 percent) of all participants say the work of original cataloging is done mostly by professional librarians. Just 6.17 percent say it is done mostly by paraprofessional support staff, with the remaining 19.75 percent saying it is done by both these groups. No MA-/PhD-granting colleges nor any research universities in the sample say original cataloging is performed mostly by paraprofessional support staff, although 26.09 percent of the former and 33.33 percent of the latter say these tasks are performed by both paraprofessionals and professional librarians, by far the highest percentages in this category. While 62.07 percent of participants in the $8,000 to $18,000 tuition range say this work is done mostly by professional librarians, 84.62 percent of those with tuition less than $8,000 say the same.

Copy Cataloging

Just 12.35 percent of survey participants say the work of copy cataloging at the library is done mostly by professional librarians. The remaining participants are split nearly evenly between the other two options: 44.44 percent say this work is done mostly by paraprofessional support staff, while 43.21 percent say it is performed by both paraprofessionals and professionals. Community colleges are the most likely to have these duties handled mostly by professional librarians, as 40 percent of them do, while the next closest percentage in this category belongs to the 4-year degree granting colleges at 15.79 percent. Broken out by public or private status, exactly half of participants in the former group say this is performed mostly by paraprofessional support staff, as compared to just 34.48 percent of the private schools in the sample. A noticeable split also arises in the annual tuition category: at least 50 percent of all those participants at schools with an annual tuition less than $18,000 say copy cataloging is performed mostly by paraprofessional support staff, while only 23.08 percent of those at schools where the tuition is more than $18,000 say the same.

Name Authority Cooperative (NACO)

The vast majority (83.95 percent) of survey participants say Name Authority Cooperative (NACO) work is done mostly by professional librarians. This is especially the case for MA-/PhD-granting colleges (95.65 percent) and community colleges (100 percent). 33.33 percent of all research universities in the sample, however, say this work is done both by professional librarians and paraprofessional support staff. Broken out by total student enrollment, the smallest schools (less than 10,000 students) are most likely to have this done by professional librarians, as 93.55 percent of them do, but that figure drops to 81.82 percent for the middle enrollment range (10,000 to 20,000 students) and then down again to 70.59 percent for the top enrollment range (more than 20,000). 92.31 percent of participants where the tuition is less than $8,000 also responded to the question in this way.

Subject Authority Cooperative (SACO)

Even more participants (92.59 percent of the sample) say the Subject Authority Cooperative (SACO) work is handled mostly by professional librarians. Just 1.23 percent says this work is handled mostly by paraprofessional support staff. The remainder says the work here is performed by both. One anomaly that stands out is in the type of college breakout, where 26.67 percent of research universities credit this work to be done by both paraprofessionals and professional librarians (no other type of college posted a percentage higher than 3 percent here). Likewise for the total student enrollment breakout: 17.65 percent of those with more than 20,000 students responded this way, while just 3.23 percent of those in the less than 10,000 students range and 3.03 percent of those in the 10,000 to 20,000 student range said the same.

Master Bibliographic Record Enhancement in OCLC

71.6 percent of all survey participants say master bibliographic record enhancement in OCLC is performed mostly by librarians, including 100 percent of community colleges, 83.89 percent of those participants with less than 10,00 students, and 80.77 percent of those with an annual tuition below $8,000. One anomaly arises in the $8,000 to $18,000 annual tuition range, where 13.79 percent of participants say this work is performed mostly by paraprofessional support staff. The next highest percentage here is 3.85 percent for the more than $18,000 range.

Participation in PCC, CONSER and BIBCO 1 Bibliographic Record Work

The vast majority (92.59 percent) of survey participants say participation in PCC, CONSER and BIBCO 1 bibliographic record work is performed mostly by professional librarians. This figure is at least 95 percent for all types of colleges in the sample except for research universities, where just 73.33 percent categorized the work responsibilities this way (20 percent say this is performed by both professional librarians and paraprofessional support staff). Similarly, just 76.47 percent of those participants with more than 20,000 students say this is mostly the job of professional librarians, while at least 96.5 percent of all other participants responded this same way.

Master Bibliographic Record Enrichment in OCLC

69.14 percent of all survey participants say master bibliographic record enhancement in OCLC (such as adding call numbers, subjects, and table of contents) is performed mostly by professional librarians, although nearly a quarter (24.69 percent) of them say this is performed by both professional librarians and paraprofessionals. This latter arrangement is more common among MA-/PhD-granting colleges (34.78 percent) and research universities (33.33 percent) as well as among participants at schools where the annual tuition is more than $18,000 (38.46 percent). The splits among public and private schools are nearly even, however, with not more than a 5.5 percent difference between the two for any one answer.

Subject Analysis and Subject Heading Application

While 59.26 percent of survey participants say subject analysis and subject heading application is performed mostly by professional librarians, 37.04 percent say it is performed by both professional librarians and paraprofessional support staff. Just 3.7 percent, however, say it is performed mostly by the latter. The splits for public and private schools are practically identical here, with no more than a 1.5 percent difference between any of the answers in this category. The middle-ranged schools in the sample—both by total student enrollment (10,000 to 20,000 students) and by annual tuition ($8,000 to $18,000)—are behind their smaller and larger counterparts here, as just 48.48 percent of the former and 48.28 percent of the latter say these tasks are performed mostly by professional librarians, while between 61.5 percent and 69.5 percent of all other categories answered this same way.

Classification

For 54.32 percent of all survey participants, the task of classification is performed mostly by professional librarians. However, 41.98 percent of participants say classification is performed by both professional librarians and paraprofessional support staff. Just more than half (51.72 percent) of the private schools in the sample reported these tasks to be handled by both professionals and paraprofessionals, while only 36.54 percent of public schools responded this same way. Likewise, just 26.92 percent of schools with annual tuitions less than $8,000 report that this is handled by both types of workers, while 48-50 percent of all other participants say the same.

Master Bibliographic Record Upgrades in OCLC

The vast majority (81.48 percent) of survey participants report that maser bibliographic record upgrades in OCLC are handled mostly by professional librarians. Just 6.17 percent say these are handled by paraprofessional support staff. However, 26.67 percent of research libraries and 23.53 percent of schools with more than 20,000 students report that these tasks are handled by both paraprofessionals and professional librarians. By comparison, 90 percent of those participants with less than 10,000 students say these tasks are performed mostly by professional librarians, as do 100 percent of the community colleges in the sample.

Establishment of Local Series, Uniform Title Headings and Authority Records

According to our survey participants, the establishment of local series, uniform title headings and authority records are handled mostly by professional librarians, with 76.54 percent of the sample citing this to be the case. For 17.28 percent of the sample, these tasks are handled by both paraprofessionals and professional librarians. There is not much deviation in this respect, as all categories in the sample lie somewhere between 13.5 and 19.5 percent for this answer, save for two: while no community colleges say these tasks are handled by paraprofessionals and professional librarians, 26.67 percent of research universities report this to be the case.

Establishment of Local Name, Corporate Body, and Conference Headings and Authority Records

A bit more than three-quarters (77.78 percent) of all participants say the establishment of local name, corporate body, and conference headings and authority records is performed mostly by professional librarians. This includes 100 percent of community colleges and 86.96 percent of MA-/PhD-granting colleges, yet just 53.33 percent of research universities, where a third of all participants say these tasks are performed by both professional librarians and paraprofessionals. The splits for public and private are nearly even, with no more than a 3.52 percent difference between the two for any answer in this category. When the data is broken out by total student enrollment, however, there appears a direct correlation between increasing enrollment numbers and the role paraprofessional support staff play in performing these tasks: while just 9.68 percent of those with less than 10,000 students say the establishment of local name, corporate body, and conference headings and authority records is handled either mostly by paraprofessionals or by both paraprofessionals and professional librarians, this figure rises to 27.27 percent for the middle enrollment range (10,000 to 20,000 students) and then up again to 35.29 percent for the top enrollment range (more than 20,000 students).

Establishment of Local Subject and Geographic Headings and Authority Records

Once again, the majority of survey participants (83.95 percent) say the establishment of local subject and geographic headings and authority records is handled mostly by professional librarians. This includes 100 percent of community colleges and 95.65 percent of MA-/PhD-granting colleges in the sample. Again the splits between public and private schools are minimal, and again the smallest schools (both by annual tuition and enrollment size) say these tasks are handled mostly by professional librarians: 92.31 percent of the former and 93.55 percent of the latter.

Change in Number of Library Support Staff

Over the last five years, the libraries in the sample gained a mean of 0.42 positions in cataloging library support staff. The median here is 0, and the range is from a loss of 5 to a gain of 10. At -0.23, research universities are the only type of college in the sample with a mean less than 0, thus losing on average 0.23 positions over the last five years. MA and PhD-granting colleges recorded the highest gains, with a mean of 1.08 and a maximum of 10, the highest maximum in the bunch. However, the medians for all types of colleges was still 0. While schools with more than 20,000 students posted a mean of 1.13, the next closest mean in this category belonged to those schools with less than 10,000 students at 0.25. As annual tuition increases, the number of positions in the cataloging library support staff steadily decreases: those participants with a tuition of less than $8,000 gained a mean of 0.90 such positions, while those in the $8,000 to $18,000 range gained a mean of less than half that at 0.42. Those in the top tuition range actually lost a mean of 0.02 over that same time span.

Change in Number of Professional Cataloging Librarians

The numbers for the change in positions of professional librarians in cataloging functions over the last five years are quite similar to those for the library support staff. The overall sample mean is a gain of 0.41, with a median of 0, and the range is from a loss of 3 to a gain of 10. This time around, however, it is the research universities who post the highest mean at 1.23, while the community colleges are the only type of college to compile a mean resulting in a loss (-0.38). In fact, no community college in the sample reporting gaining any professional cataloging librarians over the past five years. Private schools only topped out at 1, while public schools posted a mean of 0.66 and a maximum of 10. Schools with more than 20,000 students again posted the highest mean in this category at 1.04, with the next closest being those schools with less than 10,000 students with a mean of 0.29. Once again there is a sharp decline when the data is broken out by annual tuition, from a mean of 1.04 for the smallest range down to 0.29 for the mid-range and -0.15 for the top tuition range in the sample.

Recruiting Student Workers for Cataloging

44.44 percent of survey participants say their cataloging division participates in library school student mentoring and internships, or else works to recruit existing staff and student workers into the cataloging profession. This is much more common among community colleges (60 percent) than it is among 4-year degree granting colleges (39.47 percent). The largest schools (those with more than 20,000 students) are also more than likely to do so, as 64.71 percent report to this practice, as compared to just 33.33 percent of those in the 10,000 to 20,000 student enrollment range. Broken out by tuition, however, there isn't a great discrepancy, as all ranges here are between 42 and 48.5 percent.

Retiring Professional Librarians

The libraries in the sample anticipate that a mean of 0.66 professional librarians that perform mostly cataloging functions will retire in the next five years. The median here is 0, and the maximum is 5. Research universities anticipate losing a mean of 0.97 such positions over that time, while community colleges and 4-year degree granting colleges expect losing a mean of just 0.5. As could be expected, this mean increases as student enrollment increases, from a mean of 0.46 for the lowest category to a high mean of 0.97 for the top category. However, this trend does not hold true for annual tuition. While the middle range ($8,000 to $18,000) expects to lose a mean of 0.76 professional librarians, those in the top range (more than $18,000) look to lose a mean of just 0.52 due to retirement.

Retiring Paraprofessional Support Staff

Libraries in the sample expect to lose more library paraprofessional support staff due to retirement over the next five years than they do professional librarians, with a mean of 1.13 and a maximum of 10. Community colleges do not expect to lose any such personnel to retirement, although MA- and PhD-granting colleges and research universities are bracing to lose a mean of 1.59 and 1.67, respectively, over the next five years. For those schools where the annual tuition is more than $18,000, the mean is 0.76, or nearly half the mean of those schools in the middle tuition range ($8,000 to $18,000). Public schools in the sample post a mean more than twice that of their private school counterparts, 1.37 to 0.64, and no private school is expecting to lose more than 3 library paraprofessional support staff due to retirement.

SALARY ISSUES

Cataloger Salaries Comparable to Those of Public Service Librarians

62.96 percent of libraries in the sample say their catalogers have salaries comparable to public service librarians, while 13.58 percent say they do not. The remaining 23.45 percent either did not respond or were unsure. MA- and PhD-granting colleges led the pack in this respect, as 91.3 percent of them reported that their catalogers have salaries comparable to public service librarians (with the remaining 8.7 percent simply stating they were "unsure"). By comparison, 40 percent of community colleges say this is not the case, as do 26.67 percent of research universities. A great discrepancy arises when the data is broken out by total student enrollment, as 77.42 percent of schools with less than 10,000 students say these salaries are comparable, while just 41.18 percent of schools with more than 20,000 students can say the same. A similar trend can be found as annual tuition increases: whereas 73.08 percent of those in the "less than $8,000" tuition range say these salaries are comparable, just 53.85 percent of those in the "more than $18,000" range do.

The Cataloger's Pay Rate over the Past Four Years

More than half (56.79 percent) of all survey participants say the cataloger's pay rate has increased by less than 2.5 percent over the last four years. Another 30.86 percent say it has remained flat. Only two participants say the pay has been declining over this time. 20 percent of community colleges in the sample say the pay has increased between 2.5 and 5 percent, as do 13.04 percent of MA- and PhD-granting colleges. No research universities reported such an increase. While the majority (75.86 percent) of private schools report an increase of less than 2.5 percent, 40.38 percent of public schools say this pay has remained flat. Broken out by total student enrollment, the largest schools (with more than 20,000 students) are the most positive here, with 23.53 percent of them reporting an increase between 2.5 and 5 percent. No more than 6.5 percent of all other types of schools in this category reported this way.

WORK RATE COMPLETION

Turn-Around Time: From Acquisitions to Cataloging to Distribution

Only 19.75 percent of survey participants track turn-around times from acquisitions receipt to cataloging to shelf-ready distribution. This is more common among community colleges (40 percent do so) than it is among all other types of colleges (no more than 21.74 percent of them do). It is fairly standard practice not to track such statistics among private schools in the sample, as 82.76 percent do not. Less than 16.5 percent of libraries in the sample at schools with less than 20,000 students maintain these statistics, compared to 35.29 percent of those at schools with more than 20,000 students. Schools with smaller tuitions are also much more likely to keep track of such things: 34.62 percent of those libraries at schools where the annual tuition is less than $8,000 do so, compared to 17.24 percent of those in the $8,000 to $18,000 tuition range and just 7.69 percent of those where the tuition is more than $18,000.

Rating Cataloger or Staff Work Product Quotas

More than half (60.5 percent) of all survey participants find cataloger or staff work product quotas to be either "not useful" or "misleading," and another 11.11 percent find it to be altogether "detracting from quality." Outside of a meager 2.63 percent of 4-year degree granting colleges, research universities are the only type of college to find these quotas as "very useful," as 26.67 percent of them do. 13.46 percent of public schools in the sample find these quotas to be "detracting from quality," and another 38.46 percent find them to be "misleading," this compared to 6.9 percent and 20.69 percent, respectively, for the private schools.

Rating Turn-Around Time from Receipt in Cataloging to Ready for Shelf

Nearly half (49.38 percent) of all survey participants rate the turn-around time from receipt in cataloging to ready for shelf as "somewhat useful." This includes 60 percent of research universities and 57.69 percent of those participants with an annual tuition of more than $18,000. 20 percent of community colleges rate this as "very useful," as do 26.67 percent of research universities. The splits between public and private schools is fairly even across the board, although there is a gap in the "very useful" column when the data is broken out by total student enrollment: while 35.29 percent of those participants with more than 20,000 students rated the turn-around time this way, no other category here posted a figure higher than 9.09 percent.

Rating Error Rates per Bibliographic Record

59.26 percent of survey participants find error rates per bibliographic record to be "somewhat useful." Only 2.47 percent find them to be "misleading," and no one found them to be "detracting from quality." More than half (53.33 percent) of all research universities in the sample rated these error rates as "very useful," or nearly three times that of the next closest percentage in this category (20 percent for community colleges). Broken out by public and private schools, 28.85 percent of the former rate these as "very useful," compared to just 6.9 percent of the latter. Schools with larger enrollments, too, find these more useful: 35.29 percent of those with more than 20,000 students find them "very useful," while only 6.45 percent of those with less than 10,000 students say the same.

Rating the Completeness of Bibliographic Records

The completeness of bibliographic records is rated as "very useful" by 48.15 percent of survey participants, including 66.67 percent of research universities and 61.54 percent of schools with an annual tuition of more than $18,000. Overall, 37.04 percent of participants find this to be "somewhat useful." The biggest and smallest schools, both by total student enrollment and annual tuition, are more likely to find this "not useful" than those schools in the mid-range: between 11.54 and 12.9 percent of the former group rate it this way, compared to between 6 and 7 percent for the latter group.

Rating the Error Rates per Authority Record

The error rates per authority record are found to be "somewhat useful" by 40.74 percent of survey participants. However, 32.1 percent of the sample rated these as "not useful," including 52.17 percent of MA- or PhD-granting colleges and 48.39 percent of those participants with a total student enrollment less than 10,000. 60 percent of research universities found these to be "very useful," by far the highest percentage among all types of colleges in the sample (the next closest was 4-year degree granting colleges at 13.16 percent). Satisfaction in this respect generally increase as total student enrollment increases: while just 3.23 percent of those with less than 10,000 students rate error rates per authority record as "very useful," this figure jumps to 24.24 percent for the next enrollment range (10,000 to 20,000 students) and then again to 41.18 percent for the top enrollment range (more than 20,000 students).

Rating the Error Rates per Holding Record

Just about half (46.91 percent) of all survey participants find error rates per holding record to be "somewhat useful," with an identical 46.91 percent split evenly between "very useful" and "not useful." Research universities again find the most use out of these error rates, with 46.67 percent of them rating the error rates as "very useful." The next closest in this category was the MA- or PhD-granting colleges at 21.74 percent. Broken out by public and private status, 30.77 percent of public schools in the sample find these to be "very useful," as compared to just 10.34 percent of private schools. In fact, 31.03 percent of the latter find these error rates to be "not useful." 35.48 percent of survey participants with less than 10,000 students say these error rates are "not useful," while only 17.65 percent of those with more than 20,000 students say the same.

Rating the Error Rates per Physical Processing

More than half (55.56 percent) of all survey participants find the error rates per physical processing to be "somewhat useful," with another 16.05 percent finding them to be "very useful." These are again more popular with research universities, as 93.33 percent of them find them to be at least "somewhat useful." Compare this to the community colleges in the sample, where 40 percent think of them as "not useful." 37.93 percent of private schools also rated the error rates this way, as did 41.94 percent of schools with less than 10,000 total students. When the data is broken out by annual tuition, there is not much variation in the results: for each answer, the breakout categories (i.e. "less than $8,000," "$8,000 to $18,000," and "more than $18,000") differ by no more than 8.62 percent.

Rating Patron or Staff Complaints

46.91 percent of all survey participants cite patron or staff complaints as "somewhat useful," while another 33.33 percent see these as "very useful." MA-/PhD-granting colleges and research universities particularly take these complaints to heart, as 39.13 percent of the former and 46.67 percent of the latter rate them as "very useful." Schools with less than 10,000 students are less enthusiastic about this, with just 9.68 percent rating these complaints as "very useful." However, 61.29 percent of them do consider these to be "somewhat useful." Similarly, the private schools in the sample are more inclined to rate them as "somewhat useful" (58.62 percent) than they are "very useful" (20.69 percent).

Rating Patron or Staff Commendations

Almost exactly half (50.62 percent) of all survey participants find patron or staff commendations to be "somewhat useful." While less than 10 percent rated these as "not useful" or worse, 38.27 percent find them to be "very useful." Community colleges rated these commendations the least favorably, with 40 percent of them rating patron and staff commendations as "not useful." No other type of college posted a percentage higher than 6.67 percent here. The smallest schools (those with less than 10,000 students) rated these commendations as "somewhat useful" 67.74 percent of the time and "very useful" just 16. By comparison, 48.48 percent of those in the 10,000 to 20,000 enrollment range and 58.82 percent of those with more than 20,000 students rated them as "very useful."

Rating the Support or Accomplishment of Departmental or Library Goal

More than half (56.79 percent) of all survey participants find the support or accomplishment of a departmental or library goal to be "very useful," with another 35.8 percent finding it to be "somewhat useful." Most enthusiastic in this respect are the MA-/PhD-granting colleges (60.87 percent said "very useful") and research universities (66.67 percent also said "very useful"). As total student enrollment increases, so too does the participant's satisfaction with this support or accomplishment, as 76.47 percent of those institutions with more than 20,000 students rate it as "very useful," compared to 45.16 percent of those with less than 10,000 students. 73.08 percent of participants with an annual tuition of more than $18,000, too, voted this way.

OUTSOURCING

Outsourcing the Obtainment of New and Updated Authority Records

46.91 percent of all survey participants outsource the obtainment of new and updated authority records. MA-/PhD-granting colleges (56.52 percent) and research universities (60 percent) are more likely to do so than community colleges (40 percent) and 4-year degree granting colleges (36.84 percent). The splits are fairly even between public and private schools, although there is a significant difference when the data is broken out by total student enrollment: while just 35.48 percent of schools with less than 10,000 students outsource these duties, 57.58 percent of those participants in the 10,000 to 20,000 enrollment range do so. There is not a huge gap in the annual tuition breakout, as the percentages range from 42.31 percent to 51.72 percent.

Outsourcing the Updating of Headings in Bibliographic Records

35.8 percent of survey participants say they outsource the updating of headings in bibliographic records. Broken out by type of college, the biggest outsourcers here are the research universities, with 53.33 percent of them saying they outsource such activities. Community colleges are second at 40 percent, while the 4-year degree granting colleges and MA-/PhD-granting colleges lay between 30 and 32 percent. Public schools do so 34.62 percent of the time, while private schools do so 37.93 percent of the time. As annual tuition increases, so too does the likelihood of outsourcing the updating of headings in bibliographic records: whereas

26.92 percent of those with an annual tuition under $8,000 outsource here, 42.31 percent of those with annual tuition more than $18,000 do the same.

Outsourcing the Obtainment of New Bibliographic Records

46.91 percent of survey participants outsource the obtainment of new bibliographic records. This includes 73.33 percent of research universities and 70.59 percent of participants with total student enrollments over 20,000. There is a great disparity between the public schools and private schools here, as 59.62 percent of the former outsource these duties while just 24.14 percent of the latter do the same. As total student enrollment increases, so too does the likelihood of outsourcing the obtainment of new bibliographic records: 25.81 percent of those with less than 10,000 students outsource, compared to 54.55 percent of those in the 10,000 to 20,000 student range. The opposite trend occurs when the data is broken out by annual tuition. While 61.54 percent of participants with an annual tuition less than $8,000 outsource, this figure drops to 48.28 percent for the middle range ($8,000 to $18,000) and down again to 30.77 percent for the top tuition range (more than $18,000).

Outsourcing the Maintenance of Item Records and Inventory

Only 4.94 percent of the sample outsources the maintenance of item records and inventory. These participants are all affiliated with public schools and have an annual tuition of less than $18,000.

Outsourcing of Physical Processing and Barcoding

20.99 percent of survey participants say they outsource physical processing and barcoding. This is favored much more by public schools (28.85 percent) than it is by private schools (6.9 percent). No community colleges in the sample outsource these activities, while 46.67 percent of all research universities do. As total student enrollment increases, so too does the percentage of participants outsourcing physical processing and barcoding, from just 3.23 percent of those in the less than 10,000 enrollment range up to 18.18 percent for those in the middle range (10,000 to 20,000) and ballooning to 58.82 percent for those with more than 20,000 students. Whereas 27.59 percent of survey participants in the $8,000 to $18,000 annual tuition range outsource these activities, just 11.54 percent of those with tuitions higher than $18,000 do the same.

Outsourcing the Addition of Table of Contents Notes

12.35 percent of survey participants say they outsource the addition of table of contents notes, none of which were community colleges or had enrollments less than 10,000 students. While 40 percent of research universities outsource here, just 2.63 percent of 4-year degree granting colleges do the same. Public schools (15.38 percent) are more likely than private schools (6.9 percent) to do so.

Outsourcing the Addition of Book Reviews

11.11 percent of survey participants say they outsource the addition of book reviews. This is more common among private schools (20.69 percent) than it is among public schools (5.77 percent). While 26.67 percent of research universities outsource the addition of book reviews, just 4.35 percent of MA-/PhD-granting colleges and no community colleges do this. No participants with an annual tuition less than $8,000 outsources here, while just more than a quarter (26.92 percent) of all participants with annual tuitions over $18,000 do so.

Outsourcing the Addition of Book Jackets

16.05 percent of survey participants outsource the addition of book jackets. Once again community colleges do not outsource here, while 26.67 percent of research libraries do. Private schools (24.14 percent) do so at more than twice the rate of their public school counterparts (11.54 percent). Broken out by total student enrollment, there is not a great discrepancy as all the categories are within 2.5 percentage points of one another. Those with the highest annual tuitions (more than $18,000) outsource the most often here, at 23.08 percent, compared to just 7.69 percent of those participants with tuitions less than $8,000.

Outsourcing Continuing Resources

8.64 percent of survey participants say they outsource continuing resources. The greatest discrepancy arises when the data is broken out by total student enrollment: no more than 3.23 percent of participants with less than 20,000 students outsource here, while 29.41 percent of those with more than 20,000 students say they do. While no community colleges outsource these activities, 13.16 percent of 4-year degree granting colleges do, as do 13.79 percent of schools with an annual tuition in the $8,000 to $18,000 range.

Outsourcing E-Journals

28.4 percent of survey participants outsource e-journals. None of these are community colleges. 34.62 percent of public schools outsource these tasks, while just half the percentage of private schools (17.24 percent) does the same. As student enrollment increases, the percentage of participants outsourcing e-journals steadily increases as well, from 19.35 percent for the lowest range (less than 10,000 students) up to 41.18 percent for the highest range (more than 20,000). Whereas 37.93 percent of participants in the $8,000 to $18,000 annual tuition range outsource e-journals, just 19.23 percent of those with a tuition of more than $18,000 do.

Outsourcing E-Books

40.74 percent of survey participants outsource e-books, including 52.17 percent of MA-/PhD-granting colleges and 53.33 percent of research universities. Broken out by public or private status, the former is twice as likely to outsource here than the latter, 50 percent to 24.14

percent. The likelihood of outsourcing increases steadily as total student enrollment increases: 22.58 percent of those with less than 10,000 students outsources e-books, as compared to 45.45 percent of those in the middle range (10,000 to 20,000 students) and 64.71 percent of those with more than 20,000 students. The opposite trend emerges when the data is broken out by annual tuition, with 53.85 percent of those with an annual tuition under $8,000 outsourcing e-books while 26.92 percent of those with an annual tuition more than $18,000 do the same.

Outsourcing AV Formats

Just 4.94 percent of survey participants outsource AV formats. All of these are public schools with more than 20,000 students and an annual tuition less than $18,000.

Outsourcing Foreign Language Resources

8.64 percent of survey participants say they outsource foreign language resources in which they have no expertise. All of these are public schools with at least 10,000 students and an annual tuition less than $18,000.

Outsourcing Other Digital Formats

3.7 percent of participants say they outsource other digital formats. Again these are all public schools, with more than 20,000 students and annual tuition less than $18,000.

Outsourcing Materials in Cataloging Backlogs

6.17 percent of participants outsource materials in cataloging backlogs, none of which are community colleges or 4-year degree granting colleges. 23.53 percent of participants with more than 20,000 students outsource here, compare to just 3.03 percent of those in the 10,000 to 20,000 enrollment range and no participants with less than 10,000 students.

Outsourcing All Materials

Only 2.47 percent of participants say that all materials are outsourced. These are public schools (community colleges and 4-year degree granting colleges) with less than 20,000 students and annual tuitions less than $8,000.

No Outsourcing

35.8 percent of all survey participants do not outsource at all, including 39.47 percent of 4-year degree granting colleges and 47.83 percent of MA-/PhD-granting colleges. Private schools are much less likely to outsource, as 58.62 percent of them don't, compared to 76.92 percent of public schools that have outsourced. Enrollment plays a big factor, too, as 94.12 percent of schools with more than 20,000 students have outsourced, compared to 69.7 percent of those in the 10,000 to 20,000 enrollment range and 41.94 percent of those with less than 10,000 students.

Quality Control – MarcEdit

54.32 percent of survey participants use MarcEdit or some other MARC editor to preview records and globally edit to local stands prior to loading. While no community colleges use these programs, 66.67 percent of research universities and 69.57 percent of MA-/PhD-granting colleges do. Public schools (57.69 percent) are more likely to use them than private schools (48.28 percent). Schools with larger enrollments are also more apt to use MarcEdit (or a similar program): while just 38.71 percent of those with less than 10,000 students use MarcEdit, the program is used by 60.61 percent of schools in the 10,000 to 20,000 enrollment range and by 70.59 percent of those with 20,000 or more students. Also of note is that 69.23 percent of survey participants with an annual tuition of less than $8,000 use MarcEdit as a quality control method.

Quality Control – Local Integrated System

32.1 percent of survey participants use a local integrated system to review loaded records and globally edit to local standards. This is most common among research universities (53.33 percent), while just 20 percent of community colleges and 23.68 percent of 4-year degree granting colleges use these types of systems for quality control. There is not much of a difference between public and private schools (30.77 percent for the former, 34.48 percent for the latter), although there is a significant disparity when the data is broken out by total student enrollment: while 29.03 percent of those survey participants with less than 10,000 students use a local integrated system, more than twice that percentage (64.71 percent) of schools with more than 20,000 students can say the same.

Quality Control – Spot-Checking Vendor Records

38.27 percent of all survey participants say they review all vendor records whenever possible and spot-check vendor records when complete review is not possible. While no community colleges in the sample take this approach to quality control, 43.48 percent of MA-/PhD-granting colleges do, as do 53.33 percent of research universities. There is again a noticeable increase as student enrollment increases, from 36.36 percent of those in the 10,000 to 20,000 student enrollment range, up to 52.94 percent of those with more than 20,000 students. 46.15 percent of participants with an annual tuition of more than $18,000 spot-check vendor records when a complete review is not possible, the highest percentage in this category.

Just 14.81 percent of all participants say they always spot-check all vendor records. Again the most diligent in this respect are the research universities, where 33.33 percent of them participate in this practice, while the next closest percentage in this category belongs to the 4-year degree granting colleges at 13.16 percent. The participants with higher annual tuitions are more likely to spot-check all vendor records, as 23.08 percent of those with tuitions over $18,000 do so, compared to just 7.69 percent of those with tuitions less than $8,000.

Quality Control – No Review Performed

Only 8.64 percent of survey participants say they either do no perform any sort of review or else the review is minimal. Standing out in this category are the community colleges, as 20 percent of them admit to not performing a review. Just 3.85 percent of participants with an annual tuition over $18,000 do not perform such a review, not do 5.88 percent of participants with more than 20,000 students.

STATE OF CATALOGING EDUCATION IN LIBRARY SCHOOLS

RATING THE PREPAREDNESS OF RECENT LIBRARY HIRES

We asked survey participants to rate the preparedness of their recent library hires in an array of cataloging and metadata competencies, philosophies, principles, and practices. The responses offered were "not at all prepared," "minimally prepared," "prepared," and "well prepared."

Classification Systems

33.33 percent of survey participants say their recent library hires are "minimally prepared" in classification systems, while another 6.17 percent say they are "not at all prepared." For 27.16 percent, these hires are "prepared," and for 8.64 percent they are "well prepared." 40 percent of community colleges say their hires are "well prepared" in this, while 47.83 percent of MA-/PhD-granting colleges say they are "minimally prepared." The new hires at the smallest institutions seem to be the most prepared among all survey participants: whereas 70.59 percent of those institutions with more than 20,000 students say their recent hires are either "minimally prepared" or "not at all prepared," only 39.39 percent of those in the 10,000 to 20,000 enrollment range and 22.58 percent of those with less than 10,000 students say the same.

Subject/Genre Thesauri Systems

A third of all survey participants say their new library hires are "minimally prepared" in subject/genre thesauri systems. Another 23.46 percent cite them as "prepared," while 7.41 percent say they are "well prepared" and 9.88 percent say they are "not at all prepared." Community colleges are the most prepared in this respect, as 40 percent of them responded either "prepared" or "well prepared," the highest percentage in this category. Broken out by total student enrollment, the largest schools (more than 20,000 students) are the least prepared, with 17.65 percent saying their library hires are "not at all prepared" in subject/genre thesauri systems and an overwhelming 64.71 percent saying they are "minimally prepared."

Compare this to 39.39 percent of those in the 10,000 to 20,000 enrollment range who say their hires are either "prepared" or "well prepared."

Classification and Subject/Genre Analysis Principles, Rules, and Tools

32.1 percent of all survey participants rate their recent library hires as "minimally prepared" when it comes to classification and subject/genre analysis principles, rules, and tools, while 24.69 percent say they are "prepared." Hires at community colleges and 4-year degree granting colleges are better prepared than those at MA-/PhD-granting colleges and research universities, with 40 percent and 36.84 percent of the former group, respectively, saying they are either "prepared" or "well prepared," compared to just 26.09 percent and 26.67 percent of the latter group. More than half (52.94 percent) of all survey participants with more than 20,000 students say their hires are "minimally prepared" in these abilities, while 13.46 percent of public schools say they are "not at all prepared" here, compared to just 3.45 percent of private schools in the sample.

Java and PERL Script Applications

Nearly half (46.91 percent) of all survey participants say their library hires are "not at all prepared" in Java and PERL script applications, including 60 percent of research universities, 53.85 percent of public schools, and 70.59 percent of schools with more than 20,000 students. Overall, just 3.7 percent of survey participants say their hires are "prepared," and only 1.23 percent say they are "well prepared," all of which are public schools with less than 20,000 students and an annual tuition under $18,000.

Cataloging Rules and Tools (Including Descriptive Cataloging)

28.4 percent of survey participants rate their recent library hires as "prepared" when it comes to cataloging rules and tools (including descriptive cataloging). An identical 28.4 percent say they are "minimally prepared," including 47.06 percent of those schools with more than 20,000 students. Broken out by public or private status, 44.23 percent of the public schools say their hires are either "not at all prepared" or "minimally prepared," while just 24.14 percent of the private schools rated them this way. 40 percent of community colleges rate them as "well prepared," by far the highest percentage in this category (the next closest is 13.33 percent for the research universities).

Information Technology and Social Behavior in the Organizational Context

While 20.99 percent of survey participants rate their recent library hires as "prepared" when it comes to information technology and social behavior in the organizational context, 28.4 percent rate them as "minimally prepared," and another 16.05 percent rate them as "not at all prepared." Just 1.23 percent say they are "well prepared." The largest schools (those with more than 20,000 enrolled students) rate their hires as the least prepared, with 29.41 percent saying they are "not at all prepared" and 35.29 percent saying they are "minimally prepared."

Compare this to those schools with less than 10,000 students, where 25.8 percent of participants are split evenly between these two answers.

Metadata Standards for Digital Resources

Just 13.58 percent of survey participants say their library hires are "prepared" in metadata standards for digital resources, and only 2.47 percent say they are "well prepared." 25.93 percent say they are "minimally prepared" then, and 30.86 percent describe them as "not at all prepared." Broken out by public or private status, the public schools are less prepared here, as 38.46 percent of them say they are "not at all prepared," compared to just 17.24 percent of private schools. Overall preparedness seems to increase as annual tuition increases: while 42.31 percent of those participants with a tuition less than $8,000 say these hires are "not at all prepared" in terms of metadata standards, this figure drops to 31.03 percent for the middle tuition range ($8,000 to $18,000) and then down again to 19.23 percent for the top tuition bracket (more than $18,000).

Abstracting and Indexing

When it comes to abstracting and indexing, just 1.23 percent of survey participants feel their recent library hires are "well prepared," and only 9.88 percent find them to be even simply "prepared." This leaves 33.33 percent who say they are "minimally prepared" in this area, and 23.46 percent who say they are "not at all prepared." The MA-/PhD-granting colleges and research universities find their hires to be the least prepared, as just 4.35 percent of the former and none of the latter rate them as "prepared" (and none in either group rated them as "well prepared"). Hires at private schools are better prepared in this category, as just 10.34 percent of survey participants rate them as "not at all prepared" (compared to 30.77 percent of participants at public schools) while 17.24 percent say they are "prepared" (this compared to just 5.77 percent of public schools).

Electronic Delivery of Services

27.16 percent of survey participants find their recent library hires to be "minimally prepared" in electronic delivery of services, with another 16.05 percent saying they are "not at all prepared." Broken out by type of college, it is the research universities that are the least prepared here, as no such participants categorized their recent hires as either "well prepared" or even "prepared." On the other end of the spectrum, 31.58 percent of 4-year degree granting colleges categorized their hires as "prepared." Private schools were generally more prepared in this area, as 31.03 percent of them answered "prepared" and just 3.45 percent said they were "not at all prepared," while 13.46 percent of public schools answered with the former and 23.08 percent answered the latter.

Technical Services in Libraries

34.57 percent of survey participants say their recent hires are "minimally prepared" in technical services in libraries. This includes 66.67 percent of research universities and 58.82 percent of those institutions with more than 20,000 total enrolled students. 39.47 percent of 4-year degree granting colleges say their hires are "prepared," as do 34.48 percent of private schools, well above the overall sample average of 23.46 percent. While 23.53 percent of participants at schools with more than 20,000 students say these hires are "not at all prepared" in technical services in libraries, just 3.23 percent of those at schools with a total student enrollment less than 10,000 say the same.

Web and Local Network System Administration and Management

More than half (54.32 percent) of all survey participants find that their recent library hires are either "minimally prepared" or "not at all prepared" in web and local network system administration and management, including 73.33 percent of research universities, 65.22 percent of MA-/PhD-granting colleges, and 70.59 percent of schools with more than 20,000 students. 46.15 percent of participants at institutions with an annual tuition less than $8,000 say their hires are "minimally prepared," compared to just 17.24 percent of those in the $8,000 to $18,000 tuition range and 19.23 percent of those with a tuition of more than $18,000.

Cataloging Books

28.4 percent of survey participants categorize their recent library hires as "prepared" when it comes to cataloging books, while another 13.58 percent say they are "well prepared." While 23.46 percent cite them to be "minimally prepared," just 7.41 percent say they are "not at all prepared." More than half (52.94 percent) of those participants with more than 20,000 students rated these hires as either "minimally prepared" or "not at all prepared," compared to just 16.13 percent of those with less than 10,000 students. Similarly, 53.85 percent of schools with an annual tuition less than $8,000 say they are either "prepared" or "well prepared," as compared to 34.61 percent of participants with annual tuitions higher than $18,000 that can say the same.

Cataloging Digital Resources

Just about half (49.38 percent) of all survey participants say their recent library hires are either "minimally prepared" or "not at all prepared" to catalogue digital resources, including 65.22 percent of MA-/PhD-granting colleges and 70.58 percent of schools with more than 20,000 students. Just 6.17 percent of the entire sample say their hires are "well prepared" in this area. Only 7.69 percent of survey participants with more than $18,000 annual tuition say their hires are "not at all prepared," an anomaly in this breakout as no other tuition range posted a percentage lower than 19.23 percent.

Cataloging Continuing and Integrating Resources

Again, roughly half (53.09 percent) of all survey participants say their recent library hires are either "minimally prepared" or "not at all prepared" for cataloging continuing and integrating resources, including 63.46 percent of public schools and 82.35 percent of schools with more than 20,000 students. Broken out by type of college, it is the community colleges which are the most prepared here, with 40 percent of them saying "well prepared," while no MA-/PhD-granting colleges or research universities answered this way. 73.33 percent of research universities say their hires are "minimally prepared" in this respect.

Cataloging Law Materials

Just 6.17 percent of all survey participants say their recent library hires are either "prepared" or "well prepared" for cataloging law materials, with 39.51 percent saying they are "not at all prepared." This latter figure includes 60 percent of research universities and 70.59 percent of schools with more than 20,000 students. Broken out by public and private status, nearly half (48.08 percent) of the former say their hires are "not at all prepared," while about a quarter (24.14 percent) of the latter say the same. 80.77 percent of survey participants with annual tuition less than $8,000 say these hires are either "not at all prepared" or "minimally prepared," compared to 53.84 percent of those with a tuition more than $18,000.

Cataloging Music Materials

Once again, few survey participants say their recent library hires are either "prepared" or "well prepared" in cataloging music materials, only 8.64 percent of the entire sample, all of which are community colleges and 4-year degree granting colleges. Public schools in the sample seem particularly ill-prepared in this area, as 75 percent of them say they are either "not at all prepared" or "minimally prepared," as compared to just 37.93 percent of private schools. 76.47 percent of participants at schools with more than 20,000 students say their hires are "not at all prepared," while 19.35 percent of those with less than 10,000 students say the same.

Cataloging Archives and Rare Materials

As with cataloging music materials, just 8.64 percent of survey participants say their recent library hires are "prepared" or "well prepared" in cataloging archives and rare materials. Again, these are all community colleges and 4-year degree granting colleges. 40.38 percent of public libraries say they are "not at all prepared," while 17.24 percent of private libraries say the same. 64.71 percent of all survey participants with more than 20,000 students answered "not at all prepared," while none of them answered with either "prepared" or "well prepared."

XML and/or XSLT

13.58 percent of survey participants say their recent library hires are "prepared" in XML and/or XSLT, although 37.04 percent say they are "not at all prepared." Just 3.7 percent say they are "well prepared." Nearly half (47.83 percent) of MA-/PhD-granting colleges in the sample say they are "not at all prepared." Broken out by public or private status, the public schools are the least prepared, as 51.92 percent of them say these library hires are "not at all prepared" (and another 13.46 percent cite them to be "minimally prepared"). Schools with higher annual tuitions are better prepared here, as 57.69 percent of those with a tuition less than $8,000 responded with "not at all prepared," compared to just 19.23 percent of those with an annual tuition more than $18,000.

Economics and Metrics of Information

Again, only 6.17 percent of all survey participants say their library hires are either "prepared" or "well prepared" when it comes to economics and metrics of information. Private schools are better prepared than public schools here, with 46.15 percent of the latter responding with "not at all prepared," compared to just 24.14 percent of the former. As total student enrollment increases, the overall level of preparedness generally decreases: whereas 29.03 percent of participants at schools with less than 10,000 students say their hires are "not at all prepared" in these areas, this figure increases to 39.39 percent for the middle range (10.000 to 20,000 students) and all the way up to 52.94 percent for the top enrollment range (more than 20,000).

Discovery Tools and Applications

20.99 percent of all survey participants say their recent library hires are either "prepared" or "well prepared" when it comes to discovery tools and applications. 30.86 percent say they are "minimally prepared," while 17.28 percent cite them to be "not at all prepared." While only 6.9 percent of private schools believe their hires to be "not at all prepared," this is the case of 23.08 percent of public schools in the sample. More than half (53.33 percent) of all research universities in the sample say their hires are "minimally prepared" in discovery tools and applications, and just 6.67 percent say they are either "prepared" or "well prepared" in this department, by far the lowest percentage among all the types of colleges.

Authority Control

When it comes to authority control, 55.55 percent of all survey participants say their recent library hires are either "minimally prepared" or else "not at all prepared" in this respect. Only 16.05 percent say they are either "prepared" or "well prepared." Broken out by total student enrollment, it is the largest schools (those with more than 20,000 students) that appear to be the least prepared, as 47.06 percent responded with "not at all prepared." The next closest percentage in this category belonged to those with less than 10,000 students, at 19.35 percent. 50 percent of participants with an annual tuition of less than $8,000 say they are "minimally prepared," while this is the case for just 23.08 percent of those with a tuition of more than $18,000.

Web Usability, User Research, and Human Interface Design

28.4 percent of all survey participants say their recent library hires are "minimally prepared" in web usability, user research, and human interface design, while another 18.52 percent say they are "not at all prepared." Just 3.7 percent report being "well prepared" in these subjects. 57.69 percent of public schools in the sample responded with either "minimally prepared" or "not at all prepared," compared to 27.58 percent of private schools. 19.35 percent of participants with less than 10,000 students are "prepared" and just 6.45 percent are "not at all prepared," both figures a respective high in the category for the former and a low for the latter. 26.32 percent of 4-year degree granting colleges say their hires are "prepared" when it comes to web usability, user research, and human interface design.

International MARC Bibliographic , Authority and Holdings Standards

For 30.86 percent of survey participants, their recent library hires are just "minimally prepared" in terms of international MARC bibliographic, authority and holdings standards. Another 19.75 percent say they are "not at all prepared." Close to a third (29.41 percent) of all participants with more than 20,000 students say their library hires are "prepared" in this area, while the next closest percentage in this breakout belongs to the middle enrollment range (10,000 to 20,000 students) with 12.12 percent. More than half (53.85 percent) of all participants with an annual tuition of less than $8,000 categorize their hires as "minimally prepared" here, compared to just 17.24 percent of those with an annual tuition of $8,000 to $18,000 and 23.08 percent of those in the top tuition range (more than $18,000).

Data Modeling, Warehousing, Mining

40.74 percent of all survey participants say their recent library hires are "not at all prepared" when it comes to data modeling, warehousing, and mining. Another 16.05 percent say they are "minimally prepared," and just 8.64 percent say they are either "prepared" or "well prepared." Broken out by public or private status, the public schools find their hires to be less prepared, as 50 percent say they are "not at all prepared," compared to just 24.14 percent of private schools who rate their library hires the same way. While between 52.5 and 55 percent of participants with at least 10,000 enrolled students rate their hires as "not at all prepared," just 19.35 percent of those participants with less than 10,000 students say the same.

Information Systems Analysis

Just 2.47 percent of all survey participants say their recent library hires are "well prepared" in information systems analysis, with only another 7.41 percent categorizing them as "prepared." A large chunk (39.51 percent) says they are "not at all prepared" here. Hires at research universities are the least prepared, as just 6.67 percent are "minimally prepared" or better, as compared to community colleges where this figure is 40 percent. While nearly half (46.15 percent) of the public schools in the sample say their recent hires are "not at all prepared" in these abilities, just 27.59 percent of private schools say the same. A similar gap arises when the data is broken out by total student enrollment: 22.58 percent of participants with less than 10,000 students rate them as "not at all prepared," while 48-53 percent of participants with 10,000 students or more say the same.

Programming Languages and Applications

Just about half (45.68 percent) of all survey participants say their recent library hires are "not at all prepared" in terms of programming languages and applications. Only 7.41 percent say they are either "prepared" or "well prepared," none of which are research universities or MA-/PhD-granting universities. While 69.23 percent of public schools say their hires are either "not at all prepared" or "minimally prepared," only 41.38 percent of private schools in the sample categorized their hires the same way. More than half (57.69 percent) of all participants with an annual tuition of less than $8,000 responded with "not at all prepared."

Relational Database Design

Only 6.17 percent of all survey participants say their recent library hires are either "prepared" or "well prepared" when it comes to relational database design. 40.74 percent say they are "not at all prepared," including 64.71 percent of those with more than 20,000 students and 48.08 percent of public schools in the sample. 47.83 percent of MA-/PhD-granting colleges and 46.67 percent of research universities categorized their recent hires this same way, too.

OCLC Systems and Services

A respectable 22.22 percent of all survey participants say their recent library hires are "prepared" in OCLC systems and services. 23.46 percent say they are "minimally prepared," and 18.52 percent deem them to be "not at all prepared" in this area. 40 percent of all community colleges in the sample say their hires are "well prepared," by far the highest percentage among all types of colleges (the next closest was 6.67 percent for the research universities). Hires at public schools were much more prepared than those at private schools, as 36.54 percent of the former were either "prepared" or "well prepared," compared to just 13.79 percent of the latter.

Digital Libraries and Collections

23.46 percent of all survey participants say their recent library hires are "prepared" in digital libraries and collections, although just 1.23 percent say they are "well prepared." The greatest number cites them to be "minimally prepared," constituting 24.69 percent of the entire sample. Broken out by total student enrollment, it is the library hires at the largest schools in the sample (those with more than 20,000 students) that are seemingly the least prepared, as 41.18 percent of them are categorized as "not at all prepared." The next closest percentage for this answer belongs to the smallest schools (less than 10,000 students) at 16.13 percent. While 34.48 percent of participants in the $8,000 to $18,000 annual tuition range say their hires are either "prepared" or "well prepared," just 19.23 percent of those in the less than $8,000 range and an identical 19.23 percent of those in the more than $18,000 range say the same.

Practicum: Experimental Learning

The largest percentage of survey participants say their recent library hires are "minimally prepared" with an experiential learning practicum. Another 17.28 percent say they are "not at all prepared" in this respect, with just 16.05 percent saying they are either "prepared" or "well prepared." 4-year degree granting colleges seem to have the greatest experience here, as 15.79 percent answered "prepared" and 10.53 percent answered "well prepared." 47.83 percent of MA-/PhD-granting colleges and 46.67 percent of research universities answered with "minimally prepared," the two highest percentages in this category for any answer. 58.82 percent of those participants with more than 20,000 students also categorize their library hires as "minimally prepared" in this area, as compared to just 19.35 percent of those participants at schools with less than 10,000 students.

Information Storage, Retrieval, and Architecture

A third of the entire sample says their recent library hires are "minimally prepared" in information storage, retrieval, and architecture. Another 20.99 percent cites them to be "not at all prepared," leaving just 9.88 percent answering either "prepared" or "well prepared." Private schools rated significantly better here, with 17.24 percent saying their hires are at least "prepared," while just 5.77 percent of public schools answered this same way. 42.31 percent of schools with an annual tuition less than $8,000 say their hires are "minimally prepared" in this department, compared to 26.92 percent of those schools with an annual tuition of more than $18,000.

Social Networking and Information

27.16 percent of all survey participants rate their recent library hires as "prepared" when it comes to social networking, with another 11.11 percent saying they are "well prepared." Only 8.64 percent say these hires are "not at all prepared," although nearly a fifth (19.75 percent) say they are "minimally prepared." No participants with less than 10,000 students responded with "not at all prepared," while 17.65 percent of those with more than 20,000 students responded just that way. However, 32.26 percent of the former group and 29.41 percent of the latter rated their respective hires as "prepared," while "well prepared" was rated by another 9.68 and 11.76 percent, respectively. 38.46 percent of participants with an annual tuition less than $8,000 say their hires are "minimally prepared" when it comes to social networking, compared to just 3.45 percent of those participants in the $8,000 to $18,000 tuition range.

Electronic Publishing and Scholarly Communication

A third of all participants rate their recent library hires as "minimally prepared" in terms of electronic publishing and scholarly communication. Another 16.05 percent say they are "not at all prepared." While 17.28 percent say they are "prepared," just 1.23 percent says they are "well prepared." 26.32 percent of all 4-year degree granting colleges in the sample responded with "prepared," while no community colleges or research universities responded this way. Broken out by public or private status, the private schools maintain a slight edge here, with 24.14 percent saying their hires are either "prepared" or "well prepared," compared to 15.38 percent of public schools that say the same. Furthermore, 40.38 percent of the latter say their hires are "minimally prepared" in this department, while just 20.69 percent of the former answered this way.

Principles of Historical and Contemporary Bibliographic Control

Just about half (49.38 percent) of all survey participants say their recent library hires are either "minimally prepared" or "not at all prepared" in the principles of historical and contemporary bibliographic control. This includes 65.22 percent of all MA-/PhD-granting colleges in the sample and 60 percent of all research universities. While 26.92 percent of public schools say their hires are "not at all prepared" in these principles, about half that percentage (13.79 percent) of private schools say the same. Still, 21.15 percent of the former say they are either "prepared" or "well prepared," compared to just 13.79 percent of the latter.

CHAPTER 1: RESOURCES DESCRIPTION AND ACCESS

With the new Resources Description and Access (RDA) cataloging rules that will be formally adopted by the Library of Congress and other national libraries, what has your library done to prepare for this transition?

1. As the only cataloger, I am trying to get as much training and I can digest. I have also worked with our ILS vendor to ensure that RDA fields will display and so that I can work to edit the display of records.
2. Read listserves diligently.
3. I have attended a numbers of online webinar workshops provided by our consortium plus keep current via listservs.
4. Read listservs, articles, presentations, meet with each other to discuss.
5. Training for staff (webinars for all staff, sent cataloger to workshop so she could train our staff).
6. We have adapted our copy cataloging procedures so that we can accept RDA records, and have worked with our ILS vendor to make sure new MARC fields and subfields introduced to accommodate RDA function properly.
7. Training to ensure there is at least a minimum level of RDA MARC literacy by providing training on: FRBR & FRAD principles, Linked data model, MARC Standards changes (new MARC21 tags). Refresh AACR2 principles for: access points, transcribing data and chief sources of information, knowing what you are cataloguing (and ordering). Liaison and service commitment request from ILMS vendor to enable RDA associated MARC tags and indexing.
8. The District cataloging librarians discuss the transition of new rules.
9. Attended RDA webinars, update sessions at ALA, and general overview of the differences between RDA and AACR2 at state conference and at ALA pre-conference.
10. Read, coordinate a webinar and subscribe to RDA.
11. We have attended workshops and made adjustments in our ILS and cataloging procedures.
12. We have had several short training sessions for copy catalogers and public services librarians and a full week-long training for original catalogers.
13. I've taken whatever free training has been available to me.
14. Increased knowledge through research and workshop attendance and books.
15. Attended webinars.
16. The one remaining catalog librarian has taken courses. Minor display changes to the ILS. We are allowing the RDA records to come into the system via copy cataloging. Catalog Librarian will be moving to all original cataloging in RDA by the end of the fiscal year 2013, July 1, 2013. The others who are doing cataloging will be moving more slowly toward that end. All will be transitioned by March 31, 2014.
17. We've done some online workshops, but until it is fully implemented, we've not done much. As part of a larger university system, many of the cataloging protocols are decided upon as a larger group and not by individual libraries.
18. Monitor AutoCat and RDA lists. LOC RDA training materials. I also plan to take an online class.
19. We have watched several webinars on RDA rules. Also we belong to a consortium of academic libraries in IL (CARLI) which has a wikispace focused on RDA training sources. The catalogers at our library have had 1 meeting about RDA training.
20. Training.
21. Participated in Lyrasis workshops, LC sponsored online webinar courses, created a transition planning team, set up a time line for incorporating RDA in our workflows.
22. I have attended a number of workshops and webinars. My staff and I have registered for a set of 3 online classes thru our regional library cooperative. These are on original

cataloging on monographs, video recordings and electronic resources.

23. We have been looking at the RDA Toolkit. I have been doing classes and workshops on my own.
24. Online classes on RDA.
25. Had staff members attend local workshops and training when available.
26. We are already cataloging in RDA.
27. We have purchased a single-user subscription to the RDA Toolkit. The cataloger has taken numerous courses in RDA. We will also have an extensive workshop/training day in a couple of weeks to learn RDA with other librarians from institutions within our cluster/consortium.
28. Started readings a lot about the material then train the trainer then train the others.
29. I've done a little reading. We are not very prepared. Haven't seen that we have to be yet.
30. Attend webinars and start its own local RDA training in 2013.
31. Training and verifying our system can load/use the new MARC fields.
32. Attended webinars several years ago; compiling a list of sites to visit and possibly study; relying on the general academic library to lead the transition.
33. Attended online classes and workshops at conferences; purchased RDA in print; trial of RDA Toolkit; procedures LibGuide in progress. Currently in the process of getting a subscription to the Toolkit. We will likely not begin training and implementation in earnest until we have access to the Toolkit.
34. I'm the only professional cataloguer so I have been learning RDA on my own. I provided some training to the copy cataloguers and wrote up an RDA policy for our library. I've also made arrangements with our authority file vendor to get and updated RDA file later in the spring.
35. Preparing our own manuals for copy catalogers. Self-training using RDA Toolkit and list-serve responses.
36. Viewed power point presentations. Monitored listservs.
37. Attended RDA sessions, purchased RDA manuals.
38. Review of Materials; RDA Toolkit; NexGen ILS.
39. Attended webinars, made some basic policy decisions, some training, and some small updates to the ILS to validate new fields and subfields.
40. We have studied LC RDA training materials, attended webinars, drafted workflow documents and conducted training sessions.
41. Attended webinars, attended pre-conferences, attended other information sessions; provided training to all cataloging staff.
42. All training complete; have been cataloging RDA since July 1, 2012; includes all copy and original.
43. Developed a training program, prepared our LMS displays.
44. Attended a few workshops. We are accepting RDA records into the catalog, but we are NOT doing RDA cataloging.
45. Monographs Cataloger has gone to training sessions on RDA. Electronic resources librarians have monitored the progress of RDA via listservs and professional readings, but have not yet attended any formal training sessions on RDA.
46. Attended webinars, read the literature, updated our ILS load tables to accommodate changes in bib and authority records. Cataloged some materials in RDA.
47. Attended multiple workshops on RDA, purchased the RDA and access guide to the RDA.
48. In-house training, database clean-up.
49. Beginning staff training; some testing of RDA records in our ILS to be sure they display properly.
50. Mostly educational - keep current with what going on with implementation. Waiting to start using RDA.
51. Attended some training webinars.
52. Nothing.

53. Acquired books, subscribed to RDA kit, attended consortia sessions.
54. Attend webinars; will have library-wide presentations in the future.
55. Reading up on FRBR.
56. Attended online workshops, subscribe to RDA materials. Lots of discussion and training.
57. Webinar training and worked on procedures that cover how rad affects the display of records.
58. We have undergone training for catalogers, provided updates and minimal raining for public services, are in the process of researching and adjusting settings and indexing in the ILS to accommodate RDA data.
59. Attended some webnairs.
60. Nothing.
61. Very little. We've readied the changes but have not taken any steps to integrate with them at this time.
62. Set up training modules.
63. Webinars, purchased RDA Toolkit.
64. Cataloging staff has taken various courses, both online and at conferences (MLA, OLAC).
65. Webinars, purchased RDA toolkit.
66. Amended OPAC display rules; developed local practices for editing headings to be compatible with AACR2 headings.
67. Cat Dept has had RDA training (several in-depth webinars), Systems installing new release of ILS software, planning a library-wide session on RDA for non-catalogers.
68. Taken some webinars and joined a vendor based email list.
69. We have stayed updated with the latest development by email, the Library of Congress website, and by workshops.
70. Starting preliminary work on in-house copy cataloging manual.
71. Viewed webinars about RDA; read articles, books and list messages; studied training materials; attended sessions at conferences; checked ILS updates for accommodation of new rules and fields; made changes to copy cataloging procedures for acceptance of RDA records from LC and pcc; and subscribed to RDA toolkit.
72. Preliminary research, attended information sessions given by library consultants.
73. Nothing.

Table 1.1: How will RDA impact the cataloger's role in future library decisions?

	No Response	Strongly Enhance	Enhance	Not Really Enhance	Detract
Entire Sample	1.23%	2.47%	29.63%	60.49%	6.17%

Table 1.2: How will RDA impact the cataloger's role in future library decisions? Broken out by Type of College

Type of College	No Response	Strongly Enhance	Enhance	Not Really Enhance	Detract
Community College	0.00%	0.00%	60.00%	40.00%	0.00%
4-Year Degree Granting College	2.63%	0.00%	23.68%	68.42%	5.26%
MA or PHD Granting College	0.00%	4.35%	34.78%	60.87%	0.00%
Research University	0.00%	6.67%	26.67%	46.67%	20.00%

Table 1.3: How will RDA impact the cataloger's role in future library decisions? Broken out by Public or Private Status

Public or Private Status	No Response	Strongly Enhance	Enhance	Not Really Enhance	Detract
Public	1.92%	3.85%	36.54%	50.00%	7.69%
Private	0.00%	0.00%	17.24%	79.31%	3.45%

Table 1.4: How will RDA impact the cataloger's role in future library decisions? Broken out by Total Student Enrollment

Total Student Enrollment	No Response	Strongly Enhance	Enhance	Not Really Enhance	Detract
Less than 10,000	0.00%	0.00%	16.13%	77.42%	6.45%
10,000 to 20,000	3.03%	3.03%	33.33%	57.58%	3.03%
More than 20,000	0.00%	5.88%	47.06%	35.29%	11.76%

Table 1.5: How will RDA impact the cataloger's role in future library decisions? Broken out by Annual Tuition

Annual Tuition	No Response	Strongly Enhance	Enhance	Not Really Enhance	Detract
Less than $8,000	3.85%	0.00%	30.77%	50.00%	15.38%
$8,000 to $18,000	0.00%	0.00%	34.48%	65.52%	0.00%
More than $18,000	0.00%	7.69%	23.08%	65.38%	3.85%

Table 2.1: Has there been an increase in funds for your training in RDA and its effects on the library catalog?

	Yes	No
Entire Sample	7.41%	92.59%

Table 2.2: Has there been an increase in funds for your training in RDA and its effects on the library catalog? Broken out by Type of College

Type of College	Yes	No
Community College	0.00%	100.00%
4-Year Degree Granting College	7.89%	92.11%
MA or PHD Granting College	4.35%	95.65%
Research University	13.33%	86.67%

Table 2.3: Has there been an increase in funds for your training in RDA and its effects on the library catalog? Broken out by Public or Private Status

Public or Private Status	Yes	No
Public	7.69%	92.31%
Private	6.90%	93.10%

Table 2.4: Has there been an increase in funds for your training in RDA and its effects on the library catalog? Broken out by Total Student Enrollment

Total Student Enrollment	Yes	No
Less than 10,000	6.45%	93.55%
10,000 to 20,000	9.09%	90.91%
More than 20,000	5.88%	94.12%

Table 2.5: Has there been an increase in funds for your training in RDA and its effects on the library catalog? Broken out by Annual Tuition

Annual Tuition	Yes	No
Less than $8.000	15.38%	84.62%
$8,000 to $18,000	3.45%	96.55%
More than $18,000	3.85%	96.15%

What are your initial first impressions of RDA?

1. It is overwhelming.
2. RDA starts out looking simple, but it isn't. Even what might be seen as a straightforward field becomes extremely complex when the new rules are applied.
3. More work and more details.
4. Some of it makes sense, some does not.
5. A move in the right direction! Focuses more on what the user needs than on how the cataloger wants to present it.
6. The change in organization of the rules from the format-based arrangement of AARC2 makes sense; but much of the actual content seems to have been developed with little consideration of the practical implications.
7. Half-baked and unrealizable given: 1. incomplete content standards for all types of resources currently being acquired and described; 2. the resistance by ILMS vendors to develop and make available RDA data architecture and a virtual user interface (call it an OPAC for now) so staff can see the FRBRised effects of changed metadata content standards.
8. Workable.
9. Incredibly convoluted and difficult to read.
10. Too theoretical, less practical.
11. Getting a handle on the new terminology will take some time.
12. Not much has changed.
13. I appreciate its aspirations for linking data. I won't be able to partake of original cataloging using is for sometime (unfortunately) do to lack of access to RDA toolkit & training.
14. Resistance to changing an existing system that functions well.
15. It's a different paradigm. The learning curve will be significant to transition staff to RDA. It leaves a lot to cataloger's judgment so policies will need to be created for consistency but that consistency may only be internal. The real benefit of RDA will only come in a relational database with linked records.
16. Looks good on paper but implementation will be difficult.
17. Too loose interpretation of rules.
18. The rules seem not fully fleshed out, but I think the goal of more accurately reflecting the content is a good goal. I hope it will make cataloging electronic/digital items easier.
19. Too little, too late.
20. It's good that they reflect FRBR principles but the lack of the gmd (for the format) in the 245 field is a real loss and a big mistake.
21. It seems very similar to the current AACR2 instructions, much more difficult to navigate RDA Toolkit (at first blush).
22. I hope that it does work better with new data frameworks and make cataloging data more web accessible. It doesn't seem too far from our old cataloging rules of AACR2.
23. It seems like more theory than actual practical cataloging. Some of the rules are difficult to interpret.

24. Some rules are very good and the theory behind them sound but some items feel as extra work that may not ever be harnessed through discovery systems similar to the MARC codes that haven't been used well in ILS.
25. That it has some good points and some bad ones.
26. It will allow for more flexibility in the types of cataloging data; it will allow more useful information in name authority records.
27. That is was very different. Now I see it as incremental.
28. Initial first response is that it seems confusing and does not get down to the bare essentials of what catalogers will need to be doing. The language is cumbersome and not clear.
29. I like it.
30. I'm torn. I'm glad things will read easier for patrons, but it is a big imposition on all the things that go on in the background.
31. Positive. Some rules seem more natural than current AACR2 rules. To truly benefit from RDA rules, I think cataloging tools (ILS forms, OCLC's Connexion, etc) need to change more in order to deal with description of works and manifestations better. A move a way from the MARC format would be beneficial for catalogers using RDA rules too.
32. It's more complicated to use than AACR2 without a lot of benefit.
33. Confusing.
34. It will not change the current procedures of cataloging that radically, but the implications of what future systems will be able to do with the data is more radical. Until MARC is replaced we will not be able to see the full effects of RDA.
35. I think that it is a step in the right direction and long overdue.
36. The work-improvement ratio doesn't seem balanced. There's more work going into cataloging than is reflected in the improvements.
37. May be lots more data entry for the cataloger but may be less decisions to ponder.
38. Good.
39. I like some things, especially the fullness of some descriptions, but I think some things should be format specific, such as the 337, 338, and 339 should be video and audio specific.
40. Students and public service staff may like to see abbreviations spelled out.
41. Some of the rules are good, some of the rules are bad. And it is hard to come up with a good analysis until we are able to catalog in a FRBR environment.
42. Crap.
43. Not much of an improvement, and we fear some negative impact on our users.
44. Not impressed at all. We can already build relationships among entities without the sketchy instructions on how to do it in RDA.
45. Some aspects seem clear-cut while other aspects seem confusing.
46. RDA won't be worth the effort until we get the replacement for MARC, and a lot of reprogramming for library systems, and utilities such as OCLC.
47. Very confusing. I find it very hard to find the basic information I need to catalog while wading through the often abstruse verbiage.
48. Looks like it will help make library data more machine-readable and ready for the Semantic Web.
49. I don't see that it will enhance the catalog in any way, and is not worth the training time and expense to implement it.
50. We won't really see its potential until we're past MARC format.
51. Very hard to read and apply. Very different conceptual framework than AACRs. Hard to see what the benefit will be especially since we still have to use MARC encoding.
52. Premature, no vendor or schema to carry application of rules.
53. I have always been frustrated with AACR2 limiting the number of contributors to a work. to 3. RDA will let us add data with no limitations which is a marked improvement in cataloging practices since computers are much more expansive than card files.
54. Waste of time.

55. First impression a couple of years ago was negative; too different, the RDA Toolkit was hard to use, etc. That first impression has changed.
56. Reframing same issues as with AACR2.
57. Unimpressed.
58. Workable, but a little confusing.
59. Mixed. Parts are good, especially for electronic. Others seem less user friendly and patron friendly.
60. Excited about the possibilities.
61. It has great potential if an appropriate infrastructure can be created to take advantage of it. And if someone will force the ILS vendors to do more than just add display features for the new RDA data.
62. For the most part my reaction has been "mixed" with a side of "negative." I think AACR2 needed to be radically updated to reconcile cataloging with contemporary realities (print is no longer the dominant format; the card catalog is no longer in existence). So I appreciate that RDA has really tried to be a set of rules that can describe any information resource on its own terms. On the other hand I think the decision to make FRBR so central to RDA was a mistake. Relating "works" and their editions ("expressions") is important but I don't think it needed to form the basis of cataloging. FRBR may be neat to think about but it doesn't really match up with the practical reality of what catalogers actually do: create records (documents) that describe other documents. I would have preferred a set of rules that mirrored the organization of AACR2 more closely: a section on describing things (principles of description, followed by specific rules for each type of document) and a section on access. I like the fact that RDA tries to provide catalogers with a better way of recording and providing access to relationships among entities in the catalog (names to other names, names to documents, documents to other documents, etc.) but I think it was a mistake to try to encode those relationships in the rules themselves. If the language of relationship can be expressed as a thesaurus (as RDA tries to do in its appendices) I think it would be better for those relationships to live in an authority file, just like names and subjects.
63. It is a mess.
64. A standard that is not as innovative as it could have been. More like AACR3.
65. Seems about the same. Mainly improves classifications of the medium "types."
66. Professionally? What a disappointment.
67. Not an adequate solution to what they were trying to address; a poor time to consider this sort of workload change for a threatened cataloging operation.
68. Negative. Overly complicated. Language not patron-friendly.
69. I think some features will simplify cataloging and the appearance of the catalog for the user. I could see the new 3XX fields becoming useful at some point. But since I'm relatively new to cataloging (my first professional job), I am not able to give a very informed opinion about the advantages/disadvantages of RDA over AACR2. But I must admit, it will still be difficult to transition.
70. More labor-intensive; no user benefit.
71. A waste of time and effort; does not go far enough to actually improve intellectual access, e.g. nobody cares if "pages" is abbreviated or written in full.
72. Meh. It's not that different from AACR2, really. I like the addition of access points (no more rule of three), and someday the 33x fields might be useful. I'm looking forward to the Linked Data future.
73. lot of work for little benefit.
74. I first questioned the need for it, but I realized that we needed to update it so information can be better shown to the public.
75. Love it.
76. I understand the concept of having each data element stand alone so that data can be split apart and used in different ways and in by a variety of information providers. This includes the need to stop using abbreviations and to transcribe more information. However, this will greatly impact the amount of time catalogers and cataloging

assistants must spend entering the data.

77. It may help precision searching in libraries with large collections, but is of less use in smaller libraries.
78. Haven't paid any attention to it.

Who will be responsible for training staff and copy catalogers this new method of cataloging (RDA)?

1. I will.
2. Primarily the university that heads our consortium.
3. Me.
4. Head of Cataloging.
5. We will mostly use "train the trainer" model- develop expertise in one person and have that person serve as the expert and provide webinars and less detailed training for the other staff.
6. Cataloging dept head; outside training agencies (Lyrasis, Ohionet, etc)
7. In the first instance external providers; the second phase is for senior metadata staff to work closely with other experienced cataloguers to become culture changers and maintainers.
8. Me.
9. I will.
10. Me.
11. Head Cataloger and Head Technical Services Department.
12. The librarians and P&S staff.
13. I am taking a responsibility -- Head of Cataloging and Metadata Services.
14. Me.
15. Cataloguers.
16. I will.
17. Myself.
18. Department Head.
19. The Catalog Librarian.
20. Not clear, but I suspect I will have a role.
21. I will.
22. I expect it will be the Bibliographic Coordinator (in the Cataloging unit).
23. Manager, Technical Services.
24. Faculty Catalogers and Supervisors.
25. I will. Along with help from online classes and workshops from our regional library cooperative, MCLS.
26. Me.
27. Head of Technical Services.
28. The Cataloging/Metadata Librarian (me).
29. We've used webinars for all staff participation but supervisors will be front-line trainers.
30. I organized training. We used a mix of webinars, workshops, and self-teaching.
31. Cataloger.
32. Myself as the head of cataloguing department.
33. I suppose me.
34. The Cataloging & Metadata Dept Head, and Cataloging Librarians.
35. We're working together.

36. Hopefully the Collection Services and Metadata Librarian if the position is filled.
37. Director of Tech Services (who catalogs) and Catalog Librarian.
38. I will do it. I am the metadata librarian. I am teaching myself RDA.
39. Me.
40. Head of Cataloging.
41. Tech services.
42. Cataloging Librarian.
43. Head of Cataloging.
44. Cataloging unit heads.
45. I will (full time cataloger).
46. I was.
47. Librarian.
48. Catalog Librarian, i.e. ME.
49. Collection Services librarians.
50. I am responsible for training myself.
51. Myself and one other cataloger.
52. Head Librarian.
53. Catalog Librarian.
54. I will (Head of Technical Services).
55. Catalog Librarian.
56. Me.
57. Myself, Head of Discovery Enhancement.
58. Librarians.
59. Me.
60. For original cataloging, the person who has been cataloging using RDA (myself), the Dept. Head, and other faculty members. Ultimately each of our self-directed teams will take over. For copy catalogers, the two staff members who do training for copy catalogers.
61. Probably consortia resources.
62. Myself.
63. Me.
64. Collaborative among our cataloging faculty.
65. Tech services coordinator.
66. Head of Bibliographic management services.
67. Me (cataloging coordinator).
68. Me.
69. The university president; no, the cataloger of course!
70. Library Director.
71. Coordinator for TS.
72. Head of Cataloging/Cataloging Team/Authorities Librarian.
73. I will.
74. Myself, the lone cataloger.
75. Head of Cataloging Dept.
76. Staff will be expected to learn on their own, but on work time.
77. I will.
78. Webinars through Amigos and other vendors.
79. Myself.
80. Good question!
81. I am the only cataloger at my institution and will train my one copy cataloger.
82. Library cataloger.
83. ILS vendor.

Table 3.1: Has the library marketed these new cataloging rules (RDA) outside the library?

	Yes	No
Entire Sample	7.41%	92.59%

Table 3.2: Has the library marketed these new cataloging rules (RDA) outside the library? Broken out by Type of College

Type of College	Yes	No
Community College	40.00%	60.00%
4-Year Degree Granting College	2.63%	97.37%
MA or PHD Granting College	8.70%	91.30%
Research University	6.67%	93.33%

Table 3.3: Has the library marketed these new cataloging rules (RDA) outside the library? Broken out by Public or Private Status

Public or Private Status	Yes	No
Public	11.54%	88.46%
Private	0.00%	100.00%

Table 3.4: Has the library marketed these new cataloging rules (RDA) outside the library? Broken out by Total Student Enrollment

Total Student Enrollment	Yes	No
Less than 10,000	3.23%	96.77%
10,000 to 20,000	9.09%	90.91%
More than 20,000	11.76%	88.24%

Table 3.5: Has the library marketed these new cataloging rules (RDA) outside the library? Broken out by Annual Tuition

Annual Tuition	Yes	No
Less than $8,000	15.38%	84.62%
$8,000 to $18,000	0.00%	100.00%
More than $18,000	7.69%	92.31%

How does your Integrated Library System (ILS) handle these new RDA records?

1. So far so good and I was shown how to edit the display.
2. Nothing looks much different so far. A new ILS will be acquired within the next 2 years.
3. Those in charge seem to have a good handle on it by keeping updated so it seems there are no problems.
4. Without any real issue yet. Name authorities may need work.
5. Fine. We have already loaded RDA records into our system.
6. They have added the fields needed to accommodate the records, but indexing and display issues abound.
7. Passively.
8. Will implement new fields and tags.
9. New fields have been added to ILS profiles, etc. ILS displays have not changed.
10. It handles all of the fields. We are working on the display.
11. Do not know. We have Horizon 7.51.
12. We've added the new fields to the load tables and are in the process of getting the public display to work better with the new fields.
13. Most new RDA information is ignored for now.
14. It handles them but display issues have not been worked out.
15. A sample RDA record demonstrates that the ILS supports RDA to a great extent
16. It does NOT handle any of the new fields and relations established in RDA!
17. We are prepared.
18. Just as it does AACR2.
19. It does fine as long as we still have MARC.
20. Haven't downloaded many records with RDA.
21. Our ILS will upgrade our current version to incorporate new fields and assist us in local enhancements that will work with new RDA fields.
22. We use the open source ILS, Evergreen. Loading RDA records is no problem. We have made a few minor adjustments to show some of the new fields (264, etc.) and are waiting on the larger community to see how we may wish to use the new 3xx fields in our system.
23. It doesn't.
24. It imports them but most of the new fields are not indexed or displayed yet.
25. Without any re-configuration of the ILS, it either marks new MARC fields as "invalid" or deletes them entirely. RDA records do display in the OPAC but some fields, such as the 33x fields, display when perhaps they should not.
26. Badly. The 3xx fields and the 264 do not play well within Innovative Interfaces.
27. It works with them like AACR2. We have had to ask for some changes in what displays, such as the 33x fields.
28. Not started yet.
29. It does not yet.
30. There were some updates and changes made to the existing ILS system to comply with RDA, but it wasn't major.
31. No problem.
32. Our ILS is equipped to handle RDA records.
33. We updated our validation tables so it handles it better than it did at first. I think that the big problem is with the OPAC. The display is terrible.
34. Right now it doesn't - we have to adjust them accordingly. We are in a consortium and the institution that admins the ILS is hesitant to make any changes.
35. The updated version of the catalog has not been issued yet.
36. As any other - the new fields especially the 336, 337, 338 fields are not yet taken into consideration.

37. Not very well. We do not have a next gen catalog or a discovery layer, which would profit the most from RDA.
38. New fields are accepted and displayed as requested by staff.
39. We have been able to change our display to the appropriate fields are displaying. Otherwise, in terms of the catalog, there are no significant changes from AACR2, so there is no difference in how they are handled.
40. It doesn't.
41. With the new 8.2 version of Voyager, all new fields will be supported.
42. It seems to be OK. We use III--Sierra.
43. So far, our ILS has only made rudimentary adjustments for the new fields and sub-fields required. I expect they will be more responsive as the standards develop. We are able to tweak the current system for display as we see fit.
44. We have updated our load tables.
45. So far, yes.
46. No problem that we've seen so far.
47. New indexes have been added to accommodate new fields.
48. Not yet set up.
49. We currently use Millennium. We have had to turn on or off the displays of some of the new fields. Currently our ILS indexes $e and we must changes these to $4 terms instead in order to not lose the data.
50. No clue.
51. Our ILS is set up to handle the new MARC fields, though a couple still need work either in terms of being indexed or making public display decisions. Basically, our system is ready to handle the changes, though it remains to be seen how well.
52. The current ILS will not make an attempt to accommodate the changes.
53. Some fields do not display. We are adding the [gmd].
54. So far very well. There are some fields which need to be added, but in general the ILS has been proactive.
55. It does not display copyright symbols or the publication information in the 264.
56. It appears to have the ability to at least display the data. We are uncertain to what extent indexing can be updated to allow effective searching of both types of records
57. Very lightly. We created new display definitions for the 264 field. Other RDA-specific fields (36x) are currently not visible to our users (unless they choose to look at the "MARC view"). In order for these RDA-specific elements to be really useful they would have to be indexed; since that would mean applying them to the approximately 2 million records in our ILS that are pre-RDA, we have not really made an effort to make use of them.
58. Do not know yet.
59. Can accommodate new fields.
60. Inefficiently at the moment.
61. Very well ... Voyager is terrific.
62. It doesn't.
63. III Millennium: not very well.
64. Treats them same as AACR records.
65. Transparently.
66. We're about to change OPACs, so we're waiting until then to make any public changes. We do need to install a newer version of the ILS software to handle all the RDA records.
67. OK--SIRSIdynix is trying to integrated new fields into upgrades.
68. We are a Voyager Library and we are part of consortium Keystone Library Network and we have updated our Tag Tables to reflect the new MARC fields.
69. Good question!
70. Our system has updated the programming to accommodate each new field that has been added to MARC. However, I am not yet sure about how the public catalog will be

able to handle the new 336, 337, 338 fields.

71. Fields are loaded into the system; display in bibliographic records is controlled locally; no new search limits yet.

72. Unknown.

CHAPTER 2: THE FUTURE OF CATALOGING

Table 4.1: As a cataloger, how does the future of cataloging look to you?

	Good	Stable	Weak	Poor
Entire Sample	20.99%	43.21%	33.33%	2.47%

Table 4.2: As a cataloger, how does the future of cataloging look to you? Broken out by Type of College

Type of College	Good	Stable	Weak	Poor
Community College	20.00%	60.00%	20.00%	0.00%
4-Year Degree Granting College	21.05%	36.84%	36.84%	5.26%
MA or PHD Granting College	21.74%	47.83%	30.43%	0.00%
Research University	20.00%	46.67%	33.33%	0.00%

Table 4.3: As a cataloger, how does the future of cataloging look to you? Broken out by Public or Private Status

Public or Private Status	Good	Stable	Weak	Poor
Public	23.08%	44.23%	30.77%	1.92%
Private	17.24%	41.38%	37.93%	3.45%

Table 4.4: As a cataloger, how does the future of cataloging look to you? Broken out by Total Student Enrollment

Total Student Enrollment	Good	Stable	Weak	Poor
Less than 10,000	19.35%	48.39%	25.81%	6.45%
10,000 to 20,000	18.18%	42.42%	39.39%	0.00%
More than 20,000	29.41%	35.29%	35.29%	0.00%

Table 4.5: As a cataloger, how does the future of cataloging look to you? Broken out by Annual Tuition

Annual Tuition	Good	Stable	Weak	Poor
Less than$8,000	26.92%	34.62%	34.62%	3.85%
$8,000 to $18,000	17.24%	55.17%	27.59%	0.00%
More than $18,000	19.23%	38.46%	38.46%	3.85%

Table 5.1: Has the library spent more on cataloging over the past five years?

	Significantly More	Somewhat More	About the Same	Somewhat Less	Significantly Less
Entire Sample	2.47%	1.23%	48.15%	38.27%	9.88%

Table 5.2: Has the library spent more on cataloging over the past five years? Broken out by Type of College

Type of College	Significantly More	Somewhat More	About the Same	Somewhat Less	Significantly Less
Community College	20.00%	20.00%	40.00%	0.00%	20.00%
4-Year Degree Granting College	0.00%	0.00%	50.00%	39.47%	10.53%
MA or PHD Granting College	0.00%	0.00%	65.22%	30.43%	4.35%
Research University	6.67%	0.00%	20.00%	60.00%	13.33%

Table 5.3: Has the library spent more on cataloging over the past five years? Broken out by Public or Private Status

Public or Private Status	Significantly More	Somewhat More	About the Same	Somewhat Less	Significantly Less
Public	3.85%	1.92%	50.00%	34.62%	9.62%
Private	0.00%	0.00%	44.83%	44.83%	10.34%

Table 5.4: Has the library spent more on cataloging over the past five years? Broken out by Total Student Enrollment

Total Student Enrollment	Significantly More	Somewhat More	About the Same	Somewhat Less	Significantly Less
Less than 10,000	3.23%	0.00%	54.84%	32.26%	9.68%
10,000 to 20,000	0.00%	3.03%	51.52%	36.36%	9.09%
More than 20,000	5.88%	0.00%	29.41%	52.94%	11.76%

Table 5.5: Has the library spent more on cataloging over the past five years? Broken out by Annual Tuition

Annual Tuition	Significantly More	Somewhat More	About the Same	Somewhat Less	Significantly Less
Less than $8,000	7.69%	3.85%	46.15%	30.77%	11.54%
$8,000 to $18,000	0.00%	0.00%	58.62%	37.93%	3.45%
More than $18,000	0.00%	0.00%	38.46%	46.15%	15.38%

If there has been a shift in resources at the library away from cataloging to which library needs have these resources been reallocated?

1. Purchasing of electronic materials.
2. No shift so far.
3. Ours has been the opposite where our cataloging costs have gone up so funds have been taken away from other resources to cover this. Partially because our overall budget has either gone down somewhat or remained the same.
4. Electronic resources and digital collections, but this is really cataloging also.
5. Digitization projects and collections. It's not that we are doing less cataloging - more that we can batch process our work now and that we are realizing that things don't have to be perfect -- "good enough" is good enough! This has not been easy for many of our staff. Some still struggle!!
6. Monographs acquisitions and management of subscribed digital / online resources.
7. No.
8. Electronic resources.
9. Cataloging resources have been reallocated toward remote storage facilities. Our staff have spent many hours cleaning up records and packing materials to be shipped to our joint remote storage facility that we share with another university. They will start again for a new one shared by different libraries in our consortium and theirs starting this spring.
10. Not to the libraries.
11. Some staff have been shifted to public areas.
12. Digital collections.
13. Research and Instruction Librarians and Marketing staff.
14. IT... and I think this is obviously a grave mistake.
15. To electronic resources/databases, but there has also been a decrease in funding across the board, so many offices are seeing decreasing resources.
16. It is not money, it is my time. I've had to give copy cataloging to students to spend more time in class presentations and other added duties.
17. Instructional and reference areas.
18. Purchasing e-resources and working out access to them. We're trying to figure out how to deal with the "big deals" in ejournals and ebooks with limited cataloging staff.
19. To more electronic resources.
20. Budget has been cut for the library overall.
21. Electronic Resources, batch eBook purchases.
22. Vacant positions in Cataloging have been reallocated to a "pool" and considered for

use by other units (such as Research Services and Digital Initiatives).

23. No shift away from cataloging.
24. Not really.
25. Nowhere...we just don't have that money anymore.
26. Record maintenance and systems, primarily.
27. Specifically in the library, there is more of a push for greater access to e-resources and electronic services to students. Our library in general saw a reduction in staffing and collection funds this year and that trend is likely to continue due to overall shortages at our institution. The irony is that access to e-resources depends on catalogers, to a great degree.
28. Recently it has just been an overall reduction in staff, not so much a reallocation.
29. Reference
30. E-resources.
31. Library Systems, and Access Services.
32. No.
33. Digital assets and public access.
34. Databases.
35. Electronic resources
36. Materials budget - we can barely keep up with rising costs for databases and subscriptions, and yet the college would like to add new courses of study- including graduate classes!
37. There has been a general shift of resources away from personnel to space and electronic resources.
38. The majority of our resources, after salary and benefits, are going to subscription databases. We do not spend any money on cataloging services. We do all of our own copy and original cataloging.
39. Electronic resources coming in with vendor MARC records.
40. Purchase of additional library materials, especially electronic databases.
41. The cataloging unit has gradually adopted new tasks, and is gradually reducing others. Same staff doing some different things isn't exactly "reallocation," though.
42. Copy catalogers now doing mostly ILL.
43. Digital projects, electronic resource discovery system.
44. I have not noticed a shift in resources. I've seen a shift in the processing. More material is batch processed which increases workloads for all cataloging staff. Yet more and more data is requested to be added to records from outside areas.
45. As staff positions have become vacant some have been reallocated elsewhere in the Libraries but I'm unaware of their new location. Mostly they have been combined to create a new, single, position with changes of responsibility.
46. Electronic resources and digital initiatives.
47. E-resources.
48. Resources have remained stable, though the job is changing and some aspects decrease, while others increase.
49. Access services.
50. Public services.
51. Filling holes in the budget.
52. Technology, instruction.
53. Towards online databases.
54. Public services.
55. Technology, scholarly communications, digitization.
56. Reference.
57. It's not really money, it's a shift in time (which is suppose is money). In my new position, I've been given duties the other cataloger was not (more public service, liaison work). Plus we are looking at more batch processed records.

58. Archival description; metadata.
59. Still within the same department, but more record loads of vendor supplied records, less original and copy cataloging.
60. Lost to budget cuts.
61. Our library has support Cataloging. I know that there will be plenty of work ahead because of a major gift in 2008 and the cataloging of dissertations and theses.
62. Upon retirement of a copy cataloging assistant 8 years ago, the position was changed to Archives/Special Collections assistant.
63. Online full-text journal databases and related software such as citation managers, serials list managers, and OpenURL software
64. No shift.

How would you characterize the future of consortia in cataloging? Do you believe that central consortia cataloging will be the future of cataloging?

1. No.
2. I hope it will be, but I'm not optimistic. It appears that local practices will take over, with much less consistency among cataloging agencies.
3. I think this makes sense although we currently are considering pulling away from this type of cataloging but it is more due to financial reasons (keeping on-campus librarian position) and the lack of having good cataloging in the person currently in the consortia position.
4. Yes.
5. Possibly. But the resources devoted to cataloging "common" stuff are already pretty minimal, given programs like PromptCat (I know it's no longer called that) and the availability of good copy for many other commercially published materials.
6. It may - it depends in part on whether library executives appreciate that there is something distinctive and onerous about arranging and managing metadata for the highest level research institutions and their work. If executives think that vanilla flavored metadata description and workflows will meet all research universities' needs then the future is bleak. Consortia may help however one size will not fit all needs.
7. Yes.
8. I believe consortia will become more important as cataloging becomes more centralized. I think libraries might be headed in this direction.
9. It would help.
10. Consortia cataloging is a possibility but may not work in all instances.
11. Yes, we need to share more of our cataloging resources and not spend as much time with commodity resources.
12. Perhaps, but I work in a subject specific library so there is a need for customization in our catalog.
13. Acceptable and valuable for some libraries.
14. Possibly. I think every library will need to figure out how much attention they want to give to local resources. In academic institutions, there will always be unique resources and I think the best way to catalog those unique resources is by having an on-site cataloger.
15. I think it will continue until something like AI or accurate and intelligent OCR comes along. It's the foreseeable future (5-10 years).
16. Yes.
17. It is a possibility, although this is taking a huge step backwards in my opinion. I wonder if the great catalogers should be moving further up the chain -- to the publishers or CIP.
18. Unsure. I think there will always be a need for cataloging especially for unique collections/archives.

19. Probably.
20. Undecided; perhaps yes because of the advent and popularity of several types of vendors selling discovery systems; which may lead to demise of our consortia. But our consortium requires all libraries to do their own cataloging.
21. Yes.
22. I think it will speed up the process of reducing staff that are currently cataloging for individual institutions and increase the level of work for the individual cataloger.
23. I'd say they are important. We use our consortium to help us broker deals with vendors for various e-resource packages. Perhaps we could set up a way to use a central consortium to provide decent bib records for these packages as well. Here in MI they run a state-wide union catalog which is very successful, provide good training cheaply and coordinate deals between libraries of all types and vendors/publishers.
24. Not any more than currently.
25. I think consortia will dictate cataloging policy for individual libraries but that individual libraries within a consortia will need to have the option for local cataloging of special collections.
26. Yes and no. This will only work well if true union catalogs are used. III's In-reach cataloging requires local boxes / systems / catalogers.
27. Maybe. I think it depends on how libraries keep up with technology, and what libraries will be able to afford.
28. No. It may work for some systems, but not all, due to different local needs.
29. Partially this will be done by central consortia cataloging, but we are concerned about the number of mistakes in cataloging that the central consortium is making on a current cataloging project.
30. Centralized cataloging may play a greater role, yes. However, individual libraries will still need catalogers for local collections/special collections.
31. I think that there is a problem for consortia cataloguing when libraries do not want to do professional level cataloguing either locally or at the consortial level but want to outsource everything. In terms of academic libraries, I do not see there being much of a future there.
32. I don't see this changing much.
33. Yes. I think consortia cataloging will always be important.
34. No.
35. No.
36. Yes, I think that we need to stop touching the record for materials 119 ARL's own, and concentrate on our unique offerings.
37. The OCLC Online Union Catalog will remain important to catalogers around the world.
38. It would depend on the types of library involved. For mainly academic consortia, I don't see many trying to catalog at the consortial level. The MOBIUS consortium in Missouri has 60+ libraries and I don't see how a central cataloging office could be more efficient or cost effective than each library doing their own materials. Especially since many of the institutions have catalogers who do other jobs as well.
39. I hope not! But there is talk in the state about it. I just don't see Georgia Tech, Georgia State, UGA, and of course, ourselves, willingly giving up local enhancements
40. Yes.
41. Probably.
42. We need to take advantage of shared catalog records so we can focus on describing and making available special/unique collections (archival materials, institutional repositories (faculty/student scholarship), etc.)
43. It seems like consortia will be the only way to increase the value of our catalogs and make them more attractive, while not getting a bigger piece of the budgetary pie.
44. It may, but our consortium is not engaged in any such conversation.
45. I hope not.
46. It would make sense that the future would be a central consortium.
47. I think central consortial cataloging (in the cloud?) will be an important feature, but not

    the end all and be all. Also, I can imagine ways in which it could be done well, and ways in which it could be a disaster.

48. Yes, central ordering, edifact invoicing, vendor cataloging loads.

49. Perhaps. Cataloging may change its name and guise over time however you are always going to need smart people to handle the data and workflow. We have a lot of power over information and even with continual restructure and library changes, you cannot get away from the fact that you need knowledgeable people working in the database so researchers can find what is needed.

50. It will be more important. Would be very easy to have a consortia take care of almost all cataloging needs.

51. Yes, consortial/cooperative cataloging will become even stronger.

52. Initial cataloging may be consortial, with local maintenance.

53. Greater role.

54. Consortia are still central, as a source of records and maintaining standards and quality, though there function and worth will be more closely scrutinized.

55. I think that it will be even more important than in the past.

56. Possibly.

57. Yes. Not because of cataloging per se, but because eventually most everything users want will be digital, and only consortia of various types will be able to muster the purchasing power to license them. There will be less need for each library to have its own staff.

58. Do not understand the question. Currently we use OCLC which has been around since the 1970s. It is consortia cataloging.

59. Yes.

60. It is a possibility... but does not seem likely in the near future.

61. Consortia will be critical in the future, with shared cataloging as the norm.

62. Yes. It think it is natural to accept copy for most published items, and focus the work of individual catalogers in the smaller universities on special collections materials, theses, and other institutional or local items for which no copy will exist unless we create it. Let the larger libraries work on original records for mass market materials. I would also hope vendors would create better records, but I'm afraid that it will continue to be a trend to see mass-produced, poor quality vendor records.

63. Bigger role for consortia in future.

64. Cooperative cataloging is good, i.e. OCLC, but until subject cataloging is improved, enhancement at the local level will still be needed.

65. It sure seems to be a trend, particularly in public libraries. I've seen it in community colleges (and other academic libraries) too.

66. No, but vendor based cataloging records will become more common.

67. It is likely that this could happen. I feel that many will relied on their vendors to supply cataloging information.

68. Not involved in consortial cataloging. No opinion.

69. In specific situations, possibly, but not generally.

70. No.

What outreach projects can library catalogers be a part of to increase awareness of what they do?

1. Present at any opportunity to their communities (faculty, staff, patrons, etc.).
2. Have others watch/observe the whole process. We had this happen by chance recently and it opened a few eyes so that those individuals no longer think we just "slap labels on books."
3. Library newsletters,
4. We have not done a good job of that in our library and are currently working on that. I think making the rest of the library aware of changes such as RDA, discussing what it takes to create and mount metadata for digital collections, what authority records are and why (or if!!) they matter to our patrons could be some good starting places. I also think our catalogers need to get out on the public desks to see just how the patrons are using the catalog and collections that have metadata they create. They need to understand what fields really matter and to what degree of specificity they matter.
5. Participate in cross-departmental activities within institution; look for ways to pitch programs to "public-services" focused conferences or tracks within conferences.
6. Partnerships in disseminating awareness and access to their institution's research output. Partnerships with the IT Crowd in harnessing distributed and linked data.
7. Original cataloging of hidden collections.
8. Projects involving non-MARC metadata is a great way to show how our skills are transferable beyond the traditional MARC cataloging environment. Repurposing our MARC metadata is another way to demonstrate the importance of having high quality records.
9. Cataloging and digitizing of unique information resources.
10. We are doing some training sessions on cataloging and metadata across the library and opening our services to anyone who needs them.
11. Information literacy.
12. Archives.
13. Show the cataloging for their special collections that make their cataloging and their libraries unique from anyone else's.
14. I work with a volunteer retired cataloger to help elementary and secondary libraries in their cataloging.
15. Take opportunities to guest lecture in library schools' cataloging classes to present practical information on new trends like RDA. Also, try to present at univ. events (I received a grant to attend ALA conf. so the provost had a research colloquium where I presented a poster session on RDA as discussed in the ALA's CC:DA (I am a member of that committee).
16. We can be stronger activists by demanding to have a place at the table for metadata work on digital projects and institutional repositories.
17. As a tech services librarian, I also work with departments as a liaison on campus, teach classes for my departments and work with our 101 classes in oral and written rhetoric. I'm on several library teams that work with our metadata. I see firsthand how students and faculty use the resources we work on every day. I talk about controlled vocabulary in the sessions I teach and use the catalog to show students how to build better keyword searches.
18. Catalogers need to educate the rest of the staff about their job responsibilities.
19. I spend a lot of my time working with the College Archives and I think explaining how what you do can be used for other things outside of print is important
20. They can become metadata consultants for faculty and staff who have digital projects/data sets to describe.
21. We are constantly trying to insert ourselves into projects like IRs and in special collections. Mixed results.
22. Go to campus events to first promote awareness about the library, and then go into

further detail about our specific duties entail.

23. Consultacy,exchange between institutions.
24. Library catalogers could work more with programmers, web designers, and usability experts to maximize the reuse of library metadata and optimize the description of all library resources throughout our web presence.
25. Working with people creating metadata for non-library resources.
26. Don't know outside of creating metadata for digital objects.
27. Be more involved in committee work; share updates from the world of resource description with public services staff on a regular basis. Offer cataloging workshops or workshops on topics that catalogers are familiar with (searching techniques, etc.)
28. I think that the work of cataloguers can have a greater presence on the library's and university's online environment.
29. Anything that increases awareness of the collection, things that encourage browsing, usability testing of the catalog, offering workshop on trick to use the catalog in ways that are efficient to research, adding classification groups to subject guides.
30. Introduce RDA to the rest of the library.
31. Our catalogers work on the reference desk, and teach library school classes.
32. They should form committees with public service library staff to involve them in making decisions about displays in the online catalog.
33. We have to be better at communicating what we do and why. Assessment is something I'm looking into now.
34. More input in bibliographic instruction.
35. This is important--Be willing to speak up about how and why what we do is important to the reference staff and library users. Explain how information important to users (including other librarians) is incorporated in the record.
36. Maybe a project that shows how using subject terms and keywords affect one's searches or how minimal cataloging creates a lack of descriptive information.
37. Bibframe and other projects to transform catalog data into Linked Data.
38. Projects to enhance access to priority materials, to improve the catalog interface(s), to prioritize solving problems identified by reference and circulation.
39. I invite colleagues and administrators to webinars about linked data and RDF
40. Communication with all levels of your organization is crucial. The more that catalogers are recognized as database organizers and architects by the outside world the more our roles will be recognized as being necessary. We need to change how we present ourselves since few seem to understand how much our work coincides with similar work in the computer industry. At my University we also work closely with Reference staff which has helped our cause significantly.
41. Work at a reference desk and/or work jointly with reference staff to increase their level of understanding. Provide programs or attend meetings of Reference and similar staff and share their knowledge and the impact of their work.
42. Pay more attention to end users and institutional needs.
43. Work with Reference and Marketing staff on campus and conferences.
44. Collaborations with instruction librarians in the classroom.
45. I wish I knew.
46. That is a good question.
47. Link their efforts to findability and instruction.
48. Good question... probably just trying to be users themselves and working through the process of finding materials in the search systems to see how they are retrieved.
49. Working reference desk, letting reference librarians know at meetings what's changing,
50. Work with archives to create consistent metadata for digital collections, work on institutional repositories, catalog small collections around campus.
51. Needs to be integrated into Library instruction. It is easy to show how controlled vocabulary can increase hit accuracy.
52. To make sure that they let the administration know what they are doing.

53. Good questions. Don't have an answer.
54. Advanced demonstrations to our student users; presentations to faculty at teaching workshops.

Table 6.1: How much staff time in the past year did your cataloging staff expend in viewing webinars, videos, online tutorials, conferences, formal classroom training and other aids for cataloging education? (in hours)

	Mean	Median	Minimum	Maximum
Entire Sample	49.09	30.00	0.00	320.00

Table 6.2: How much staff time in the past year did your cataloging staff expend in viewing webinars, videos, online tutorials, conferences, formal classroom training and other aids for cataloging education? Broken out by Type of College

Type of College	Mean	Median	Minimum	Maximum
Community College	35.00	45.00	0.00	60.00
4-Year Degree Granting College	58.69	30.00	0.00	320.00
MA or PHD Granting College	32.03	25.75	0.00	100.00
Research University	54.25	35.00	13.00	200.00

Table 6.3: How much staff time in the past year did your cataloging staff expend in viewing webinars, videos, online tutorials, conferences, formal classroom training and other aids for cataloging education? Broken out by Public or Private Status

Public or Private Status	Mean	Median	Minimum	Maximum
Public	43.55	27.50	0.00	300.00
Private	59.90	35.00	0.00	320.00

Table 6.4: How much staff time in the past year did your cataloging staff expend in viewing webinars, videos, online tutorials, conferences, formal classroom training and other aids for cataloging education? Broken out by Total Student Enrollment

Total Student Enrollment	Mean	Median	Minimum	Maximum
Less than 10,000	46.34	26.25	0.00	320.00
10,000 to 20,000	40.98	20.00	0.00	200.00
More than 20,000	73.05	50.00	24.00	300.00

Table 6.5: How much staff time in the past year did your cataloging staff expend in viewing webinars, videos, online tutorials, conferences, formal classroom training and other aids for cataloging education? Broken out by Annual Tuition

Annual Tuition	Mean	Median	Minimum	Maximum
Less than $8,000	44.05	25.00	0.00	200.00
$8,000 to $18,000	46.90	32.00	0.00	300.00
More than $18,000	56.68	23.75	0.00	320.00

What should library administrators understand about cataloging that they do not seem to understand?

1. The importance of it! They need to understand that it is not automatic, that it is not a simple task that just any person can do. It takes skill, practice, and attention to detail.
2. The time and detail involved.
3. That quality cataloging is not easy or cheap.
4. There is a need for completeness in the record and accuracy. You have to balance what the patron wants and uses with what will stand the test of time.
5. That publishers aren't going to get into the cataloging business in a meaningful way; that machines can't do everything that needs to be done; that cataloging/providing metadata for the unique/scarce materials we all want to focus on requires more time, and higher level skills which many institutions have lost in pushing "routine" cataloging down to paraprofessionals.
6. That there is a professional and ethical imperative to ensure that information resources held out in the name of supporting a university's work (research, teaching, ongoing learning) are in fact: accessible (the URL/URI are active); accurately described (transcribed accurately); contain appropriate metadata to support discovery and organisation; give best possible support for the world-wide (and local) discovery of research output (such as well formed authorities for names of faculty, departments and centers; representative of the best work of employees who have bought into the university's vision, goals, mission; not outsourced to third parties who do not have the intellectual, and other associations to do the best possible job for the institution and its varied needs.
7. Cataloging class should be required in any Library schools.
8. The analytical work of cataloging must be done by humans.

9. They don't understand why it is so complex or why cataloging training would take so long. To them, discoverability and access is important to users, and they have little patience for the accuracy of what they perceive as minutiae. Quick access by keyword is what matters to them, and they understand little about the need for authority control or what that is in the first place. They also don't understand the division between monographs and serials catalogers, and how one cannot necessarily do the job of the other. They also don't understand why not every cataloger is trained to do all different types of formats and why there is not more cross-training and sharing of these responsibilities.

10. That machines cannot do authority control, controlled vocabulary, accurate description and quality control.

11. That it is a public service and we serve more people than the public desks.

12. It takes more time than they think to catalog an item.

13. The catalog is only as good as the data that goes into it.

14. It is a time-consuming task and continuous professional development is required

15. That cataloging requires judgment based on understanding the rules and the bibliographic universe. Anyone doing cataloging needs to be well-trained and the training needs to be on-going so they stay trained with current practice. Without that, you get a dirty database which makes reports and batch processes very difficult.

16. All data for the OPAC starts in cataloging.

17. That the catalog matters! Catalogers make our catalogs more useable. Catalogers are a vital part of making our resources discoverable.

18. That it IS professional work, and is more than just data input. That, without cataloging, the CIRC and OPAC parts of our ILS would not work.

19. It is important to have accurate access points to aid in research and discovery, and that it takes a significant commitment to provide staff time to do this type of work. Also, keywords are not good enough. A recent discovery system vendor rep stressed the importance of controlled vocabulary in making the system robust and provide opportunities for better search results

20. Takes time to do careful, detailed work.

21. The work we provide assists users to find resources in our collection and that it takes time to produce records that will facilitate this process. The current trend is to provide minimal information for our records, which in turn creates hidden collections and frustration for our library users as they waste time attempting locate resources in our collection.

22. My administrator is very supportive but we are getting more and more squeezed by costs and budget cuts.

23. Cataloging in house is necessary and needs to be done by people who are trained in it. It is not an area that can be outsourced.

24. That it is as important as the public services such as reference and circulation and interlibrary loan.

25. That it can be time consuming and it is for the end user to be able to find things not a single staff member.

26. That authority control as an activity and an operation cannot just be dispensed with in the name of saving money.

27. Its value. As we move to an ever more online environment the catalog becomes public services.

28. That catalogers are essential to the success of a library. If something is not searchable in the online catalog, or if there are catalog problems, that onus is on the cataloger.

29. The intricacy of the job.

30. That you don't just "do it" like flipping a switch or pushing a button or checking something "yes" on a computer screen.

31. It depends on the administrators.

32. Cataloging is a public service, just like reference. Not everyone visiting a library asks questions at the reference/information desk; almost everyone uses the catalog at some point.

33. That good results from searching in the local ILS, local federated catalog (One Search), OCLC, Google, etc. is dependent on good cataloging (GIGO - garbage in, garbage out)
34. That it is critical for resource discovery and that the "devil is in the details"! Things about cataloging that seem arcane and overly particular to some are often very important for resource discovery.
35. In an electronic environment, cataloguing is even more important than ever because users rely on good quality and user-appropriate metadata in order to discover resources that they previously could have found by browsing the shelves or asking at the reference desk (our users don't want to do that anymore). Users want to find and use information on their cell phones and good cataloguing (metadata) is essential for supporting their needs.
36. Access points of a cataloging record are essential to discovery.
37. Everything.
38. The learning curve involved in switching systems. The impact the cataloging records have on the OPAC (hence the students).
39. Discovery layers cannot replace the catalog, because the information they ingest comes from the catalog.
40. Cataloging requires educated staff who exercise their judgment in applying rules and local standards.
41. What we do DOES impact resource discovery.
42. Successful keyword searching depends good cataloging.
43. How labor-intensive the work is. We can't drop what we are doing to move on to the latest "project/publicity opportunity" of the day.
44. Our administrators are very understanding and appreciative of what our catalogers do. They know that cataloging aids discoverability of resources.
45. That bibliographic description and subject analysis are important for web materials as well as tangible materials.
46. That it is essential to creating searchable content that makes searching OPACS more productive for patrons. That taking the time to enter publisher's description, TOC, additional authors, etc creates a better search results for patrons. That cataloging should be done on site to ensure the quality of the records as well as allowing library catalogers to view the materials and use this information in Readers's advisory.
47. The metadata catalogers create is the basis for much of the underlying metadata on the Web, a model for vendor records, and contributes to the future of the Semantic Web
48. It takes time to do it right, and it needs to be done right in order to provide good access to library materials.
49. If I had to pick one thing, it's that shared cataloging doesn't work if every library tries to be a parasite. Records won't be available if nobody is making them.
50. It is integral to the future of linked data on the Internet. Catalogers produce the data elements; they don't just magically appear from some unseen source in the sky.
51. They need to understand that we cannot rely on outsourcing and batch loading to replace the work we do. The more they recognize the specific service we offer, especially tailoring it to our own university population, they will begin to see us as vital. My favorite phrase to tell people is, "Databases don't work without authority control." I've discovered that improving our turnaround time and service to the public has completely changed the mind of our administrators and we are now beginning to be recognized as vital.
52. First, that cataloging and metadata creation are mostly synonymous. Both are working with data to elucidate what a library has and what a library has access to. Second, that cataloging is a core value in the success of making our students, faculty, staff, and other users better educated.
53. Public services sit on top of technical services. If cataloging is underfunded, then eventually public services will deteriorate.
54. A library catalog is only as good as the information that goes into it. Garbage in; garbage out.
55. Not everything can or should be automated.

56. As material types keep expanding, cataloging is more complicated.
57. If they want cataloging to be as effective as it should be then it should be done by catalogers who are familiar with the patrons of the library.
58. Cataloging is continually changing and there is a need for support for continuing education. Everything can't be automated, and the quality of the data does affect the services provided by other areas of the library.
59. That an institution's catalog is part of its information infrastructure.
60. It is time consuming if done correctly. We can should not accept any record and push the button.
61. That catalogers enhance records, increase findability--linked to student retention
62. Its all about end user discovery and not the bottom line.
63. Hmm...our dean is a former cataloger ...
64. The value of quality bibliographic information for discovery of resources.
65. My administrators are catalog-friendly.
66. I think my library administration understands cataloging very well. But I would guess most do not appreciate how time-consuming it is to do it right, and that we have a responsibility to fulfill a national standard (not just a locally defined practice). And that an expensive discovery service won't take the place of a well-built catalog.
67. Catalogers will never be productive if they are not required to meet quotas.
68. Catalogers are saddled with national standards that are out of touch with how today's patrons want to find information.
69. Not my dean of course, but many administrators don't realize the complexity involved in original or copy cataloging. Sometimes they think outsourcing cataloging can be cheaper than handling it in-house, but typically what ends up in the backlog needing cataloging is very complex and doesn't lend itself to outsourcing.
70. That irretrievable material is the same as non-existent material and that one size fits all searching (i.e. discovery) is less likely to get the best results which could come from trained searching of different databases.
71. I feel that they do not understand that it takes longer to catalog books and other resources than they realized.
72. Though my administrator understands, others do not seem to understand that good metadata is necessary for the retrieval of information, especially for in depth needs for information, such as for scholars and researchers. This includes authority data, which not only collects items, but provides keywords for searching. Full-text searching has its uses, but in most cases, does not allow for the precise retrieval that good metadata has. We should not base our decisions solely on the practices of the general public and freshmen students, though this seems to be what we are doing.
73. Good cataloging is still a demanding task, even if the numbers of cataloged items declines. The change is not proportional. One has to keep familiar with all cataloging rules, procedures, and software, whether processing 5 or 500 items.
74. Library administrator is the cataloger.

To what extent has technology usurped the need for catalogers and the library catalog?

1. I don't think technology has/can replace a cataloger or the library catalog. If anything technology is a reason for better cataloging.
2. I don't think that it has.
3. Very little, although that may not be a common perception. There is continuous need for both.
4. Lots. Computerized keyword searching has been a game changer, and not everyone wants to admit it. The card catalog is gone, gone, gone, and we don't need to be as precise as we were in the golden days of cataloging, when every item had to be

handled "just so." Couple that with the ability to batch load hundreds if not thousands of records into your catalog at once...you can do so much more now with so many fewer people. It can be a very scary time for catalogers who are afraid to let go of the old model.

5. It hasn't. It does make it more efficient to do some processes for common materials, and batch changes needed for authority control, etc. But the process remains an intellectual one that needs to be done by talented human beings.
6. There has been no usurpation; however, there is a vacuum where catalogers have expected to carry on with work as though there has been no technological change. As if catalogers are not consumers of ICT products? Go figure. Catalogers who understand how metadata in certain contexts should behave and how it is optimally arranged / organized and sourced are required. There is no substitute at this time for an experienced and interested human being's judgment. I'm still waiting for the semantic web (but not holding my breath).
7. Ability to rely on information from automated sources.
8. Discovery layers like Primo are the current trend. We recently implemented Primo and were told that it would eventually replace the catalog as our public interfaace. So this will eventually happen. But it has not usurped the need for catalogers because we're getting rid of MetaLib, so that people will only discover databases if they are in our catalog. Technology has not usurped catalogers or the need for catalogs yet, at least not in my library.
9. About 75%.
10. Some, but the information needs to be input before the technology can use it.
11. Keyword searching makes some cataloging tasks seem not as valuable.
12. Technology compliments the need for cataloguers and the library catalogue rather than replace this specialized service.
13. In some ways it's made catalogers need to be savvier with technology, learning how to use new tools and new ways to use the tools we have.
14. I think the need is still there but cataloging and catalogs must change.
15. We now are able to use student assistants to do low level cataloging.
16. Our library administration and our Head of IT certainly *think* that technology has completely replaced the need for cataloger; however, I say they are dead wrong.
17. The MarcEdit software has made it easier for staff to work with catalog records and could result in administrators thinking catalogers aren't needed; that lower-level staff can load those records & few if any original catalog work needs doing.
18. I don't see that technology has hurt catalogers.
19. It is a two-edged sword. Technology has increased the efficiency that an individual can do in cataloging, however it gives the false impression that it is good data (if we provide minimal work). This will have the effect of redirecting our frustrated users from our collections to other places to find their information.
20. I don't think that's true. I do think we may need to get our data out to our users in a different manner than the traditional catalog. We need mobile apps that search library resources, and display them in an accessible manner. We need to show students how they need to use a variety of resources in their papers and projects. But the metadata that runs all these technology driven tools is still needed. Better ways to link publisher data, library specific data and input from our students, faculty, etc. is really needed.
21. It hasn't - it has actually made our jobs more important.
22. There has been some but if you can adapt and fill in with other roles such as batch uploads, system management or archives then you will be fine.
23. I think the technology is being misused. Vendors provide publisher-supplied metadata for electronic books, but the data does not fill our needs because it does not follow our standards. Discovery systems are largely built on publisher metadata, relegating the library catalog data to a second and sometimes never found layer of discovery. The catalog is becoming an inventory tool rather than a discovery tool.
24. We can share work with each other. We can batch process records.

25. I don't think it has usurped the need for catalogers. If anything, catalogers are still need to sort through the all of the library data and edit electronic records so the everyday user can find what they are searching for.
26. It didn't.
27. It hasn't. Cataloguers are still the reason patrons and library faculty and staff find the items for which they are looking.
28. It hasn't "usurped" the need, just changed our focus form creating records to managing data from a variety of sources, most of which seem to follow different (or no) standards.
29. Technology may have usurped the need for cataloging and the library catalog in some people's minds, but it is a fallacy to believe that catalogers and the catalog should go away. I think libraries who are getting rid of catalogers are paying the price now, or that they will pay eventually in hindered access.
30. It hasn't really. Perhaps old fashioned OPACs have been usurped but our bibliographic databases will continue to be the way that we connect our users with our resources - that includes moving forward into the realm of linked data.
31. Technology has made it easier to share cataloging and to increase access points, but the need is still there for controlled and consistent access points.
32. More available ready-made marc records.
33. To a much smaller extent than projected. Technology can handle the materials everyone owns, but not the unique items.
34. Online catalog technology has eliminated the need to use typewriters to prepare catalog cards, and the need to use people to file cards in card catalogs.
35. I don't think technology has usurped the need for a catalog. I also wouldn't say that it has usurped the need for catalogers, but it has allowed fewer people to do more work.
36. It has made some administrations think that catalogers are not necessary.
37. Somewhat.
38. Not at all. It has made many parts of the job more complex.
39. Technology has reduced the need for catalogers to spend time on repetitive tasks and allowed them to spend more time on complex projects, such as special collections and institutional repositories.
40. Technology has not yet completely obviated the need for local catalogs, and therefore local catalogers. Eventually, something like WorldCat local, plugged into something like Google Books may eliminate us, along with physical libraries.
41. I wouldn't say that it has usurped the need for catalogers, it has shifted our focus to database clean up projects.
42. It has not. Catalogers are the ones who recognize discrepancies and errors, who are willing and able to search further to have the most complete accurate record for patrons. The library is also essential because it allows for local information to be added and for authority control to reside with librarians not workers for outsourcing companies.
43. Services such as Promptcat and vendor-supplied MARC records has eliminated most of the "easy" jobs. Catalogers have had to upgrade their skills to focus on special formats, rare materials, and archival finding aids.
44. It hasn't -- But many administrators don't understand that.
45. No at all - only in the minds of uninformed and ignorant.
46. Our library collection now 90 digital resources, ebooks, digital articles, databases, etc. My work has changed though I still do some original cataloging - mostly websites & some special local materials like academic technology equipment. Also do editing of batch files of ebook records. Catalog still critical as we have federated Primo interface but mostly accessing online materials.
47. Full-text crawling in vendor databases--which still does not meet the need for authority control or cataloging for materials not in full text.
48. I only see technology as increasing the need for catalogers. We have become more efficient and often need less staff than previously but the work our staff do now is much more complicated and difficult than previously. You have to have someone handling the data and the data must be controlled. That's what we do.

49. Technology has both usurped the need for persons to do the work but also made the tasks involved more efficient. I would estimate that the "negative" impact of losing positions due to technological enhancements has been a minimal role, if anything it has allowed institutions to push cataloging responsibilities down into hands of non-professionals such as student assistants. I don't think there is a direct correlation between technology uptick and job loss, rather I think that those making choices about jobs have used technological efficiencies as a reason to do things like no longer fill some kinds of cataloging positions. Perhaps the biggest "technological" impact towards job loss was when the idea of "shelf-ready materials" became widely implemented because the bib. Records come with the materials.

50. Technology has initiated a different set of problems where cataloging has absorbed some acquisitions functions and some public services functions.

51. Not as much as people think.

52. It is illusion to think the need for catalogers and catalogs have been usurped. We need to work with the technologies and we need to market ourselves and the value of libraries better. Users assume less need for libraries because they don't always understand what libraries provide.

53. To the extent that it is easily accessible and most people have a search engine as their homepage.

54. not much

55. I wouldn't say "usurped" but transformed. Just like we no longer require librarians to have perfect handwriting, we no longer need catalogers who just painstakingly create record after record and file it away forever. They need to be able to understand the implications of controlled, bibliographic metadata, and how to manage it over the long term.

56. It has not usurped the need for us. Our administrators seem to think so, because of OCLC, outsourcing, etc. They fail to recognize that a cataloger is needed to create the record in OCLC, etc.

57. Quite a bit....

58. Common records and beyond that the assumption that "its all out there somewhere" to download or Google.

59. Users tend to grab whatever comes first not necessarily what is the best resource.

60. The library catalog is still essential, but with outsourcing and shared cataloging, the need for catalogers has decreased.

61. Your question implies that it already has, to some degree, usurped catalogers and the catalog--an implication not everyone will agree with. I think technology has allowed catalogers to work more efficiently, and has freed their time (to some extent) to do even more cataloging, to add hundreds of records at a time, and alter them all with the press of a button. I think it has made us, to some extent, database managers, and not the same, traditional catalogers. So in this sense, technology has not usurped catalogers, it has just altered their roles. The catalog is still the inventory of the physical, and in many cases, the inventory of the purchased electronic items. As an inventory database, it is still the same. Discovery systems still need it as a foundation to locate items 'owned'. Its role also has changed--it's no longer the discovery tool it used to be. But it is still necessary to connect those other tools/layers/what-have-you to the items we actually own. It can be as useful and necessary as we make it to be. But doing so involves our time, effort, and expertise. Hard to justify when all that knowledge and experience dies or retires, and it seems easier and cheaper to replace with a 'service'. But it only seems that way.

62. To a great extent.

63. Very little; garbage in, garbage out. In theory full-text indexing of every book could supplant the library catalog, but has not been achieved and access to those books is limited. Use of Google Books diverts attention away from hardcopy resources that are readily available.

64. More routine tasks are no longer needed (like filing catalog cards), plus the catalog is no longer the only database containing library materials. I think catalogers are still

needed, but in a variety of settings beyond the book catalog.

65. In some ways, it has made them more important, especially in being able to understand and troubleshoot retrieval issues.
66. I feel that technology has enable us to do a better job with our work and we can more done than we did in the past prior to computers and online systems.
67. I don't think it has.
68. Very significantly. Keyword searching of full text is very helpful for most users. Keyword searching in Google Books or Amazon, accompanied by interlibrary loan, often gives better results for users than OPAC searching. Journal access via licensed databases is becoming more important in academic environments. Access provided by bibliographic records and the Web OPAC is woefully outdated in comparison with other online searches.
69. No usurpation.

Table 7.1: How do other librarians view catalogers?

	Essential	Needed	Somewhat Needed	Not Needed
Entire Sample	25.93%	39.51%	30.86%	3.70%

Table 7.2: How do other librarians view catalogers? Broken out by Type of College

Type of College	Essential	Needed	Somewhat Needed	Not Needed
Community College	20.00%	60.00%	0.00%	20.00%
4-Year Degree Granting College	28.95%	26.32%	42.11%	2.63%
MA or PHD Granting College	21.74%	47.83%	30.43%	0.00%
Research University	26.67%	53.33%	13.33%	6.67%

Table 7.3: How do other librarians view catalogers? Broken out by Public or Private Status

Public or Private Status	Essential	Needed	Somewhat Needed	Not Needed
Public	25.00%	38.46%	30.77%	5.77%
Private	27.59%	41.38%	31.03%	0.00%

Table 7.4: How do other librarians view catalogers? Broken out by Total Student Enrollment

Total Student Enrollment	Essential	Needed	Somewhat Needed	Not Needed
Less than 10,000	32.26%	38.71%	25.81%	3.23%
10,000 to 20,000	21.21%	45.45%	33.33%	0.00%
More than 20,000	23.53%	29.41%	35.29%	11.76%

Table 7.5: How do other librarians view catalogers? Broken out by Annual Tuition

Annual Tuition	Essential	Needed	Somewhat Needed	Not Needed
Less than $8,000	26.92%	38.46%	26.92%	7.69%
$8,000 to $18,000	24.14%	44.83%	27.59%	3.45%
More than $18,000	26.92%	34.62%	38.46%	0.00%

CHAPTER 3: PERSONNEL ISSUES

At your institution, what basic responsibilities and job requirements are listed in a cataloger's job description?

1. Adding and deleting records as needed, reviewing records to ensure they are correct & to make changes as needed, use copy cataloging when possible to avoid time spent on original cataloging, and then do original cataloging when time permits.
2. MLS, knowledge of cataloging rules, knowledge of evolving technologies and rules, continuing education, attending workshops & Webinars.
3. Original and copy cataloging, metadata creation, supervise students.
4. Copy catalogers (paraprofessionals) identify usable records in OCLC, edit those records as needed, assign classification if necessary. If a full record is not available for the format in hand, but complete record can be found for the same work in another format (VHS for DVD, for example), copy catalogers may derive a new record for the new format. Department head is only MLS in the unit; does original cataloging and upgrading of minimal records; does batch loads of records for electronic packages, government documents, etc.
5. Accurate bibliographic description; Headings conform to local / international authority file; know what you are describing (what is in your hand); knowledge of relevant standards (AACR2, MARC21, local MARC standards, LCRI, LC Authorities, BIBCO minimum record, conventions for cataloging in network such as Worldcat).
6. Reference skills --- odd but that's how they bulletin the jobs.
7. Original cataloging, copy cataloging, understanding of accepted standards, ability to make good judgments.
8. Cataloging and classification schemes and rules are required. Catalogers are responsible for original cataloging: description, subject assignment, authorities creation and classification.
9. Cataloging, authority work, answer questions, work with others.
10. Cataloging physical collections Creating metadata records for digital collections
11. MLIS, but cataloger must wear many hats so it's wide ranging in terms of library responsibilities.
12. MLS.
13. Staff: 4 year college degree, 2 years general office experience, analytical ability, attention to detail, organizational skills, accuracy, and ability to prioritize. Keyboarding and data entry. 25+ WPM typing speed. They do copy cataloging.
14. Responsible for original and copy cataloging, maintain ILS database and operation, develop workflow and processing (physical and electronic) routines. Instruct staff in use of OCLC connexion for copy cataloging.
15. Able to interpret MARC, knowledge of OCLC, knowledge of assigning subjects, working knowledge of using Voyager ILS.
16. 1. Perform original and copy cataloging of monographic and serial materials in all formats. 2. Provide authorized name and Library of Congress Subject Heading access points, which are the basis for end user access to materials in the Library's online catalog. 3. Classify (provide call numbers for) materials using the Library of Congress classification system. 4. Revise (review and correct for accuracy and adherence to policies and procedures) copy cataloging done by Library Assistants. 5. Train Library Assistants and others on cataloging and classification standards and processes. 6. Draft new cataloging policies and procedures. Review and update current cataloging policies and procedures. ** Must be able to use OCLC, III Millennium, Cataloger's Desktop, Classification Web, and have a thorough understanding of MARC 21 and AACR2.
17. Copy cataloging, original cataloging, metadata and digital collection development including institutional repository.

18. Catalog all gifts and purchased materials, provide statistical information, keep authority files and database MARC records, deal with issues that might come up concerning our ILS.
19. Original & complex cataloging of material in various formats (& theses) using OCLC and Voyager. Plan to integrate metadata into current library practices; share duties for authority control. Work with bibliographic control coordinator in staff training, database maintenance, quality control and assessment of cataloging policies. Requires knowledge of cataloging rules & standards (AACR2, MARC21, LCRI, LCSH, LC classification, experience with OCLC & metadata standards.
20. Cataloging, classifying, maintaining the accuracy of records in ILS.
21. Attention to detail, ability to communicate effectively, knowledge of current cataloging rules and practices, knowledge of ILS.
22. Original and copy cataloging in all formats. Database maintenance of the catalog. Knowledge of AACR2 (now RDA training). Ability to work with OCLC, LCSH and LC classification. As the Cataloging librarian, I also teach ENG101 classes, liaison with 2 departments, teach classes for them as requested, do collection development and work the reference desk in the evenings (1x every 3 weeks and 2 Saturdays a semester). All professional librarians have these same duties.
23. Cataloging all materials whether through copy cataloging or original records.
24. Cataloging, authority control.
25. OCLC Connexion, System Management, Work with ILS Vendor, Manage Contentdm, Help at Circ/Ref Desk when needed, Serve on faculty committees, Cataloging with MARC Standard Cataloging with other standards, i.e Dublin Core.
26. Cataloging librarians do not have job descriptions per se. However, I would include original cataloging of items in a particular format; sometimes complex copy cataloging if needed; supervision; project management; problem solving.
27. Performs original and complex copy cataloging. Serves as a professional resource. Works to develop the in-sourcing of cataloging operations. Supervises, trains and evaluates students Participates in policy development
28. Masters of Library Science or equivalent from an ALA accredited institution preferred. Knowledge of AACR2, MARC21, and LC classification and subject headings are essential. Experience with an automated library system such as Innovative Interfaces Inc.'s Millennium/Sierra system preferred.
29. Cataloguing all sorts of material including iPads, Kindles, etc.
30. Cataloguing responsibilities, staff work load responsibilities, acquisitions responsibilities, reference responsibilities, collection management responsibilities.
31. Performs original and complex copy cataloging of library materials. Serves as a liaison to a certain dept/division/branch library and catalogs all materials from that same dept/division/branch library. Participates in original cataloging of all formats and various languages, as well as metadata creation activities in the library as needed. Establishes and revises practices and procedures for providing bibliographic access through various discovery tools in conjunction with other departmental faculty/staff. Identifies, develops, and oversees special cataloging projects, working closely with other library faculty/staff. These duties may include: developing and documenting policies & procedures; maintaining statistics; directing, training, and supervising library and student assistants in project assignments. Responsible for the resolution of cataloging and authority problems to ensure bibliographic and authority records meet local and national standards. Supervises, trains, and helps evaluate cataloging staff. May work with the Metadata Librarians and Digital Library staff to aid in resource description of unique materials. Maintains awareness of general cataloging issues and standards, metadata standards, and librarianship. Demonstrates commitment to user-centered library service and the ability to work flexibly and creatively in a changing and fast-paced environment with a culturally diverse population. Evidence of continued professional development, involvement, and contribution. Serves on/participates in University and Library committees, task forces, and teams as appropriate. Networks, collaborates and actively participates in local, regional, national, or international

organizations regarding issues in librarianship, cataloging, and metadata creation.

32. creating and editing bibliographic records; creating and updating authority records; maintenance of authority and bibliographic records; loading and reviewing purchased cataloging for physical items and firm-ordered ebooks

33. Varies depending on the position - we currently don't have anyone whose job is only cataloging.

34. Performs original and complex copy cataloging of library materials, mostly English-language monographs, serials, audiovisuals, and electronic resources. Performs descriptive and subject cataloging based on LC Classification and Subject Headings, using OCLC bibliographic utility and local cataloging system, Voyager. Edits bibliographic records and is responsible for bibliographic database maintenance program and authority control in an OCLC/Voyager environment. Catalogs continuations (standing orders for annuals, multipart items, etc.). Adds new holdings and item records to existing bibliographic records. Maintains serials holdings, updates holdings information on OCLC for all GPC campus libraries. Trains students, paraprofessional staff and librarians in the use of OCLC and Voyager, reviews and revises their cataloging work. Assists in writing cataloging procedures, participates in setting policies and regulations for cataloging department. Serves on library and campus committees. Belongs to professional associations and seeks appropriate professional development opportunities. Serves as contact person for questions and concerns of Public Services staff regarding the catalog. Miscellaneous duties as assigned by the Coordinator of Technical Services.

35. Mostly copy cataloguing, processing, simple bulk record processing.

36. We don't have job descriptions.

37. 1. Performs original and complex copy cataloging of all library materials in all formats. 2. Works with the department head in establishing priorities for the cataloging of new materials. 3. Maintains awareness of new developments in the field of librarianship relative to cataloging, bibliographic control, and cost-effective operations. 4. Participates in on-going professional development to meet job responsibilities and to meet requirements of tenure and promotion. 5. Serves as library liaison to one or more academic departments as appointed. 6. Serves on library and university committees as appointed. 7. May teach bibliographic instruction classes. 8. Performs other duties as required.

38. Cataloging in all formats; supervision of professional staff; training in current trends; scholarship and service in the area of librarianship.

39. Our academic catalogers have MLS degrees. They are expected to perform original cataloging, complex copy, cataloging, supervision, research, and service.

40. catalog and classify library materials using AACR2 or RDA, LC classification, LC subject headings, OCLC and our local online catalog; perform authority work

41. Catalog all types of materials using OCLC, MARC21, and LCSH, classifying in either LCC or DDC. Includes general cataloging of books, other print materials, music materials, and various non-book formats. Participates in teaching rotation for graduate level cataloging course. Assists with departmental training and database cleanup projects. Must meet faculty requirements for librarianship, professional development, research, and service.

42. Computer skills, knowledge of MARC and cataloging rules, knowledge of AACR2 and RDA.

43. Original cataloging, overseeing copy cataloging, database management (and other duties, as needed).

44. perform original and complex cataloging of a variety of materials//perform database maintenance and authority control//stay abreast of trends in cataloging//serve as library liaison to one or more academic departments//serve on library committees//

45. Basically, get the records into the local system; I think that the job description includes supervising the physical processing of materials. Anything else is up to me (including seeing to it that the catalog works)

46. Bibliograhic description, subject analysis, database cleanup, authority work.

47. We only have 2.5 FTE employees, so the library assistant does the cataloging, library instruction, helping with work study students, circulation, reference questions, collection development, gathering statistical information, and anything else that comes up and the head librarian assigns.

48. Performs original and complex copy cataloging for special and traditional formats. Creates metadata for digital resources. Interpret name, subject, series and uniform title records to establish accurate and consistent indexing in the OCLC and library databases. Provide data needed to establish names and concepts not yet represented in the databases for other libraries to use.

49. Original and copy cataloging, catalog maintenance, loading batches of records for electronic resources, authority work, processing new materials.

50. Librarian or staff? For catalog librarian: Specific duties of the position: • Develop and implement policies, standards, goals, and procedures to continuously improve cataloging and processing workflow • Apply knowledge of current issues and trends in cataloging and processing to improve services and enhance the library's catalog • Provide descriptive metadata for all physical and digital formats, including monographs, serials, government publications, theses, audio and visual materials, and online resources • Resolve bibliographic and holdings problems • Ensure that all cataloging and database maintenance activities are completed in a timely, efficient, and accurate manner • Coordinate with colleagues in the MINITEX region and in the MnPALS Consortium • Coordinate with other members of the collection management team, specifically the E-Resources/Serials Librarian, the Collection Management Librarian, and the Systems Librarian • Oversee the work of staff and student employees • Provide leadership in adoption of new methods, technologies, and resources in a rapidly changing academic library environment • Provide leadership for administration, technical services, and collection maintenance of government publications • Serve on the reference desk   Qualifications and Experience: Required: • ALA-accredited master's degree in library or information science • Minimum of 2 years experience doing original cataloging of multiple formats • Knowledge of current and emerging trends of technical services in academic library services/resources • Knowledge and proficiency in using AACR2r, LC Classification, LCSH, • SuDoc organization, MARC21 formats and OCLC Connexion • Knowledge of FRBR, RDA, Dublin Core and other emerging practices and standards • Demonstrated ability to work with persons from culturally diverse backgrounds • Ability to communicate effectively, both orally and in writing Preferred: • Second graduate degree • Academic library experience • Teaching experience • Training and/or supervisory experience

51. Tech Services Coordinator: 1. Maintain the accuracy and usability of the library's online catalog, including overseeing authority control and efficient display of holdings information.   2. Perform copy and original cataloging of materials, train staff, write procedures, and recommend policies. Maintain cataloging statistics on collections, oversee cataloging projects, and promote efficient cataloging workflow. 3.Oversee the areas of acquisitions and serials control including coordinating workflow, training staff, writing procedures, and recommending policies. 4, Supervise Library Technicians who perform copy cataloging and ILL. 5. Act as backup for the Systems Librarian as needed.

52. Supply data that describes library materials in all formats across multiple data input schema as assigned. Find, edits, and creates data, then transfer it into a variety of library discovery systems. Job Requirements: MLS from accredited institution. Ability to independently plan, coordinate, organize, schedule, and manage multiple work assignments. Ability to understand and implement complex written and oral instructions. Logical thinking skills with the ability to extrapolate from prior learning to new situations. Flexibility and ability to adapt to constant change in technologies and standards. Oral and written communication skills adequate to plan collaborative workflows with supervisors and peers. Ability to establish and maintain effective working relationships and train or supervise the workflows of others. Manual ability to operate equipment such as a computer keyboard, copier, media player, microfiche reader, etc. Must be able to retrieve materials from shelves and move materials around

on book trucks.

53. Cataloging, Authority Control, Collection & database maintenance, Management & workflow, Documentation, Supervision & appraisal, Communication & Consulting, Professional Development, Special projects

54. Depends on the grade level of the position. The few individuals who only do copy cataloging are responsible for knowing how to search OCLC for copy, evaluate the copy found, make necessary changes, and pass the items on to our Marking Unit. Everyone else must have at least a Bachelor's degree in a subject area, learn and apply AACR2, LCRIs, create authority records, work with a host of languages, and be flexible in working with either editing copy or creating original records. Faculty members do all of the above, of course must have an ALA-accredited MLS or similar, plus be active in leadership roles, service, and research/publications.

55. original cataloging, catalog maintenance, resource person for copy catalogers, participate in consortial events

56. All copy cataloging, original cataloging for all formats and all languages; management of import/export for electronic MARC records

57. Original and copy cataloging. Database maintenance.

58. Experience with cataloging tools (OCLC, ILS, etc.) Computer skills, attention to detail...

59. Catalog materials in all formats Train copy-catalogers Write procedures for cataloging

60. oversight of cataloging/metadata processes, oversight of acquisitions, e-resources, cataloging, service, research, collection development, reference desk, teaching

61. Familiarity with cataloging rules, LCSH, LC classification, Voyager and OCLC.

62. Copy-catalog and original cataloging; some serials; binding

63. analyzing library materials, assigning an appropriate Dewey decimal classification, determining subject headings, and standardizing records

64. need computer skills, work with bib records

65. Skills with bibliographic description, knowledge of standards and practices

66. MLS. Experience with OCLC, current cataloging standards, Library of Congress classification and subject headings, authority control, Innovative Millennium

67. Manage train other copy-catalogers and technical services staff. Perform original cataloging for monographs and special formats. Provide liaison and collection development assistance to subject faculty. Perform Reference duties.

68. Authority work, original cataloging, LCSH, LCC, satisfy requirements for tenure and promotion through research, committee work, etc.

69. Responsibilities include: cataloging in all formats and languages, resolving complicated cataloging problems, etc. Requirements include: MLS, cataloging experience, excellent oral, written and interpersonal skills.

70. Original and copy cataloging using OCLC, LC subject headings, Marc and RDA. Cleaning up and loading vendor mac records into catalog

71. The cataloging of books and other resources acquired by the library by purchase and gift using Library of Congress classification and subject heading. We do Reference duties as needed.

72. Original cataloging of all types of materials--monographs, serials, audio-visual, electronic, archival, etc. Classification, shelflisting, assigning of subject headings. Authority control and maintenance of the catalog database.

73. Supervise student book processors and cataloging assistants, maintain OCLC cataloging software, troubleshoot and maintain cataloging software, troubleshoot and maintain library OPAC, troubleshoot and maintain library server for the library database, troubleshoot and maintain integrated library software modules for all staff and liaison with vendor, run authority control.

If your institution has a metadata librarian/cataloguer, what basic responsibilities and job requirements are listed in the job description?

1. Institutional Repository Librarian, collecting and organizing faculty and student research, work with faculty, create forms and write policy and procedures.
2. Create metadata, train others, defines elements.
3. Manage scaled description and access of digital resources; manage holdings information in catalog, WorldCat, web-scale discovery platforms and services; staff training; troubleshoot and give policy / workflow advice to executive and technical services staff.
4. All catalogers do MARC cataloging as well as metadata creation.
5. Librarian: MLS, 2 years experience, knowledge of LCC, MARC, AACR2 and RDA, OCLC WorldCat and Connexion, and LCSH. I do original cataloging, problem-solving, name authority records, planning and implementing innovations, etc.
6. We are just beginning to delve into metadata with baby steps. As the cataloger, I am in the process of needing to learn Dublin Core Content DM and DSpace for our institutional repository.
7. Same as above.
8. Knowledge in Dublin Core or related metadata schema, knowledge of current cataloging rules and practices, catalog electronic resources, provide descriptive metadata for digital projects, catalog archival materials, catalog serials analytics.
9. Same as above.
10. There is no real job description for the metadata librarian/cataloger, but that person provides metadata for digital projects as well as for electronic books; troubleshoots connection problems for ebooks; supervises a staff member; recommends policies for metadata creation and electronic books cataloging.
11. Perform complex copy and original cataloging according to Anglo-American Cataloging Rules (AACR2rev), OCLC, Library of Congress Subject Headings (LCSH) and Library of Congress (LC) Classification standards using the integrated library system and OCLC. Recommends cataloging procedures and keeps current on developments in cataloging by attending professional meetings and reading the literature. Maintains bibliographic and item records in the local and state catalog, and makes changes as required. Performs or oversees the processing and repair of materials. Collects and reports statistical information about the materials collection. Assists and advises Library Technical Services Manager, Library Public Services Manager, and Reference Librarians on matter relating to cataloging, circulation, and reference services. Perform other technical processing duties as needed (e.g. interlibrary loan, checking in serials).
12. Creates, reviews, and edits metadata for digital collections and assists in the development and application of metadata crosswalks and data conversion routines; trains & revises library faculty, staff, and/or interns in the application of metadata. Participates in the development, evaluation, and implementation of metadata policies, standards, goals, procedures, and workflows in cooperation with Digital Scholarship & Programs and necessary stakeholders; Oversees quality control for non-MARC metadata processes and projects as assigned. Collaborates in the selection, design, and adaptation of metadata schema, controlled vocabularies, and data dictionaries. Participates in the evaluation of the effectiveness of catalog data and metadata for resource discovery. Assists in other departmental training initiatives by developing training material or providing instruction to library staff as needed. May perform original and copy cataloging and assist with catalog database maintenance activities as needed. Remains current with metadata and cataloging standards and digital library development; Participates in library professional associations and other appropriate venues for professional development. Other duties as assigned by Supervisor. Networks, collaborates and actively participates in local, regional, national, or

international organizations regarding related issues. Represents and promotes the University of Miami Libraries in local, state-wide, regional, national, or international organizations as appropriate. Serves on Cataloging Policy Board and participates in Libraries and University organizations.

13. Managing large record sets for ebook and e-journal packages; managing records for streaming video and audio; creating MARC records from non-MARC data; coordinating with library staff managing the institutional repository.

14. Supervision; collection management and assessment; liaison to 2 other library departments and to the general academic library; committee memberships; medical cataloging; collection development; authority control; may include reference desk duties

15. Original cataloguing, bulk record work (eBooks), metadata work, developing and customizing metadata schema, crosswalking, authority work, metadata consultation with other campus organizations, digitization

16. We don't have job descriptions.

17. Cataloging in all formats; supervision of professional staff; training in current trends; scholarship and service in the area of librarianship.

18. We do not have a metadata librarian. Metadata is distributed among our catalogers.

19. Coordinating oversight of our Institutional Repository, chairing our Cataloging Standards Committee.

20. Descriptive metadata for materials in the digital collections and the institutional repository.

21. Essential and assigned professional work of the faculty librarian for the unit   a. Oversee the creation of complex and original cataloging and classification in a variety of subjects, languages and formats and general cataloging support for the University Libraries, including authority work and database maintenance   b. Oversee cataloging functions in the integrated library system   c. Maintains integrity of database using national standards (e.g. MARC 21, RDA, AACR2 revised, ISBDs, LCSH, LC Rule Interpretations and LC classification and subject headings)   d. Track developments in and maintains knowledge of existing and developing national metadata standards and schemas (e.g. DC, MARC, VRA Core, CDWA, CCO, TEI, EAD in compliance with OAI, Linked Data)   e. Participate in the Libraries' digital projects, planning metadata creation and maintenance, interpreting/adapting schema, and creatintg metadata templates and collections for local, statewide and national projects   f. Oversee the creation of and create metadata for the Libraries' digital projects

22. Same as above.

23. Produce and manage MARC and non-MARC metadata. Select metadata schema and standards, document procedures and processes, train staff in descriptive metadata production. Job Requirements: ALA-accredited MLS, broad understanding of digital metadata management, creation of metadata dictionaries, and authority control. Familiarity with emerging cataloging theories and concepts, proficiency with global editing tools, ability to learn new technologies and metadata standards, ability to multitask and priorities both independently and as part of a team.

24. Management & workflow, Digital collection description, Collection & database maintenance and authority control, Documentation, Digital object processing, Communication & Consulting, Special projects, Professional Development

25. We lost our metadata librarian recently and the position description is being re-evaluated and rewritten.

26. Do original cataloging, assist copy catalogers and catalog maintenance, do authority work, work with librarians in other areas

27. Original and copy cataloging. Database maintenance.

28. Metadata is part of what all catalogers deal with, not a separate responsibility

29. We have a digital assets librarian ... haven't begun metadata stuff yet ...

30. Knowledge of metadata practices and systems; satisfy requirements for tenure and promotion through research, committee work, etc.

31. I am just a cataloger. Responsible for running the Cataloging Department and catalog and withdraw books and other resources from the collection.

List briefly the cataloging and authority tasks, concepts, and cataloguing tools used to train catalogers.

1. Training by the library director, graduate school course, and consortium training.
2. Classification Web (LC), RDA Toolkit, LTI authority loading, AACR2, Written procedures, Links to helpful websites, webinars.
3. This question isn't very clear to me -- we use webinars, send some people to training, etc.
4. Training provided by online and in person workshops, access to Catalogers Desktop, meetings and promulgation of procedures by dept head.
5. Restricted sources for copy cataloguing; Skills in minimal and accurate bibliographic description; Original cataloging; Daily new headings report and import / creation of name authority records; Support university research output by maintaining name records; Support new research output through SACO submissions; Classification web; Catalogers desktop; BIBCO standard records; LC Authorities; OCLC bibliographic formats; MARC Standards; RDA Toolkit;
6. Analyze content, assign classification and subject headings, understand international descriptive standards. Tools: OCLC, LC authority database, Cataloger's Desktop, Classification Web, RDA Toolkit, LCSH database.
7. AACR2, Dewey, LC Classification, LCSH, Catalogers Desktop, LC Rule Interpretations, Worldcat, Government Documents, Dictionaries and Encyclopedias, Google
8. Cataloger's Desktop, Classification Web, local policies and procedures
9. Class Web
10. AACR2, Bibliographic formats and standards, in-house policies and procedures.
11. Self-trained
12. ALCTS, OCLC, Lyrasis webinars and in-house worksheets
13. Tools: OCLC, III Millennium, Cataloger's Desktop, Classification Web, and have a thorough understanding of MARC 21 and AACR2, must have a thorough understanding of authority control.
14. I only have two students to help with copy cataloging. I give them a cheat sheet and monitor them closely for the first semester. They are asked to bookmark LOC authorities and a few other sites.
15. Tasks: OCLC Connexion: searching, identifying, and downloading/importing catalog records into Voyager; Use Access software to run reports for bibliographic maintenance work; Tools: LC Cutter table; AACR2, LCSH, LC Subject Headings Manual; LC Shelflisting Manual;
16. AACRII, LCSH, LCRI, OCLC Bibliographic standards
17. Must already have current knowledge of basic cataloging tools. Department head will instruct local cataloging practices to train new catalogers. Supervisors will train non-faculty catalogers in all forms of cataloging tools and local practices.
18. We work with our regional consortium and the workshops it offers either online or at its site in Lansing to train our staff. I work with each staff member as needed as well. We've set up a Google docs site to hold procedures, manuals and so on.
19. OCLC Connexion and ILS
20. Online classes through OCLC, Cataloger's Desktop, Calssification Web, LTI
21. Original catalogers are trained in the MARC format for their specialty, OCLC searching and inputting techniques; AACR2 and RDA instructions. Tools: OCLC, Cataloger's Desktop, ClassWeb.
22. OCLC Bib Formats & Standards Cataloger's Desktop OCLC Dates Classification Web LC Cutter Tables Differences Between, Changes Within / ALCTS Roman Numeral Calculator Copy Cataloging Fields to Check   Item Record Documentation Millennium Materials Understanding MARC Bibliographic MARC21 Tutorial Connexion Client Set Up Connexion Central at KSU OCLC Connexion Client: Searching WorldCat Cataloger's Desktop Webinars from CD3 2009 Touring

Technical Services (streaming video from KentLINK; or DVD 0718) TMQ MARC21 in Your Library Part 1: MARC & Bibliographic Info Fundamentals (Self-Paced) (Free but need to register with OCLC)

23. Webinars, conferences, workshops.
24. All Library of Congress tools ply Dewey Decimal Classification.
25. They already knew what to do when I came in. I'm screwed if they retire or leave. I had three but one passed away. We just plain old lost some of what she did because she'd been here for almost 30 years and there were just some things she did that I don't think were written down. :(
26. Tools: AACR2/RDA, LCRIs/LC-PCC PSs, LCSH, Subject Cataloging Manual, Descriptive Cataloging Manual (esp. DCM Z1), a local cataloging manual; training materials from the Library of Congress
27. NLM cataloging site LC cataloging site
28. Overview provided by readings (M. Yee's text) and LC MARC bib and authorities tutorials online. Overview of local procedures, which are based on national cataloging rules and guidelines. Side-by-side training until comfortable, then review records until error rate is low. Release and spot check periodically if necessary
29. I mostly just design things that I use for training or borrow things that I get from ALCTS or other metadata librarians I know.
30. MARC 21, AACR2, LOC website, OCLC Bibliographic Standards
31. MARC, subject headings
32. Webinars, in-person training from consortia, professional conferences
33. LC/PCC copy, member copy, working up to original work; we check authorities, then move up to creating original, authorities. We use local policies and procedures, OCLC Connexion, and Cataloger's Desktop.
34. AACR2, RDA, LC classification, LC subject headings, OCLC; Cataloger's Desktop; Classification Web, OCLC Bibliographic Formats and Standards, LC Catalogers' Learning Workshop
35. one-on-one training for daily/routine tasks; workshops and webinars for format or subject specific information
36. One-on-one training, with use of standards documents. Independent research.
37. OCLC Bib. Formats and Standards, plus local practices
38. Basic authority maintenance, Classweb, RDA Toolkit, trial and error
39. We have one catalog librarian- me. I try to find free or inexpensive webinars or local workshops. I read Autocat, and rely on their aid, and local catalogers in our small consortium.
40. Authority work is done separately for most cataloging.   Original catalogers are trained to use AACR2, the subject manual and other LC tools to perform authority work.
41. Our library assistants have had their MLIS or extensive work in the library. There is only training for the specifics of Maki Library, local codes and DDC 19 usage.
42. Local documentation, RDA Toolkit, AACR2, LCSH, Classweb (call numbers, subject headings, etc.), OCLC bib formats, Cataloger's desktop
43. I drew on my experiences at a larger institution, read widely, attended consortial events, and paid attention to public services librarians. The incoming cataloger has been doing reference and instruction, and works with me one-on-one to understand limits of existing ILS and consortial participation. Most importantly, understanding balancing competing needs and tolerate ambiguity.
44. OCLC webinars
45. All catalogers took cataloging during their MLS. They also take OCLC training courses.
46. online Dewey, OCLC training , Cataloger's desktop, classification web, ALCTS webinars, AACR2, RDA tooklit, most of our training is all in house with more experienced people teaching newer employees
47. Connexion, Cutter-Sanborn table
48. We're still on oral tradition
49. We have an extremely detailed procedures manual that takes a new cataloger step-by-

step through the cataloging process.
50. No one has time to list 'briefly' these things.   Here's a list of manuals we consult to do our work: RDA toolkit/AACR2 Bibliographic formats and standards Authorities: formats and indexes Maxwell's guide to authority work Cataloging of Audiovisual Materials and other Special Formats. Subject Headings Manual (LC) MARC 21 formats And many others.
51. RDA Toolkit, Catalogers Desktop, Classweb, SHM, Training materials on LC and PCC websites, webinars.
52. The position required a Masters in Library Science and some experience in the cataloging. We use authority records supplied by LTI which annually update the authority file.
53. We use in house information documents for training.
54. We expect their library school to have trained them.

Table 8.1.1: Is original cataloging performed mostly by library paraprofessional support staff, by professional librarians, or by both?

	Mostly paraprofessional support staff	Mostly professional librarians	Performed by both
Entire Sample	6.17%	74.07%	19.75%

Table 8.1.2: Is original cataloging performed mostly by library paraprofessional support staff, by professional librarians, or by both? Broken out by Type of College

Type of College	Mostly paraprofessional support staff	Mostly professional librarians	Performed by both
Community College	20.00%	80.00%	0.00%
4-Year Degree Granting College	10.53%	76.32%	13.16%
MA or PHD Granting College	0.00%	73.91%	26.09%
Research University	0.00%	66.67%	33.33%

Table 8.1.3: Is original cataloging performed mostly by library paraprofessional support staff, by professional librarians, or by both? Broken out by Public or Private Status

Public or Private Status	Mostly paraprofessional support staff	Mostly professional librarians	Performed by both
Public	5.77%	76.92%	17.31%
Private	6.90%	68.97%	24.14%

Table 8.1.4: Is original cataloging performed mostly by library paraprofessional support staff, by professional librarians, or by both? Broken out by Total Student Enrollment

Total Student Enrollment	Mostly paraprofessional support staff	Mostly professional librarians	Performed by both
Less than 10,000	9.68%	77.42%	12.90%
10,000 to 20,000	3.03%	75.76%	21.21%
More than 20,000	5.88%	64.71%	29.41%

Table 8.1.5: Is original cataloging performed mostly by library paraprofessional support staff, by professional librarians, or by both? Broken out by Annual Tuition

Annual Tuition	Mostly paraprofessional support staff	Mostly professional librarians	Performed by both
Less than $8,000	3.85%	84.62%	11.54%
$8,000 to $18,000	10.34%	62.07%	27.59%
More than $18,000	3.85%	76.92%	19.23%

Table 8.2.1: Is copy cataloging performed mostly by library paraprofessional support staff, by professional librarians, or by both?

	Mostly paraprofessional support staff	Mostly professional librarians	Performed by both
Entire Sample	44.44%	12.35%	43.21%

Table 8.2.2: Is copy cataloging performed mostly by library paraprofessional support staff, by professional librarians, or by both? Broken out by Type of College

Type of College	Mostly paraprofessional support staff	Mostly professional librarians	Performed by both
Community College	40.00%	40.00%	20.00%
4-Year Degree Granting College	50.00%	15.79%	34.21%
MA or PHD Granting College	34.78%	8.70%	56.52%
Research University	46.67%	0.00%	53.33%

Table 8.2.3: Is copy cataloging performed mostly by library paraprofessional support staff, by professional librarians, or by both? Broken out by Public or Private Status

Public or Private Status	Mostly paraprofessional support staff	Mostly professional librarians	Performed by both
Public	50.00%	7.69%	42.31%
Private	34.48%	20.69%	44.83%

Table 8.2.4: Is copy cataloging performed mostly by library paraprofessional support staff, by professional librarians, or by both? Broken out by Total Student Enrollment

Total Student Enrollment	Mostly paraprofessional support staff	Mostly professional librarians	Performed by both
Less than 10,000	35.48%	25.81%	38.71%
10,000 to 20,000	51.52%	6.06%	42.42%
More than 20,000	47.06%	0.00%	52.94%

Table 8.2.5: Is copy cataloging performed mostly by library paraprofessional support staff, by professional librarians, or by both? Broken out by Annual Tuition

Annual Tuition	Mostly paraprofessional support staff	Mostly professional librarians	Performed by both
Less than $8,000	50.00%	7.69%	42.31%
$8,000 to $18,000	58.62%	6.90%	34.48%
More than $18,000	23.08%	23.08%	53.85%

Table 8.3.1: Is Name Authority Cooperative work (NACO) performed mostly by library paraprofessional support staff, by professional librarians, or by both?

	Mostly paraprofessional support staff	Mostly professional librarians	Performed by both
Entire Sample	6.17%	83.95%	9.88%

Table 8.3.2: Is Name Authority Cooperative work (NACO) performed mostly by library paraprofessional support staff, by professional librarians, or by both? Broken out by Type of College

Type of College	Mostly paraprofessional support staff	Mostly professional librarians	Performed by both
Community College	0.00%	100.00%	0.00%
4-Year Degree Granting College	10.53%	84.21%	5.26%
MA or PHD Granting College	0.00%	95.65%	4.35%
Research University	6.67%	60.00%	33.33%

Table 8.3.3: Is Name Authority Cooperative work (NACO) performed mostly by library paraprofessional support staff, by professional librarians, or by both? Broken out by Public or Private Status

Public or Private Status	Mostly paraprofessional support staff	Mostly professional librarians	Performed by both
Public	5.77%	80.77%	13.46%
Private	6.90%	89.66%	3.45%

Table 8.3.4: Is Name Authority Cooperative work (NACO) performed mostly by library paraprofessional support staff, by professional librarians, or by both? Broken out by Total Student Enrollment

Total Student Enrollment	Mostly paraprofessional support staff	Mostly professional librarians	Performed by both
Less than 10,000	3.23%	93.55%	3.23%
10,000 to 20,000	6.06%	81.82%	12.12%
More than 20,000	11.76%	70.59%	17.65%

Table 8.3.5: Is Name Authority Cooperative work (NACO) performed mostly by library paraprofessional support staff, by professional librarians, or by both? Broken out by Annual Tuition

Annual Tuition	Mostly paraprofessional support staff	Mostly professional librarians	Performed by both
Less than $8,000	0.00%	92.31%	7.69%
$8,000 to $18,000	13.79%	75.86%	10.34%
More than $18,000	3.85%	84.62%	11.54%

Table 8.4.1: Is Subject Authority Cooperative work (SACO) performed mostly by library paraprofessional support staff, by professional librarians, or by both?

	Mostly paraprofessional support staff	Mostly professional librarians	Performed by both
Entire Sample	1.23%	92.59%	6.17%

Table 8.4.2: Is Subject Authority Cooperative work (SACO) performed mostly by library paraprofessional support staff, by professional librarians, or by both? Broken out by Type of College

Type of College	Mostly paraprofessional support staff	Mostly professional librarians	Performed by both
Community College	0.00%	100.00%	0.00%
4-Year Degree Granting College	2.63%	94.74%	2.63%
MA or PHD Granting College	0.00%	100.00%	0.00%
Research University	0.00%	73.33%	26.67%

Table 8.4.3: Is Subject Authority Cooperative work (SACO) performed mostly by library paraprofessional support staff, by professional librarians, or by both? Broken out by Public or Private Status

Public or Private Status	Mostly paraprofessional support staff	Mostly professional librarians	Performed by both
Public	1.92%	90.38%	7.69%
Private	0.00%	96.55%	3.45%

Table 8.4.4: Is Subject Authority Cooperative work (SACO) performed mostly by library paraprofessional support staff, by professional librarians, or by both? Broken out by Total Student Enrollment

Total Student Enrollment	Mostly paraprofessional support staff	Mostly professional librarians	Performed by both
Less than 10,000	0.00%	96.77%	3.23%
10,000 to 20,000	3.03%	93.94%	3.03%
More than 20,000	0.00%	82.35%	17.65%

Table 8.4.5: Is Subject Authority Cooperative work (SACO) performed mostly by library paraprofessional support staff, by professional librarians, or by both? Broken out by Annual Tuition

Annual Tuition	Mostly paraprofessional support staff	Mostly professional librarians	Performed by both
Less than $8,000	0.00%	96.15%	3.85%
$8,000 to $18,000	3.45%	89.66%	6.90%
More than $18,000	0.00%	92.31%	7.69%

Table 8.5.1: Is master bibliographic record enhancement in OCLC performed mostly by library paraprofessional support staff, by professional librarians, or by both?

	Mostly paraprofessional support staff	Mostly professional librarians	Performed by both
Entire Sample	6.17%	71.60%	22.22%

Table 8.5.2: Is master bibliographic record enhancement in OCLC performed mostly by library paraprofessional support staff, by professional librarians, or by both? Broken out by Type of College

Type of College	Mostly paraprofessional support staff	Mostly professional librarians	Performed by both
Community College	0.00%	100.00%	0.00%
4-Year Degree Granting College	10.53%	73.68%	15.79%
MA or PHD Granting College	4.35%	60.87%	34.78%
Research University	0.00%	73.33%	26.67%

Table 8.5.3: Is master bibliographic record enhancement in OCLC performed mostly by library paraprofessional support staff, by professional librarians, or by both? Broken out by Public or Private Status

Public or Private Status	Mostly paraprofessional support staff	Mostly professional librarians	Performed by both
Public	5.77%	69.23%	25.00%
Private	6.90%	75.86%	17.24%

Table 8.5.4: Is master bibliographic record enhancement in OCLC performed mostly by library paraprofessional support staff, by professional librarians, or by both? Broken out by Total Student Enrollment

Total Student Enrollment	Mostly paraprofessional support staff	Mostly professional librarians	Performed by both
Less than 10,000	0.00%	83.87%	16.13%
10,000 to 20,000	12.12%	63.64%	24.24%
More than 20,000	5.88%	64.71%	29.41%

Table 8.5.5: Is master bibliographic record enhancement in OCLC performed mostly by library paraprofessional support staff, by professional librarians, or by both? Staff Broken out by Annual Tuition

Annual Tuition	Mostly paraprofessional support staff	Mostly professional librarians	Performed by both
Less than $8,000	0.00%	80.77%	19.23%
$8,000 to $18,000	13.79%	68.97%	17.24%
More than $18,000	3.85%	65.38%	30.77%

Table 8.6.1: Is participation in PCC, CONSER and BIBCO 1 bibliographic record work performed mostly by library paraprofessional support staff, by professional librarians, or by both?

	Mostly paraprofessional support staff	Mostly professional librarians	Performed by both
Entire Sample	3.70%	92.59%	3.70%

Table 8.6.2: Is participation in PCC, CONSER and BIBCO 1 bibliographic record work performed mostly by library paraprofessional support staff, by professional librarians, or by both? Broken out by Type of College

Type of College	Mostly paraprofessional support staff	Mostly professional librarians	Performed by both
Community College	0.00%	100.00%	0.00%
4-Year Degree Granting College	2.63%	97.37%	0.00%
MA or PHD Granting College	4.35%	95.65%	0.00%
Research University	6.67%	73.33%	20.00%

Table 8.6.3: Is participation in PCC, CONSER and BIBCO 1 bibliographic record work performed mostly by library paraprofessional support staff, by professional librarians, or by both? Broken out by Public or Private Status

Public or Private Status	Mostly paraprofessional support staff	Mostly professional librarians	Performed by both
Public	5.77%	90.38%	3.85%
Private	0.00%	96.55%	3.45%

Table 8.6.4: Is participation in PCC, CONSER and BIBCO 1 bibliographic record work performed mostly by library paraprofessional support staff, by professional librarians, or by both? Broken out by Total Student Enrollment

Total Student Enrollment	Mostly paraprofessional support staff	Mostly professional librarians	Performed by both
Less than 10,000	3.23%	96.77%	0.00%
10,000 to 20,000	0.00%	96.97%	3.03%
More than 20,000	11.76%	76.47%	11.76%

Table 8.6.5: Is participation in PCC, CONSER and BIBCO 1 bibliographic record work performed mostly by library paraprofessional support staff, by professional librarians, or by both? Broken out by Annual Tuition

Annual Tuition	Mostly paraprofessional support staff	Mostly professional librarians	Performed by both
Less than $8,000	3.85%	96.15%	0.00%
$8,000 to $18,000	6.90%	89.66%	3.45%
More than $18,000	0.00%	92.31%	7.69%

Table 8.7.1: Is master bibliographic record enrichment (adding call numbers, subjects, tables of contents) in OCLC performed mostly by library paraprofessional support staff, by professional librarians, or by both?

	Mostly paraprofessional support staff	Mostly professional librarians	Performed by both
Entire Sample	6.17%	69.14%	24.69%

Table 8.7.2: Is master bibliographic record enrichment (adding call numbers, subjects, tables of contents) in OCLC performed mostly by library paraprofessional support staff, by professional librarians, or by both? Broken out by Type of College

Type of College	Mostly paraprofessional support staff	Mostly professional librarians	Performed by both
Community College	0.00%	100.00%	0.00%
4-Year Degree Granting College	10.53%	71.05%	18.42%
MA or PHD Granting College	4.35%	60.87%	34.78%
Research University	0.00%	66.67%	33.33%

Table 8.7.3: Is master bibliographic record enrichment (adding call numbers, subjects, tables of contents) in OCLC performed mostly by library paraprofessional support staff, by professional librarians, or by both? Broken out by Public or Private Status

Public or Private Status	Mostly paraprofessional support staff	Mostly professional librarians	Performed by both
Public	7.69%	67.31%	25.00%
Private	3.45%	72.41%	24.14%

Table 8.7.4: Is master bibliographic record enrichment (adding call numbers, subjects, tables of contents) in OCLC performed mostly by library paraprofessional support staff, by professional librarians, or by both? Broken out by Total Student Enrollment

Total Student Enrollment	Mostly paraprofessional support staff	Mostly professional librarians	Performed by both
Less than 10,000	0.00%	77.42%	22.58%
10,000 to 20,000	12.12%	60.61%	27.27%
More than 20,000	5.88%	70.59%	23.53%

Table 8.7.5: Is master bibliographic record enrichment (adding call numbers, subjects, tables of contents) in OCLC performed mostly by library paraprofessional support staff, by professional librarians, or by both? Broken out by Annual Tuition

Annual Tuition	Mostly paraprofessional support staff	Mostly professional librarians	Performed by both
Less than $8,000	0.00%	80.77%	19.23%
$8,000 to $18,000	13.79%	68.97%	17.24%
More than $18,000	3.85%	57.69%	38.46%

Table 8.8.1: Is subject analysis and subject heading application performed mostly by library paraprofessional support staff, by professional librarians, or by both?

	Mostly paraprofessional support staff	Mostly professional librarians	Performed by both
Entire Sample	3.70%	59.26%	37.04%

Table 8.8.2: Is subject analysis and subject heading application performed mostly by library paraprofessional support staff, by professional librarians, or by both? Broken out by Type of College

Type of College	Mostly paraprofessional support staff	Mostly professional librarians	Performed by both
Community College	20.00%	80.00%	0.00%
4-Year Degree Granting College	5.26%	55.26%	39.47%
MA or PHD Granting College	0.00%	65.22%	34.78%
Research University	0.00%	53.33%	46.67%

Table 8.8.3: Is subject analysis and subject heading application performed mostly by library paraprofessional support staff, by professional librarians, or by both? Broken out by Public or Private Status

Public or Private Status	Mostly paraprofessional support staff	Mostly professional librarians	Performed by both
Public	3.85%	59.62%	36.54%
Private	3.45%	58.62%	37.93%

Table 8.8.4: Is subject analysis and subject heading application performed mostly by library paraprofessional support staff, by professional librarians, or by both? Broken out by Total Student Enrollment

Total Student Enrollment	Mostly paraprofessional support staff	Mostly professional librarians	Performed by both
Less than 10,000	3.23%	67.74%	29.03%
10,000 to 20,000	6.06%	48.48%	45.45%
More than 20,000	0.00%	64.71%	35.29%

Table 8.8.5: Is subject analysis and subject heading application performed mostly by library paraprofessional support staff, by professional librarians, or by both? Broken out by Annual Tuition

Annual Tuition	Mostly paraprofessional support staff	Mostly professional librarians	Performed by both
Less than $8,000	3.85%	69.23%	26.92%
$8,000 to $18,000	3.45%	48.28%	48.28%
More than $18,000	3.85%	61.54%	34.62%

Table 8.9.1: Is classification performed mostly by library paraprofessional support staff, by professional librarians, or by both?

	Mostly paraprofessional support staff	Mostly professional librarians	Performed by both
Entire Sample	3.70%	54.32%	41.98%

Table 8.9.2: Is classification performed mostly by library paraprofessional support staff, by professional librarians, or by both? Broken out by Type of College

Type of College	Mostly paraprofessional support staff	Mostly professional librarians	Performed by both
Community College	20.00%	80.00%	0.00%
4-Year Degree Granting College	5.26%	47.37%	47.37%
MA or PHD Granting College	0.00%	65.22%	34.78%
Research University	0.00%	46.67%	53.33%

Table 8.9.3: Is classification performed mostly by library paraprofessional support staff, by professional librarians, or by both? Broken out by Public or Private Status

Public or Private Status	Mostly paraprofessional support staff	Mostly professional librarians	Performed by both
Public	3.85%	59.62%	36.54%
Private	3.45%	44.83%	51.72%

Table 8.9.4: Is classification performed mostly by library paraprofessional support staff, by professional librarians, or by both? Broken out by Total Student Enrollment

Total Student Enrollment	Mostly paraprofessional support staff	Mostly professional librarians	Performed by both
Less than 10,000	3.23%	61.29%	35.48%
10,000 to 20,000	6.06%	42.42%	51.52%
More than 20,000	0.00%	64.71%	35.29%

Table 8.9.5: Is classification performed mostly by library paraprofessional support staff, by professional librarians, or by both? Broken out by Annual Tuition

Annual Tuition	Mostly paraprofessional support staff	Mostly professional librarians	Performed by both
Less than $8,000	3.85%	69.23%	26.92%
$8,000 to $18,000	3.45%	48.28%	48.28%
More than $18,000	3.85%	46.15%	50.00%

Table 8.10.1: Are master bibliographic record upgrades in OCLC performed mostly by library paraprofessional support staff, by professional librarians, or by both?

	Mostly paraprofessional support staff	Mostly professional librarians	Performed by both
Entire Sample	6.17%	81.48%	12.35%

Table 8.10.2: Are master bibliographic record upgrades in OCLC performed mostly by library paraprofessional support staff, by professional librarians, or by both? Broken out by Type of College

Type of College	Mostly paraprofessional support staff	Mostly professional librarians	Performed by both
Community College	0.00%	100.00%	0.00%
4-Year Degree Granting College	7.89%	84.21%	7.89%
MA or PHD Granting College	4.35%	82.61%	13.04%
Research University	6.67%	66.67%	26.67%

Table 8.10.3: Are master bibliographic record upgrades in OCLC performed mostly by library paraprofessional support staff, by professional librarians, or by both? Broken out by Public or Private Status

Public or Private Status	Mostly paraprofessional support staff	Mostly professional librarians	Performed by both
Public	9.62%	78.85%	11.54%
Private	0.00%	86.21%	13.79%

Table 8.10.4: Are master bibliographic record upgrades in OCLC performed mostly by library paraprofessional support staff, by professional librarians, or by both? Broken out by Total Student Enrollment

Total Student Enrollment	Mostly paraprofessional support staff	Mostly professional librarians	Performed by both
Less than 10,000	0.00%	90.32%	9.68%
10,000 to 20,000	9.09%	81.82%	9.09%
More than 20,000	11.76%	64.71%	23.53%

Table 8.10.5: Are master bibliographic record upgrades in OCLC performed mostly by library paraprofessional support staff, by professional librarians, or by both? Broken out by Annual Tuition

Annual Tuition	Mostly paraprofessional support staff	Mostly professional librarians	Performed by both
Less than $8,000	3.85%	88.46%	7.69%
$8,000 to $18,000	13.79%	72.41%	13.79%
More than $18,000	0.00%	84.62%	15.38%

Table 8.11.1: Is the establishment of local series, uniform title headings and authority records performed mostly by library paraprofessional support staff, by professional librarians, or by both?

	Mostly paraprofessional support staff	Mostly professional librarians	Performed by both
Entire Sample	6.17%	76.54%	17.28%

Table 8.11.2: Is the establishment of local series, uniform title headings and authority records performed mostly by library paraprofessional support staff, by professional librarians, or by both? Broken out by Type of College

Type of College	Mostly paraprofessional support staff	Mostly professional librarians	Performed by both
Community College	0.00%	100.00%	0.00%
4-Year Degree Granting College	7.89%	76.32%	15.79%
MA or PHD Granting College	0.00%	82.61%	17.39%
Research University	13.33%	60.00%	26.67%

Table 8.11.3: Is the establishment of local series, uniform title headings and authority records performed mostly by library paraprofessional support staff, by professional librarians, or by both? Broken out by Public or Private Status

Public or Private Status	Mostly paraprofessional support staff	Mostly professional librarians	Performed by both
Public	7.69%	73.08%	19.23%
Private	3.45%	82.76%	13.79%

Table 8.11.4: Is the establishment of local series, uniform title headings and authority records performed mostly by library paraprofessional support staff, by professional librarians, or by both? Broken out by Total Student Enrollment

Total Student Enrollment	Mostly paraprofessional support staff	Mostly professional librarians	Performed by both
Less than 10,000	0.00%	83.87%	16.13%
10,000 to 20,000	6.06%	75.76%	18.18%
More than 20,000	17.65%	64.71%	17.65%

Table 8.11.5: Is the establishment of local series, uniform title headings and authority records performed mostly by library paraprofessional support staff, by professional librarians, or by both? Broken out by Annual Tuition

Annual Tuition	Mostly paraprofessional support staff	Mostly professional librarians	Performed by both
Less than $8,000	0.00%	80.77%	19.23%
$8,000 to $18,000	13.79%	68.97%	17.24%
More than $18,000	3.85%	80.77%	15.38%

Table 8.12.1: Is the establishment of local name, corporate body, and conference headings and authority records performed mostly by library paraprofessional support staff, by professional librarians, or by both?

	Mostly paraprofessional support staff	Mostly professional librarians	Performed by both
Entire Sample	6.17%	77.78%	16.05%

Table 8.12.2: Is the establishment of local name, corporate body, and conference headings and authority records performed mostly by library paraprofessional support staff, by professional librarians, or by both? Broken out by Type of College

Type of College	Mostly paraprofessional support staff	Mostly professional librarians	Performed by both
Community College	0.00%	100.00%	0.00%
4-Year Degree Granting College	7.89%	78.95%	13.16%
MA or PHD Granting College	0.00%	86.96%	13.04%
Research University	13.33%	53.33%	33.33%

Table 8.12.3: Is the establishment of local name, corporate body, and conference headings and authority records performed mostly by library paraprofessional support staff, by professional librarians, or by both? Broken out by Public or Private Status

Public or Private Status	Mostly paraprofessional support staff	Mostly professional librarians	Performed by both
Public	5.77%	76.92%	17.31%
Private	6.90%	79.31%	13.79%

Table 8.12.4: Is the establishment of local name, corporate body, and conference headings and authority records performed mostly by library paraprofessional support staff, by professional librarians, or by both? Broken out by Total Student Enrollment

Total Student Enrollment	Mostly paraprofessional support staff	Mostly professional librarians	Performed by both
Less than 10,000	0.00%	90.32%	9.68%
10,000 to 20,000	9.09%	72.73%	18.18%
More than 20,000	11.76%	64.71%	23.53%

Table 8.12.5: Is the establishment of local name, corporate body, and conference headings and authority records performed mostly by library paraprofessional support staff, by professional librarians, or by both? Broken out by Annual Tuition

Annual Tuition	Mostly paraprofessional support staff	Mostly professional librarians	Performed by both
Less than $8,000	0.00%	88.46%	11.54%
$8,000 to $18,000	10.34%	72.41%	17.24%
More than $18,000	7.69%	73.08%	19.23%

Table 8.13.1: Is the establishment of local subject and geographic headings and authority records performed mostly by library paraprofessional support staff, by professional librarians, or by both?

	Mostly paraprofessional support staff	Mostly professional librarians	Performed by both
Entire Sample	4.94%	83.95%	11.11%

Table 8.13.2: Is the establishment of local subject and geographic headings and authority records performed mostly by library paraprofessional support staff, by professional librarians, or by both? Broken out by Type of College

Type of College	Mostly paraprofessional support staff	Mostly professional librarians	Performed by both
Community College	0.00%	100.00%	0.00%
4-Year Degree Granting College	5.26%	84.21%	10.53%
MA or PHD Granting College	0.00%	95.65%	4.35%
Research University	13.33%	60.00%	26.67%

Table 8.13.3: Is the establishment of local subject and geographic headings and authority records performed mostly by library paraprofessional support staff, by professional librarians, or by both? Broken out by Public or Private Status

Public or Private Status	Mostly paraprofessional support staff	Mostly professional librarians	Performed by both
Public	5.77%	82.69%	11.54%
Private	3.45%	86.21%	10.34%

Table 8.13.4: Is the establishment of local subject and geographic headings and authority records performed mostly by library paraprofessional support staff, by professional librarians, or by both? Broken out by Total Student Enrollment

Total Student Enrollment	Mostly paraprofessional support staff	Mostly professional librarians	Performed by both
Less than 10,000	0.00%	93.55%	6.45%
10,000 to 20,000	6.06%	78.79%	15.15%
More than 20,000	11.76%	76.47%	11.76%

Table 8.13.5: Is the establishment of local subject and geographic headings and authority records performed mostly by library paraprofessional support staff, by professional librarians, or by both? Broken out by Annual Tuition

Annual Tuition	Mostly paraprofessional support staff	Mostly professional librarians	Performed by both
Less than $8,000	0.00%	92.31%	7.69%
$8,000 to $18,000	10.34%	75.86%	13.79%
More than $18,000	3.85%	84.62%	11.54%

Table 9.1: How many positions in cataloging library support staff has your organization gained or lost in the past five years?

	Mean	Median	Minimum	Maximum
Entire Sample	0.42	0.00	-5.00	10.00

Table 9.2: How many positions in cataloging library support staff has your organization gained or lost in the past five years? Broken out by Type of College

Type of College	Mean	Median	Minimum	Maximum
Community College	0.13	0.00	-0.50	1.00
4-Year Degree Granting College	0.31	0.00	-3.00	5.00
MA or PHD Granting College	1.08	0.00	-3.00	10.00
Research University	-0.23	0.00	-5.00	6.00

Table 9.3: How many positions in cataloging library support staff has your organization gained or lost in the past five years? Broken out by Public or Private Status

Public or Private Status	Mean	Median	Minimum	Maximum
Public	0.62	0.00	-5.00	10.00
Private	0.08	0.00	-3.00	4.00

Table 9.4: How many positions in cataloging library support staff has your organization gained or lost in the past five years? Broken out by Total Student Enrollment

Total Student Enrollment	Mean	Median	Minimum	Maximum
Less than 10,000	0.25	0.00	-3.00	5.00
10,000 to 20,000	0.15	0.00	-4.00	5.00
More than 20,000	1.13	1.00	-5.00	10.00

Table 9.5: How many positions in cataloging library support staff has your organization gained or lost in the past five years? Broken out by Annual Tuition

Annual Tuition	Mean	Median	Minimum	Maximum
Less than $8,000	0.90	0.00	-2.00	5.00
$8,000 to $18,000	0.42	0.00	-4.00	10.00
More than $18,000	-0.02	0.00	-5.00	4.00

Table 10.1: How many positions for professional librarians in cataloging functions has your organization gained or lost in the past five years?

	Mean	Median	Minimum	Maximum
Entire Sample	0.41	0.00	-3.00	10.00

Table 10.2: How many positions for professional librarians in cataloging functions has your organization gained or lost in the past five years? Broken out by Type of College

Type of College	Mean	Median	Minimum	Maximum
Community College	-0.38	0.00	-1.50	0.00
4-Year Degree Granting College	0.25	0.00	-2.00	5.00
MA or PHD Granting College	0.35	0.00	-3.00	5.00
Research University	1.23	0.00	-2.00	10.00

Table 10.3: How many positions for professional librarians in cataloging functions has your organization gained or lost in the past five years? Broken out by Public or Private Status

Public or Private Status	Mean	Median	Minimum	Maximum
Public	0.66	0.00	-3.00	10.00
Private	-0.06	0.00	-2.00	1.00

Table 10.4: How many positions for professional librarians in cataloging functions has your organization gained or lost in the past five years? Broken out by Total Student Enrollment

Total Student Enrollment	Mean	Median	Minimum	Maximum
Less than 10,000	0.29	0.00	0.00	5.00
10,000 to 20,000	0.23	0.00	-3.00	5.00
More than 20,000	1.04	0.00	-2.00	10.00

Table 10.5: How many positions for professional librarians in cataloging functions has your organization gained or lost in the past five years? Broken out by Annual Tuition

Annual Tuition	Mean	Median	Minimum	Maximum
Less than $8,000	1.04	0.00	-2.00	10.00
$8,000 to $18,000	0.29	0.00	-2.00	3.00
More than $18,000	-0.15	0.00	-3.00	2.00

Table 11.1: Does your cataloging division participate in library school student mentoring or internships, or recruiting existing staff and student workers into the cataloging profession?

	No Response	Yes	No
Entire Sample	1.23%	44.44%	54.32%

Table 11.2: Does your cataloging division participate in library school student mentoring or internships, or recruiting existing staff and student workers into the cataloging profession? Broken out by Type of College

Type of College	No Response	Yes	No
Community College	0.00%	60.00%	40.00%
4-Year Degree Granting College	2.63%	39.47%	57.89%
MA or PHD Granting College	0.00%	47.83%	52.17%
Research University	0.00%	46.67%	53.33%

Table 11.3: Does your cataloging division participate in library school student mentoring or internships, or recruiting existing staff and student workers into the cataloging profession? Broken out by Public or Private Status

Public or Private Status	No Response	Yes	No
Public	0.00%	46.15%	53.85%
Private	3.45%	41.38%	55.17%

Table 11.4: Does your cataloging division participate in library school student mentoring or internships, or recruiting existing staff and student workers into the cataloging profession? Broken out by Total Student Enrollment

Total Student Enrollment	No Response	Yes	No
Less than 10,000	3.23%	45.16%	51.61%
10,000 to 20,000	0.00%	33.33%	66.67%
More than 20,000	0.00%	64.71%	35.29%

Table 11.5: Does your cataloging division participate in library school student mentoring or internships, or recruiting existing staff and student workers into the cataloging profession? Broken out by Annual Tuition

Annual Tuition	No Response	Yes	No
Less than $8,000	0.00%	42.31%	57.69%
$8,000 to $18,000	0.00%	48.28%	51.72%
More than $18,0000	3.85%	42.31%	53.85%

Table 12: How many of each of the following do you believe will be retiring from your institution within the next five years?

Table 12.1.1: Professional Librarians performing mostly cataloging functions

	Mean	Median	Minimum	Maximum
Entire Sample	0.66	0.00	0.00	5.00

Table 12.1.2: Professional Librarians performing mostly cataloging functions Broken out by Type of College

Type of College	Mean	Median	Minimum	Maximum
Community College	0.50	0.50	0.00	1.00
4-Year Degree Granting College	0.50	0.00	0.00	3.00
MA or PHD Granting College	0.75	0.00	0.00	5.00
Research University	0.97	1.00	0.00	5.00

Table 12.1.3: Professional Librarians performing mostly cataloging functions Broken out by Public or Private Status

Public or Private Status	Mean	Median	Minimum	Maximum
Public	0.74	0.00	0.00	5.00
Private	0.50	0.00	0.00	2.00

Table 12.1.4: Professional Librarians performing mostly cataloging functions Broken out by Total Student Enrollment

Total Student Enrollment	Mean	Median	Minimum	Maximum
Less than 10,000	0.46	0.00	0.00	1.00
10,000 to 20,000	0.68	0.00	0.00	5.00
More than 20,000	0.97	0.50	0.00	5.00

Table 12.1.5: Professional Librarians performing mostly cataloging functions Broken out by Annual Tuition

Annual Tuition	Mean	Median	Minimum	Maximum
Less than $8,000	0.69	0.00	0.00	5.00
$8,000 to $18,000	0.76	1.00	0.00	3.00
More than $18,000	0.52	0.00	0.00	2.00

Table 12.2.1: Library Paraprofessional Support Staff Performing mostly cataloging functions

	Mean	Median	Minimum	Maximum
Entire Sample	1.13	1.00	0.00	10.00

Table 12.2.2: Library Paraprofessional Support Staff Performing mostly cataloging functions Broken out by Type of College

Type of College	Mean	Median	Minimum	Maximum
Community College	0.00	0.00	0.00	0.00
4-Year Degree Granting College	0.70	0.00	0.00	3.00
MA or PHD Granting College	1.59	1.00	0.00	10.00
Research University	1.67	2.00	0.00	4.00

Table 12.2.3: Library Paraprofessional Support Staff Performing mostly cataloging functions Broken out by Public or Private Status

Public or Private Status	Mean	Median	Minimum	Maximum
Public	1.37	1.00	0.00	10.00
Private	0.64	0.00	0.00	3.00

Table 12.2.4: Library Paraprofessional Support Staff Performing mostly cataloging functions Broken out by Total Student Enrollment

Total Student Enrollment	Mean	Median	Minimum	Maximum
Less than 10,000	0.48	0.00	0.00	3.00
10,000 to 20,000	1.31	1.00	0.00	10.00
More than 20,000	1.84	2.00	0.00	5.00

Table 12.2.5: Library Paraprofessional Support Staff Performing mostly cataloging functions Broken out by Annual Tuition

Annual Tuition	Mean	Median	Minimum	Maximum
Less than $8,000	1.24	0.00	0.00	10.00
$8,000 to $18,000	1.33	1.00	0.00	5.00
More than $18,000	0.76	1.00	0.00	3.00

CHAPTER 4: SALARY ISSUES

Table 13.1: Do catalogers at your institution have salaries comparable to public service librarians?

	No Response	Yes	No	Unsure
Entire Sample	1.23%	62.96%	13.58%	22.22%

Table 13.2: Do catalogers at your institution have salaries comparable to public service librarians? Broken out by Type of College

Type of College	No Response	Yes	No	Unsure
Community College	0.00%	60.00%	40.00%	0.00%
4-Year Degree Granting College	2.63%	60.53%	13.16%	23.68%
MA or PHD Granting College	0.00%	91.30%	0.00%	8.70%
Research University	0.00%	26.67%	26.67%	46.67%

Table 13.3: Do catalogers at your institution have salaries comparable to public service librarians? Broken out by Public or Private Status

Public or Private Status	No Response	Yes	No	Unsure
Public	0.00%	65.38%	17.31%	17.31%
Private	3.45%	58.62%	6.90%	31.03%

Table 13.4: Do catalogers at your institution have salaries comparable to public service librarians? Broken out by Total Student Enrollment

Total Student Enrollment	No Response	Yes	No	Unsure
Less than 10,000	3.23%	77.42%	9.68%	9.68%
10,000 to 20,000	0.00%	60.61%	9.09%	30.30%
More than 20,000	0.00%	41.18%	29.41%	29.41%

Table 13.5: Do catalogers at your institution have salaries comparable to public service librarians? Broken out by Annual Tuition

Annual Tuition	No Response	Yes	No	Unsure
Less than $8,000	0.00%	73.08%	19.23%	7.69%
$8,000 to $18,000	0.00%	62.07%	13.79%	24.14%
More than $18,000	3.85%	53.85%	7.69%	34.62%

Table 14.1: Which phrase best describes the trend in pay rates for catalogers at your institution over the past four years?

	No Response	Increases between 2.5% and 5%	Increases of less than 2.5%	Pay has remained flat	Pay has been declining
Entire Sample	1.23%	8.64%	56.79%	30.86%	2.47%

Table 14.2: Which phrase best describes the trend in pay rates for catalogers at your institution over the past four years? Broken out by Type of College

Type of College	No Response	Increases between 2.5% and 5%	Increases of less than 2.5%	Pay has remained flat	Pay has been declining
Community College	0.00%	20.00%	40.00%	40.00%	0.00%
4-Year Degree Granting College	2.63%	7.89%	60.53%	28.95%	0.00%
MA or PHD Granting College	0.00%	13.04%	56.52%	26.09%	4.35%
Research University	0.00%	0.00%	53.33%	40.00%	6.67%

Table 14.3: Which phrase best describes the trend in pay rates for catalogers at your institution over the past four years? Broken out by Public or Private Status

Public or Private Status	No Response	Increases between 2.5% and 5%	Increases of less than 2.5%	Pay has remained flat	Pay has been declining
Public	0.00%	11.54%	46.15%	40.38%	1.92%
Private	3.45%	3.45%	75.86%	13.79%	3.45%

Table 14.4: Which phrase best describes the trend in pay rates for catalogers at your institution over the past four years? Broken out by Total Student Enrollment

Total Student Enrollment	No Response	Increases between 2.5% and 5%	Increases of less than 2.5%	Pay has remained flat	Pay has been declining
Less than 10,000	3.23%	6.45%	64.52%	25.81%	0.00%
10,000 to 20,000	0.00%	3.03%	54.55%	39.39%	3.03%
More than 20,000	0.00%	23.53%	47.06%	23.53%	5.88%

Table 14.5: Which phrase best describes the trend in pay rates for catalogers at your institution over the past four years? Broken out by Annual Tuition

Annual Tuition	No Response	Increases between 2.5% and 5%	Increases of less than 2.5%	Pay has remained flat	Pay has been declining
Less than $8,000	0.00%	11.54%	42.31%	42.31%	3.85%
$8,000 to $18,000	0.00%	10.34%	58.62%	27.59%	3.45%
More than $18,000	3.85%	3.85%	69.23%	23.08%	0.00%

CHAPTER 5: WORK RATE COMPLETION

Does your cataloging agency have cataloging quotas, and please explain why, or why not.

1. No because my director does not understand cataloging.
2. No. I am the primary cataloguer and I keep working at my own pace until everything has been catalogued! I set my own priorities and goals.
3. No quotas. Small department. No backlogs. Many other projects which we prioritize.
4. No. It is too difficult to predict the work that will come through and how long it will take. Quotas don't tell the whole story. You can do lots of easy work, or a few pieces that take forever to do.
5. No. We have no backlog, so we have no need for quotas. We catalog what comes in/becomes available.
6. No quotas because the majority of staff are seriously challenged to produce an accurate bibliographic description. A quota would paralyze the majority of staff who are already struggling.
7. No quotas since incoming materials are unstable.
8. Yes. To maintain productivity levels and for evaluation purposes.
9. No, we used to have, but the practice was discontinued, maybe because of external problems (physical facilities, strike, etc) which which were an obstacle to achieving the quotas.
10. No. We have no backlog so we catalog materials as they arrive
11. Yes, we need to show that we are completing the necessary work for items coming into the library.
12. No, we don't have the need as there is a high volume of output for the size of cataloging staff & yearly accessions.
13. Yes in order to evaluate performance objectives.
14. No. I don't find quotas to be meaningful or useful.
15. No.
16. No.
17. No. We do not have enough people to have quotas! We are lucky to get done what we get done.
18. No.
19. No. I just need to keep up with the purchases.
20. No. Catalog all the new and gift books.
21. No, we do not believe quotas indicate the level of work by individual catalogers.
22. No. I don't feel this is useful. I ask my staff to try to move easy copy cataloging out of our department from time of receipt to finish of processing in 3 days. Materials that do not have DLC copy cataloging may take longer.
23. No.
24. No, not relevant.
25. No.
26. No. We don't have enough to do to have a quota. We do have qualititative expectations for cataloging.
27. No.
28. We do not because we are a small institution. If there is a rush, we get it done immediately.
29. We used to have but then staff became resentful so we stopped it.
30. No, we try to maintain a no backlog policy, but numerical cataloging quotas are not as important as long as the cataloging service to our users and branch libraries is good.
31. No quotas; catalogers are engaged in a variety of tasks related to cataloging (e.g.,

maintenance, creating authority records) which precludes using quotas. Catalogers are expected to provide quality as well as quantity; quotas "encourage" speed to the detriment of quality. We monitor statistics, but our primary goal is to provide high-quality records.

32. No.

33. No. We are not a production shop - at this point our philosophy is quality over quantity. That being said, we do not have a backlog and our materials get to the shelves quickly.

34. Only those that are related to the cataloguing that we outsource. If we don't send them a certain amount of cataloguing, we get charged extra per unit.

35. No.

36. Yes, because staff were being very lazy!

37. OCLC quota.

38. Yes. Only as a means to track productivity for annual reviews.

39. Quotas have not been the norm, but we are considering instituting goals.

40. We have realistic quotas to encourage staff to be productive.

41. No. It is assumed that everyone is an adult and can manage their own time. It is expected that items will make it through the department in a timely manner and we have never had a problem doing this.

42. No.

43. No.

44. No quotas.

45. No, nobody is available to enforce them (and we hardly have enough material coming through for it to matter).

46. We have never hit upon a reasonable metric to establish quotas.

47. No.

48. We dropped cataloging quotas and are now focusing on quality of metadata created as working with rare and special materials takes more time.

49. No. We recognize that there are many factors that affect the number of items each person can catalog in a given period, such as other responsibilities in addition to cataloging, level of difficulty of cataloging different types of materials, etc., so setting quotas can not be done fairly.

50. No - we don't have a backlog, so quotas wouldn't make any sense.

51. No.

52. No; so few staff, keeping up with backlog is enough

53. We used to set monthly quotas but after eliminating all backlogs we have moved to a turnaround time metric.

54. No, it all gets done, no excuses.

55. No. Apparently this has been a longstanding culture, though it may have been put in place in the mid-1990s when we went from a traditionally top-down heirarchy to self-directed teams. If there were cataloging quotas expected before then I am not aware of them.

56. No quotas. We can only do what we acquire.

57. No.

58. No, much is outsourced.

59. No quotas, but back logs are discouraged. We do monitor quantity and quality.

60. No.

61. No, we evaluate effectiveness by time it takes for materials to move through the department rather than by numbers of items completed.

62. No.

63. No, because nobody has set any. Personally I set a quota for myself each year.

64. No agency used.

65. No ... it wouldn't do any good.

66. No, it upsets the staff and undermines productivity to set quotas for them.

67. No. We have no backlog, so it's never been an issue.
68. Not that I am aware of. If I had to take a guess about "quotas" or lack thereof, I would say it's because cataloging is variable work that is impacted by purchases and complexity/type/ and rarity of materials. I think quotas are a bad idea.
69. No - too cumbersome to manage.
70. Not formally, but our goal is to stay current on new material--i.e. get it on the shelf with 1 month.
71. No.
72. No. We're too "nice" and wouldn't want to hurt anybody's feelings.
73. No. We have not had the need to establish quotas since we are so small.
74. No.
75. No. That's their business model.

Table 15.1: Does your technical services area track turn-around time from Acquisitions receipt to Cataloging to shelf-ready distribution?

	No Response	Yes	No	Don't Know
Entire Sample	8.64%	19.75%	70.37%	1.23%

Table 15.2: Does your technical services area track turn-around time from Acquisitions receipt to Cataloging to shelf-ready distribution? Broken out by Type of College

Type of College	No Response	Yes	No	Don't Know
Community College	0.00%	40.00%	60.00%	0.00%
4-Year Degree Granting College	10.53%	18.42%	71.05%	0.00%
MA or PHD Granting College	4.35%	21.74%	69.57%	4.35%
Research University	13.33%	13.33%	73.33%	0.00%

Table 15.3: Does your technical services area track turn-around time from Acquisitions receipt to Cataloging to shelf-ready distribution? Broken out by Public or Private Status

Public or Private Status	No Response	Yes	No	Don't Know
Public	9.62%	25.00%	63.46%	1.92%
Private	6.90%	10.34%	82.76%	0.00%

Table 15.4: Does your technical services area track turn-around time from Acquisitions receipt to Cataloging to shelf-ready distribution? Broken out by Total Student Enrollment

Total Student Enrollment	No Response	Yes	No	Don't Know
Less than 10,000	9.68%	16.13%	74.19%	0.00%
10,000 to 20,000	9.09%	15.15%	75.76%	0.00%
More than 20,000	5.88%	35.29%	52.94%	5.88%

Table 15.5: Does your technical services area track turn-around time from Acquisitions receipt to Cataloging to shelf-ready distribution? Broken out by Annual Tuition

Annual Tuition	No Response	Yes	No	Don't Know
Less than $8,000	11.54%	34.62%	53.85%	0.00%
$8,000 to $18,000	0.00%	17.24%	79.31%	3.45%
More than $18,000	15.38%	7.69%	76.92%	0.00%

Table 16: How would you rate the use of the following quality indicators in Cataloging work

Table 16.1.1: Cataloger or staff work product quotas

	No Response	Very Useful	Somewhat Useful	Not Useful	Misleading	Detracting from Quality
Entire Sample	1.23%	6.17%	20.99%	28.40%	32.10%	11.11%

Table 16.1.2: Cataloger or staff work product quotas Broken out by Type of College

Type of College	No Response	Very Useful	Somewhat Useful	Not Useful	Misleading	Detracting from Quality
Community College	0.00%	0.00%	0.00%	60.00%	20.00%	20.00%
4-Year Degree Granting College	2.63%	2.63%	23.68%	28.95%	28.95%	13.16%
MA or PHD Granting College	0.00%	0.00%	13.04%	26.09%	52.17%	8.70%
Research University	0.00%	26.67%	33.33%	20.00%	13.33%	6.67%

Table 16.1.3: Cataloger or staff work product quotas Broken out by Public or Private Status

Public or Private Status	No Response	Very Useful	Somewhat Useful	Not Useful	Misleading	Detracting from Quality
Public	0.00%	7.69%	19.23%	21.15%	38.46%	13.46%
Private	3.45%	3.45%	24.14%	41.38%	20.69%	6.90%

Table 16.1.4: Cataloger or staff work product quotas Broken out by Total Student Enrollment

Total Student Enrollment	No Response	Very Useful	Somewhat Useful	Not Useful	Misleading	Detracting from Quality
Less than 10,000	3.23%	0.00%	22.58%	41.94%	25.81%	6.45%
10,000 to 20,000	0.00%	3.03%	15.15%	24.24%	39.39%	18.18%
More than 20,000	0.00%	23.53%	29.41%	11.76%	29.41%	5.88%

Table 16.1.5: Cataloger or staff work product quotas Broken out by Annual Tuition

Annual Tuition	No Response	Very Useful	Somewhat Useful	Not Useful	Misleading	Detracting from Quality
Less than $8,000	0.00%	7.69%	19.23%	30.77%	30.77%	11.54%
$8,000 to $18,000	0.00%	6.90%	17.24%	17.24%	44.83%	13.79% .
More than $18,000	3.85%	3.85%	26.92%	38.46%	19.23%	7.69%

Table 16.2.1: Turn-around time from receipt in Cataloging to ready for shelf

	No Response	Very Useful	Somewhat Useful	Not Useful	Misleading	Detracting from Quality
Entire Sample	1.23%	11.11%	49.38%	18.52%	17.28%	2.47%

Table 16.2.2: Turn-around time from receipt in Cataloging to ready for shelf Broken out by Type of College

Type of College	No Response	Very Useful	Somewhat Useful	Not Useful	Misleading	Detracting from Quality
Community College	0.00%	20.00%	40.00%	20.00%	0.00%	20.00%
4-Year Degree Granting College	2.63%	7.89%	47.37%	18.42%	21.05%	2.63%
MA or PHD Granting College	0.00%	4.35%	47.83%	21.74%	26.09%	0.00%
Research University	0.00%	26.67%	60.00%	13.33%	0.00%	0.00%

Rate as an Indicator of Quality

Table 16.2.3: Turn-around time from receipt in Cataloging to ready for shelf Broken out by Public or Private Status

Public or Private Status	No Response	Very Useful	Somewhat Useful	Not Useful	Misleading	Detracting from Quality
Public	0.00%	11.54%	50.00%	17.31%	19.23%	1.92%
Private	3.45%	10.34%	48.28%	20.69%	13.79%	3.45%

Table 16.2.4: Turn-around time from receipt in Cataloging to ready for shelf Broken out by Total Student Enrollment

Total Student Enrollment	No Response	Very Useful	Somewhat Useful	Not Useful	Misleading	Detracting from Quality
Less than 10,000	3.23%	0.00%	51.61%	22.58%	19.35%	3.23%
10,000 to 20,000	0.00%	9.09%	48.48%	18.18%	21.21%	3.03%
More than 20,000	0.00%	35.29%	47.06%	11.76%	5.88%	0.00%

Table 16.2.5: Turn-around time from receipt in Cataloging to ready for shelf Broken out by Annual Tuition

Annual Tuition	No Response	Very Useful	Somewhat Useful	Not Useful	Misleading	Detracting from Quality
Less than $8,000	0.00%	15.38%	50.00%	19.23%	15.38%	0.00%
$8,000 to $18,000	0.00%	6.90%	41.38%	20.69%	27.59%	3.45%
More than $18,000	3.85%	11.54%	57.69%	15.38%	7.69%	3.85%

Table 16.3.1: Error rates per bibliographic record

	Very Useful	Somewhat Useful	Not Useful	Misleading
Entire Sample	20.99%	59.26%	17.28%	2.47%

Rate As An Indicator Of Quality

Table 16.3.2: Error rates per bibliographic record Broken out by Type of College

Type of College	Very Useful	Somewhat Useful	Not Useful	Misleading
Community College	20.00%	60.00%	20.00%	0.00%
4-Year Degree Granting College	13.16%	60.53%	21.05%	5.26%
MA or PHD Granting College	13.04%	69.57%	17.39%	0.00%
Research University	53.33%	40.00%	6.67%	0.00%

Table 16.3.3: Error rates per bibliographic record Broken out by Public or Private Status

Public or Private Status	Very Useful	Somewhat Useful	Not Useful	Misleading
Public	28.85%	53.85%	15.38%	1.92%
Private	6.90%	68.97%	20.69%	3.45%

Table 16.3.4: Error rates per bibliographic record Broken out by Total Student Enrollment

Total Student Enrollment	Very Useful	Somewhat Useful	Not Useful	Misleading
Less than 10,000	6.45%	67.74%	22.58%	3.23%
10,000 to 20,000	27.27%	57.58%	15.15%	0.00%
More than 20,000	35.29%	47.06%	11.76%	5.88%

Table 16.3.5: Error rates per bibliographic record Broken out by Annual Tuition

Annual Tuition	Very Useful	Somewhat Useful	Not Useful	Misleading
Less than $8,000	19.23%	57.69%	23.08%	0.00%
$8,000 to $18,000	24.14%	58.62%	13.79%	3.45%
More than $18,000	19.23%	61.54%	15.38%	3.85%

Table 16.4.1: Completeness of bibliographic record

	No Response	Very Useful	Somewhat Useful	Not Useful	Misleading
Entire Sample	1.23%	48.15%	37.04%	9.88%	3.70%

Table 16.4.2: Completeness of bibliographic record Broken out by Type of College

Type of College	No Response	Very Useful	Somewhat Useful	Not Useful	Misleading
Community College	0.00%	40.00%	40.00%	20.00%	0.00%
4-Year Degree Granting College	2.63%	44.74%	36.84%	7.89%	7.89%
MA or PHD Granting College	0.00%	43.48%	47.83%	8.70%	0.00%
Research University	0.00%	66.67%	20.00%	13.33%	0.00%

Table 16.4.3: Completeness of bibliographic record Broken out by Public or Private Status

Public or Private Status	No Response	Very Useful	Somewhat Useful	Not Useful	Misleading
Public	0.00%	44.23%	44.23%	7.69%	3.85%
Private	3.45%	55.17%	24.14%	13.79%	3.45%

Table 16.4.4: Completeness of bibliographic record Broken out by Total Student Enrollment

Total Student Enrollment	No Response	Very Useful	Somewhat Useful	Not Useful	Misleading
Less than 10,000	3.23%	54.84%	25.81%	12.90%	3.23%
10,000 to 20,000	0.00%	45.45%	45.45%	6.06%	3.03%
More than 20,000	0.00%	41.18%	41.18%	11.76%	5.88%

Table 16.4.5: Completeness of bibliographic record Broken out by Annual Tuition

Annual Tuition	No Response	Very Useful	Somewhat Useful	Not Useful	Misleading
Less than $8,000	0.00%	34.62%	50.00%	11.54%	3.85%
$8,000 to $18,000	3.45%	48.28%	37.93%	6.90%	3.45%
More than $18,000	0.00%	61.54%	23.08%	11.54%	3.85%

Rate as an Indicator of Quality

Table 16.5.1: Error rates per authority record

	No Response	Very Useful	Somewhat Useful	Not Useful	Misleading
Entire Sample	4.94%	19.75%	40.74%	32.10%	2.47%

Table 16.5.2: Error rates per authority record Broken out by Type of College

Type of College	No Response	Very Useful	Somewhat Useful	Not Useful	Misleading
Community College	20.00%	0.00%	60.00%	20.00%	0.00%
4-Year Degree Granting College	5.26%	13.16%	44.74%	31.58%	5.26%
MA or PHD Granting College	4.35%	8.70%	34.78%	52.17%	0.00%
Research University	0.00%	60.00%	33.33%	6.67%	0.00%

Table 16.5.3: Error rates per authority record Broken out by Public or Private Status

Public or Private Status	No Response	Very Useful	Somewhat Useful	Not Useful	Misleading
Public	1.92%	23.08%	42.31%	30.77%	1.92%
Private	10.34%	13.79%	37.93%	34.48%	3.45%

Table 16.5.4: Error rates per authority record Broken out by Total Student Enrollment

Total Student Enrollment	No Response	Very Useful	Somewhat Useful	Not Useful	Misleading
Less than 10,000	6.45%	3.23%	38.71%	48.39%	3.23%
10,000 to 20,000	3.03%	24.24%	51.52%	21.21%	0.00%
More than 20,000	5.88%	41.18%	23.53%	23.53%	5.88%

Table 16.5.5: Error rates per authority record Broken out by Annual Tuition

Annual Tuition	No Response	Very Useful	Somewhat Useful	Not Useful	Misleading
Less than $8,000	3.85%	15.38%	42.31%	38.46%	0.00%
$8,000 to $18,000	6.90%	20.69%	41.38%	27.59%	3.45%
More than $18,000	3.85%	23.08%	38.46%	30.77%	3.85%

Rate as an Indicator of Quality

Table 16.6.1: Error rates per holdings record

	No Response	Very Useful	Somewhat Useful	Not Useful	Misleading
Entire Sample	3.70%	23.46%	46.91%	23.46%	2.47%

Table 16.6.2: Error rates per holdings record Broken out by Type of College

Type of College	No Response	Very Useful	Somewhat Useful	Not Useful	Misleading
Community College	20.00%	20.00%	40.00%	20.00%	0.00%
4-Year Degree Granting College	0.00%	15.79%	55.26%	26.32%	2.63%
MA or PHD Granting College	8.70%	21.74%	43.48%	26.09%	0.00%
Research University	0.00%	46.67%	33.33%	13.33%	6.67%

Table 16.6.3: Error rates per holdings record Broken out by Public or Private Status

Public or Private Status	No Response	Very Useful	Somewhat Useful	Not Useful	Misleading
Public	3.85%	30.77%	42.31%	19.23%	3.85%
Private	3.45%	10.34%	55.17%	31.03%	0.00%

Table 16.6.4: Error rates per holdings record Broken out by Total Student Enrollment

Total Student Enrollment	No Response	Very Useful	Somewhat Useful	Not Useful	Misleading
Less than 10,000	3.23%	12.90%	48.39%	35.48%	0.00%
10,000 to 20,000	3.03%	27.27%	54.55%	15.15%	0.00%
More than 20,000	5.88%	35.29%	29.41%	17.65%	11.76%

Table 16.6.5: Error rates per holdings record Broken out by Annual Tuition

Annual Tuition	No Response	Very Useful	Somewhat Useful	Not Useful	Misleading
Less than $8,000	3.85%	23.08%	42.31%	26.92%	3.85%
$8,000 to $18,000	6.90%	27.59%	44.83%	17.24%	3.45%
More than $18,000	0.00%	19.23%	53.85%	26.92%	0.00%

Rate as an Indicator of Quality

Table 16.7.1: Error rates per physical processing

	Very Useful	Somewhat Useful	Not Useful	Misleading
Entire Sample	16.05%	55.56%	27.16%	1.23%

Table 16.7.2: Error rates per physical processing Broken out by Type of College

Type of College	Very Useful	Somewhat Useful	Not Useful	Misleading
Community College	20.00%	40.00%	40.00%	0.00%
4-Year Degree Granting College	13.16%	50.00%	34.21%	2.63%
MA or PHD Granting College	8.70%	65.22%	26.09%	0.00%
Research University	33.33%	60.00%	6.67%	0.00%

Table 16.7.3: Error rates per physical processing Broken out by Public or Private Status

Public or Private Status	Very Useful	Somewhat Useful	Not Useful	Misleading
Public	19.23%	57.69%	21.15%	1.92%
Private	10.34%	51.72%	37.93%	0.00%

Table 16.7.4: Error rates per physical processing Broken out by Total Student Enrollment

Total Student Enrollment	Very Useful	Somewhat Useful	Not Useful	Misleading
Less than 10,000	6.45%	51.61%	41.94%	0.00%
10,000 to 20,000	24.24%	57.58%	18.18%	0.00%
More than 20,000	17.65%	58.82%	17.65%	5.88%

Table 16.7.5: Error rates per physical processing Broken out by Annual Tuition

Annual Tuition	Very Useful	Somewhat Useful	Not Useful	Misleading
Less than $8,000	15.38%	57.69%	26.92%	0.00%
$8,000 to $18,000	13.79%	58.62%	24.14%	3.45%
More than $18,000	19.23%	50.00%	30.77%	0.00%

Rate as an Indicator of Quality

Table 16.8.1: Patron or staff complaints

	Very Useful	Somewhat Useful	Not Useful	Misleading	Detracting from Quality
Entire Sample	33.33%	46.91%	9.88%	8.64%	1.23%

Table 16.8.2: Patron or staff complaints Broken out by Type of College

Type of College	Very Useful	Somewhat Useful	Not Useful	Misleading	Detracting from Quality
Community College	20.00%	40.00%	40.00%	0.00%	0.00%
4-Year Degree Granting College	26.32%	50.00%	10.53%	10.53%	2.63%
MA or PHD Granting College	39.13%	39.13%	8.70%	13.04%	0.00%
Research University	46.67%	53.33%	0.00%	0.00%	0.00%

Table 16.8.3: Patron or staff complaints Broken out by Public or Private Status

Public or Private Status	Very Useful	Somewhat Useful	Not Useful	Misleading	Detracting from Quality
Public	40.38%	40.38%	9.62%	9.62%	0.00%
Private	20.69%	58.62%	10.34%	6.90%	3.45%

Table 16.8.4: Patron or staff complaints Broken out by Total Student Enrollment

Total Student Enrollment	Very Useful	Somewhat Useful	Not Useful	Misleading	Detracting from Quality
Less than 10,000	9.68%	61.29%	12.90%	12.90%	3.23%
10,000 to 20,000	45.45%	33.33%	12.12%	9.09%	0.00%
More than 20,000	52.94%	47.06%	0.00%	0.00%	0.00%

Table 16.8.5 Patron or staff complaints Broken out by Annual Tuition

Annual Tuition	Very Useful	Somewhat Useful	Not Useful	Misleading	Detracting from Quality
Less than $8,000	23.08%	50.00%	15.38%	11.54%	0.00%
$8,000 to $18,000	41.38%	41.38%	10.34%	6.90%	0.00%
More than $18,000	34.62%	50.00%	3.85%	7.69%	3.85%

Rate as an Indicator of Quality

Table 16.9.1: Patron or staff commendation

	No Response	Very Useful	Somewhat Useful	Not Useful	Misleading	Detracting from Quality
Entire Sample	1.23%	38.27%	50.62%	6.17%	2.47%	1.23%

Table 16.9.2: Patron or staff commendation Broken out by Type of College

Type of College	No Response	Very Useful	Somewhat Useful	Not Useful	Misleading	Detracting from Quality
Community College	0.00%	0.00%	60.00%	40.00%	0.00%	0.00%
4-Year Degree Granting College	0.00%	34.21%	57.89%	2.63%	2.63%	2.63%
MA or PHD Granting College	4.35%	47.83%	39.13%	4.35%	4.35%	0.00%
Research University	0.00%	46.67%	46.67%	6.67%	0.00%	0.00%

Table 16.9.3: Patron or staff commendation Broken out by Public or Private Status

Public or Private Status	No Response	Very Useful	Somewhat Useful	Not Useful	Misleading	Detracting from Quality
Public	1.92%	44.23%	46.15%	7.69%	0.00%	0.00%
Private	0.00%	27.59%	58.62%	3.45%	6.90%	3.45%

Table 16.9.4: Patron or staff commendation Broken out by Total Student Enrollment

Total Student Enrollment	No Response	Very Useful	Somewhat Useful	Not Useful	Misleading	Detracting from Quality
Less than 10,000	0.00%	16.13%	67.74%	6.45%	6.45%	3.23%
10,000 to 20,000	3.03%	48.48%	42.42%	6.06%	0.00%	0.00%
More than 20,000	0.00%	58.82%	35.29%	5.88%	0.00%	0.00%

Table 16.9.5: Patron or staff commendation Broken out by Annual Tuition

Annual Tuition	No Response	Very Useful	Somewhat Useful	Not Useful	Misleading	Detracting from Quality
Less than $8,000	0.00%	30.77%	61.54%	7.69%	0.00%	0.00%
$8,000 to $18,000	0.00%	44.83%	44.83%	10.34%	0.00%	0.00%
More than $18,000	3.85%	38.46%	46.15%	0.00%	7.69%	3.85%

Rate as an Indicator of Quality

Table 16.10.1: Support or accomplishment of departmental or library goal

	No Response	Very Useful	Somewhat Useful	Not Useful	Misleading
Entire Sample	1.23%	56.79%	35.80%	4.94%	1.23%

Table 16.10.2: Support or accomplishment of departmental or library goal Broken out by Type of College

Type of College	No Response	Very Useful	Somewhat Useful	Not Useful	Misleading
Community College	0.00%	40.00%	40.00%	20.00%	0.00%
4-Year Degree Granting College	2.63%	52.63%	42.11%	2.63%	0.00%
MA or PHD Granting College	0.00%	60.87%	30.43%	4.35%	4.35%
Research University	0.00%	66.67%	26.67%	6.67%	0.00%

Table 16.10.3: Support or accomplishment of departmental or library goal Broken out by Public or Private Status

Public or Private Status	No Response	Very Useful	Somewhat Useful	Not Useful	Misleading
Public	0.00%	53.85%	36.54%	7.69%	1.92%
Private	3.45%	62.07%	34.48%	0.00%	0.00%

Table 16.10.4: Support or accomplishment of departmental or library goal Broken out by Total Student Enrollment

Total Student Enrollment	No Response	Very Useful	Somewhat Useful	Not Useful	Misleading
Less than 10,000	3.23%	45.16%	45.16%	3.23%	3.23%
10,000 to 20,000	0.00%	57.58%	39.39%	3.03%	0.00%
More than 20,000	0.00%	76.47%	11.76%	11.76%	0.00%

Table 16.10.5: Support or accomplishment of departmental or library goal Broken out by Annual Tuition

Annual Tuition	No Response	Very Useful	Somewhat Useful	Not Useful	Misleading
Less than $8,000	0.00%	53.85%	42.31%	3.85%	0.00%
$8,000 to $18,000	3.45%	44.83%	37.93%	10.34%	3.45%
More than $18,000	0.00%	73.08%	26.92%	0.00%	0.00%

How does your cataloging department define quality?

1. It is my own judgment.
2. Good records acquired in the minimum amount of time that serve our students well. We do not spend extra time scrutinizing subject headings or call numbers.
3. Providing the best representation of an item in our catalog.
4. Rush items dealt with immediately. We are all trained well which enables us to provide quality cataloging.
5. That's a good question -- the department would probably say accuracy and completeness...a "perfect record" whereas I would say, "material is in the catalog or database and discoverable." Getting everyone to agree and work towards the same definition is a challenge.
6. Honestly, have not given this thoughtful consideration in several years.
7. Quality has been replaced by quantity with the expectation that the most senior and experienced professional librarians will silently edit and correct and maintain minimum network and bibliographic standards without ever making the extent of the problems overt.
8. Above average.
9. Materials are easily and correctly found in our OPAC, and materials are acquired, cataloged, and processed in a timely manner.
10. Productivity, minimal error rate (errors affecting retrieval most important), timeliness-- we have target turnaround times for certain "Rush" categories of materials
11. Quality means cataloging thoroughness and efficiency with the least mistakes.
12. The materials are processed in a timely manner and are able to be found.
13. The surrogate record accurately represents the item and there is not any hindrance to access for patrons
14. Quality is defined by a high level of accuracy of bibliographic and holdings information in order to maintain the integrity of the catalog.
15. I would like staff to be able to get a decent number of materials cataloged and processed with minimal errors. I'm working with a staff who was poorly trained and one staff member who really can't do the work so I'm trying to move everyone (staff and students) to a higher level of productivity and capability gently.
16. Not defined.
17. Providing the best records to our ability.
18. With the MARC record loads (a.k.a. dumps), our online catalog is now filled with foreign records of various qualities. We can control our own cataloging, however. We do strive for our original records to be as perfect as possible. After all is said and done, however, "faster and cheaper" has won out over quality, in this administration's eyes.
19. A clean, correct database and purchased materials "shelf ready" in a month or less.
20. Accurate access points.
21. Provide accurate information for users.
22. Adherence to current cataloging rules in the creation of a bibliographic and authority records.
23. Materials are accessible within a reasonable amount of time (65 in 4 days or less). Materials can be found in the catalog, located in the shelves, or electronically. Cataloging rules are followed to the best of our ability, level K or higher. Call numbers and subject headings are accurate and lead users to similar materials. 2-3 headings are assigned to each item. Classification rules are followed correctly. Table of contents is added if useful.
24. The resources are properly entered into the catalog and processed correctly.
25. Records with little or no errors, fully cataloged with several access points.
26. By the completeness of the record and how findable it is for the end user.
27. Quality = general completeness of cataloging copy that meets standards, with an emphasis on access points that facilitate discovery.

28. Accurate and useful access and identification.
29. That the material or item is searchable in the catalog.
30. With perfect authority records.
31. Quality is an excellence in service to our users by being timely, without errors, and complete.
32. A complete bibliographic record with all appropriate access points, no errors in indexed fields and discoverable in our library catalog.
33. Don't know.
34. Adherence to established goals and procedures. Also, level of public service staff (and to some degree, patron) satisfaction with our product.
35. We consider quality two part. The first is if we meet standards (i.e. MARC 21) and the second is if we meet the needs of our users as defined in annual user surveys of quality.
36. I rarely have time to check copy cataloging.
37. Historically, quality=perfection. Our new trend is to look at production and error rates more holistically.
38. A quality record is complete and accurate with information that will help the user find the resource.
39. We do not have a formal definition. However, it is assumed that all work will be done to current cataloging standards and that everyone will take the time and care necessary to ensure these standards are met.
40. Access Points match (using OPAC searching); All RDA specific data in record); Relationships recorded properly; and most of all, the right record was used to begin with (acquisitions will/do make this type of error)
41. Can the user find the materials and do we catalog books as an acceptable rate with acceptable quality.
42. It depends on the director's judgment.
43. Records that aid discoverability.
44. We don't.
45. Clear, accurate bibliographic records with rational subject analysis.
46. Completeness of record, no errors, adheres to standards of LOC, AACR2, DDC 19, MARC, etc.
47. Following standards, completeness of record, usefulness to local and international patrons.
48. Materials are cataloged as quickly as possible, with accurate catalog records.
49. Finding a good balance between quickness and attention to detail.
50. Being dedicated to the highest standards of accuracy and usefulness of the records in the OPAC and for staff side processes.
51. Meets minimal standard on QC checklist; does not impede user access to material
52. Quality is access. Increasing access by adding all authors and tracing all authors will help future researchers. We are concerned with note information (keyword hits) and linking access points. A typo in a note field or a semicolon in the wrong place does not affect searches in the database.
53. It doesn't.
54. Cataloging and Metadata Services enjoys the skills and expertise of a diverse group of people committed to processing materials efficiently while maintaining the highest possible standards of cataloging excellence.
55. Quality is ultimately being able to present information that enhances access and use of resources.
56. The department has no formal quality statement.
57. Getting materials out in a timely efficient manner.
58. Complete cataloging records with few errors.
59. We use OCLC validation in conjunction with a full record level of cataloging.
60. We don't specifically.

61. There is not, as far as I know, a single agreed upon definition in our department.
62. We define in an error ration of less than 3.
63. Findability.
64. Precision when known, captured essence if not.
65. We really don't.
66. Patrons able to find materials easily.
67. Catalog record is as complete as possible & correct according to standards. Class number is accurate and unique, subject headings are appropriate. No typos in record. All authority work done.
68. Major access points correct and present. No typos or bibliographic errors Materials processed correctly (labeled/stamped) Materials processed and available to the patron in a timely manner. Materials tracked and located at every step in the process from acquisitions to shelf.
69. Record must be completely full and error-free.
70. In accord with national and/or local standards and practice.
71. Records meeting OCLC standards that are easily retrieved by our patrons, and completely retrievable by those who have received library instruction.
72. We demand the highest quality possible. Errors are corrected intermediately upon discovery.
73. Getting along with one another.
74. We don't use any metrics to define quality. We strive to create high quality records with few errors.
75. Accuracy of bibliographic information for the item in hand, clarity and usefulness for the user, efficient use of staff time.
76. If the college administration tells us to keep coming to work, we've achieved quality.

CHAPTER 6: TECHNOLOGY

Please explain any difficulties your area has face in improving and upgrading staff use of hardware and software technology.

1. I am fighting for new technologies to use for cataloging. I have a hard time explaining why they are important because I feel they are essentials to my job.
2. New versions of Microsoft have created issues working with our ILS.
3. Some staff members seem afraid to fail and turn to one or two "experts" and rely too heavily on them to solve their problems. This creates silos of expertise and subsequently bottlenecks in the workflow in the department. Newer technology and programs/scripting require new skill sets and our older staff are reluctant to get on board. Our paraprofessional staff are by far more willing to learn and experiment.
4. Staff's flexible attitude.
5. Getting the hardware needed.
6. Financial.
7. Personal capability.
8. Training and time to train
9. No problem, we are in a University wide rotation for hardware and supported by our Dean for needed software.
10. We have problems communicating with Purchasing, which has trouble getting our vendors paid. That's been the biggest problem.
11. I have good support from my director in purchasing needed hardware and software if finances are available. The difficulty is finding finances.
12. Sometimes budget is not enough for this.
13. Lack of funds.
14. We lack personnel in our Systems Department to provide support for our work.
15. We use the open source ILS, Evergreen. Exciting to be part of the open-source movement but system needs continual work and tweaking by local programming staff. Vital modules like serials, Acq and circ could use enhancements and further development. Programming staff time is limited for all these.
16. Lack of money.
17. There is always apprehension to trying something new but if it proves it can make their job easier they will be happy with it in the end.
18. Hardware is not a problem; cataloging staff have equipment similar to other library staff. Software technology is a problem because we have not had adequate local ILS support since the retirement of our systems librarian a few years ago. We cannot explore technological innovations (such as CatQC) that would streamline workflow because of this lack of support. Catalogers do not have the time to learn skills that would help with this.
19. Communications between systems and us could be improved. Overall service is good. Staff are change-resistant. We are working on that.
20. Technical services is often the last area to receive new hardware, although that is starting to change. Individual staff members don't have control over what software is available on their computers; if someone identifies a useful program, we have to request it from our IT department. IT staff are also the only ones who can perform updates to software, so we often end up using older versions for quite awhile.
21. Few difficulties.
22. I think that the biggest one is that we have some staff who have used the same hardware and software for many years. They have a hard time changing when necessary.
23. Budget approval and consortium restrictions are a big problem.
24. To date we have not had any difficulties with hardware and software.

25. Older generation staff with few tech skills.
26. Due to budget constraints, we do not have much system support, so upgrades were often delayed or not done.
27. We generally have not had any problems, at least that originate in our department or the library has a whole. The problems mainly come from the technology itself (e.g. not working how it is supposed to).
28. Windows has not always been our friend; software for label printers has been an issue too; lack of serial port on upgraded computers was/is an issue with label printers
29. Not much.
30. Dealing with ebook cataloging and database management has become very complex. There are too many ebook formats and maintaining links for large numbers of ebooks is nearly impossible with our small staff.
31. Paraprofessional staff have been hesitant about learning new technology that would reduce the amount of repetitive tasks they have to do, but have been willing to learn.
32. Most of our staff have not trouble improving and upgrading their use of technology.
33. Lack of funds.
34. Lack of unit expertise.
35. We have concerns about maintaining access to ClassWeb, Cataloger's Desktop and the RDA Toolkit.
36. Little or no training available; as dept head, I not only catalog but must teach mysel and train staff.
37. Our library is part of the IT division and we have not had many difficulties improving our hardware or software technologies. The computer support staff have sometimes run into issues with the hardware/software themselves due to the nature of computers, but we have not had trouble acquiring these improvements.
38. Money.
39. The only big difficulty is the level of security imposed on systems in general, thus sometimes preventing us from being more flexible in our work.
40. Budget limitations from state appropriations.
41. Some incompatibility between current versions of OCLC software and latest version of Windows. We also have strong firewalls, which interfere at times.
42. Funding only allows computers to upgraded on a 4 year cycle. Volunteer and student employee computers are much older and slow and inhibits their ability to work efficiently
43. Our staff are all pretty technologically savvy.
44. Most of it has just been with people who have been in certain systems for long periods of time not wanting to or having difficulty in learning the new systems.
45. Money.
46. Difficulty in getting system vendor to make improvements; some communication problems with learning about improvements and their implementation.
47. We are stuck with Innovative Millennium for 2 more years because we recently bought a new server.
48. Steep learning curve for older folks.
49. Reluctance of some staff to give up current duties to learn new things.
50. We often have to use computers for 5 to 10 years.
51. Changes in operating systems make traditional label printing on dedicated printers outdated. Hard to find staff time for learning new software beyond required routines.
52. Just the usual.

Briefly list and explain what you consider the most useful new technologies (hardware, software, etc.) in cataloging and metadata today, such as wikis, blogs, harvesting software, Dspace for institutional repositories, any OCLC or vendor products or services, etc.

1. OCLC batch load services OCLC connexion client
2. OCLC FirstSearch for use in copy cataloging.
3. Digital Commons and other software for institutional repositories, blogs, cloud storage of information
4. Batch processes and any utility that can streamline the workflow. Online training sources have been helpful too. Digital Libraries have helped spark interest in metadata in new ways and made it more relevant to a wider audience of both catalogers and public service librarians.
5. OCLC's Collection Manager looks promising (significant upgrade of Bibliographic Notification Service): MARCedit - software which allows batch-processing of records outside ILS;
6. Terry Reese's MARCedit and Deborah Fritz's MARC REPORT. Hands down. ILMS vendors should be embarrassed by the, in comparison, mediocre offerings they sell as cataloging / metadata clients. MARC Standards linked entries. PCC / LC training materials.
7. OCLC catexpress bibliographic record sources
8. Blogs are useful for keeping up with the profession Macros in OCLC Connexion and use of MacroPro are useful to minimize keystrokes and speed up tasks Access reports MARCedit used in conjunction with Excel spreadsheets for spot checking record quality and making batch edits Online videos and slides for training
9. Worldcat is the best cataloging database, Content DM is the best metadata and digitation tool and OCLC´s Worldshare is a promising ILS which can streamline the workflow of libraries like mine, getting out the most of cataloging, metadata and integrating description with content.
10. Blogs for sharing information, vendor services such as OCLC and shelf-ready items
11. Integrated searching of various platforms, such as a Union Catalogue; content management tools
12. MarcEdit. I'm investigating OCLC's WorldShare Metadata platform and haven't used it enough to know if it's helpful or not.
13. Listservs, OCLC connexion and OCLC ILLiad, electronic document delivery and MARCedit
14. OCLC bibliographic services continues to reign supreme
15. Since finances are a problem, my most valuable resources are the listservs and MarcEdit.
16. ContentDM is clunky, but it's the only tool for catalogers I know of to represent digital data. I think wikis and blogs are very useful also. I've heard of DSpace but not used it. I think it could be useful. One of the best OCLC software updates was the "control headings" feature to facilitate accurate access points in bibliographic records
17. Latest discovery tools (Summon, etc.) show promise, but needs more work for these products to do what they are intended to do.
18. I'm very interested in the new OCLC Worldshare Metadata service for ebooks. We use Google docs to store local procedures, manuals, etc. MARCedit is handy to help work with large batches of bib records cheaply. RSS feeds and Twitter are great for professional development in a timely manner.
19. OCLC, wikis, blogs
20. MarcEdit-it makes batch editing of vendor records a breeze
21. Web-based, cloud-based management solutions for library data--these could allow telecommuting and reallocation of library "systems" resources to other endeavors.
22. MarcEdit, Connexion

23. I think wikis and blogs are beneficial in the support of lone catalogers being able to find additional information or support when they have questions that cannot be answered by in-house staff.
24. Maybe with authorization of original records.
25. I'm lucky to get stuff done with what I have much less know what is better or worse than what I have.
26. RDA Toolkit, XML software like oXygen, Cataloger's desktop, MARCedit, wikis.
27. The ability to research people, places, topics and corporations on the web enables catalogers to add to names to the authority file and propose new subjects, without leaving one's work area.
28. Wikis
29. MARCEdit! This saves my life. I use it for all sorts of things. I also like my metadata contacts on FaceBook. They also save my life from time to time.
30. ClassWeb and OCLC Bibliographic Standards,
31. oclc
32. I would like to see wikis used for procedures, so that they can be updated and kept current by the staff who perform the tasks, rather than having to be vetted and converted to HTML by supervisors. We are investigating using the OCLC Knowledge Base to download records for ebook packages and 360 Link for ejournal records.
33. MarcEdit
34. DSpace, Marcive, OCLC, online cataloging resources.
35. OCLC has the potential to improve our workflow; we just haven't had the time to make it happen. Most of the other things listed above just add complexity to already-complex tasks.
36. We are planning to experiment with OCLC Worldshare Metadata Collection Manager this year. Bepress for institutional repositories
37. batch MARC records for electronic resources   MARCedit
38. So far, the most useful technology has been an in-house program that reduces the amount of routine checking and correcting of MARC coding and item record creation. Improvements to OCLC connexion have been very helpful. Vendor records are useful for getting a large amount of records into the database.
39. We use our Library Wiki extensively to record procedures and share useful resources
40. MarcEdit!!!
41. MARCEdit program is critical to what I do with ebooks records.
42. MarcEdit
43. DSpace, Internet, OCLC web services
44. Access to online tools outside of the traditional ones such as Cataloger's Desktop (but also including them), such as Klokan Technologies' Bounding Box tool.
45. The most useful technologies depends on meeting needs when they can be articulated
46. Our consortial office handles batchloading of purchased records.
47. MarcEdit is useful tool for bulk loading records and ensuring quality.
48. Oclc
49. MarkEdit, hardware, ability to bulk process and load records
50. Without a doubt MARCEdit and Z39.5.
51. OCLC Connexion
52. Worldcat, standards posted by LOC on their pages.
53. Dspace, ILSs, OCLC, online information for authority work
54. Automated work tools for catalogers; batch records for automated loads; automated authority control
55. WorldCat Local has the potential to become a major improvement over other ILSs, because OCLC is always as up-to-date as possible with the changes in standards, while other companies are always playing catch-up.
56. I think the ILS has come a long way from where I started with a telnet interface 10 years ago. Downloading and batch-processing records is a great tool. Wikis and blogs--

that's good for documenting and sharing procedures, I guess. And what do you meant by harvesting software? I think having most of our documentation online is a great innovation.

57. Classweb, Catalogers Desktop, RDA Toolkit
58. ClassWeb, MARC-edit, Connexion Client (compared to previous OCLC interfaces).
59. Cataloging listservs, webinars on marc, cataloging and RDA aren't necessarily new, but they are the most useful to us.
60. I subscribe to several listservs which keep me updated with latest developments: Auto Cat and OCLC Cataloging.
61. OCLC, ClassWeb, WebDewey, Cataloger's Desktop,
62. OCLC resources, Vendor manuals and listservs
63. Vendor services

CHAPTER 7: OUTSOURCING

Table 17: What functions or value-added services, if any, does your agency outsource to any degree? Please select all that apply.

Table 17.1.1: Does your division outsource the obtainment of new and updated authority records to any extent?

	Yes	No
Entire Sample	46.91%	53.09%

Table 17.1.2: Does your division outsource the obtainment of new and updated authority records to any extent? Broken out by Type of College

Type of College	Yes	No
Community College	40.00%	60.00%
4-Year Degree Granting College	36.84%	63.16%
MA or PHD Granting College	56.52%	43.48%
Research University	60.00%	40.00%

Table 17.1.3: Does your division outsource the obtainment of new and updated authority records to any extent? Broken out by Public or Private Status

Public or Private Status	Yes	No
Public	48.08%	51.92%
Private	44.83%	55.17%

Table 17.1.4: Does your division outsource the obtainment of new and updated authority records to any extent? Broken out by Total Student Enrollment

Total Student Enrollment	Yes	No
Less than 10,000	35.48%	64.52%
10,000 to 20,000	57.58%	42.42%
More than 20,000	47.06%	52.94%

Table 17.1.5: Does your division outsource the obtainment of new and updated authority records to any extent? Broken out by Annual Tuition

Annual Tuition	Yes	No
Less than $8,000	42.31%	57.69%
$8,000 to $18,000	51.72%	48.28%
More than $18,000	46.15%	53.85%

Table 17.2.1: Does your division outsource the updating of headings in bibliographic records to any extent?

	Yes	No
Entire Sample	35.80%	64.20%

Table 17.2.2: Does your division outsource the updating of headings in bibliographic records to any extent? Broken out by Type of College

Type of College	Yes	No
Community College	40.00%	60.00%
4-Year Degree Granting College	31.58%	68.42%
MA or PHD Granting College	30.43%	69.57%
Research University	53.33%	46.67%

Table 17.2.3: Does your division outsource the updating of headings in bibliographic records to any extent? Broken out by Public or Private Status

Public or Private Status	Yes	No
Public	34.62%	65.38%
Private	37.93%	62.07%

Table 17.2.4: Does your division outsource the updating of headings in bibliographic records to any extent? Broken out by Total Student Enrollment

Total Student Enrollment	Yes	No
Less than 10,000	29.03%	70.97%
10,000 to 20,000	42.42%	57.58%
More than 20,000	35.29%	64.71%

Table 17.2.5: Does your division outsource the updating of headings in bibliographic records to any extent? Broken out by Annual Tuition

Annual Tuition	Yes	No
Less than $8,000	26.92%	73.08%
$8,000 to $18,000	37.93%	62.07%
More than $18,000	42.31%	57.69%

Table 17.3.1: Does your division outsource the obtainment of new bibliographic records to any extent?

	Yes	No
Entire Sample	46.91%	53.09%

Table 17.3.2: Does your division outsource the obtainment of new bibliographic records to any extent? Broken out by Type of College

Type of College	Yes	No
Community College	40.00%	60.00%
4-Year Degree Granting College	36.84%	63.16%
MA or PHD Granting College	47.83%	52.17%
Research University	73.33%	26.67%

Table 17.3.3: Does your division outsource the obtainment of new bibliographic records to any extent? Broken out by Public or Private Status

Public or Private Status	Yes	No
Public	59.62%	40.38%
Private	24.14%	75.86%

Table 17.3.4: Does your division outsource the obtainment of new bibliographic records to any extent? Broken out by Total Student Enrollment

Total Student Enrollment	Yes	No
Less than 10,000	25.81%	74.19%
10,000 to 20,000	54.55%	45.45%
More than 20,000	70.59%	29.41%

Table 17.3.5: Does your division outsource the obtainment of new bibliographic records to any extent? Broken out by Annual Tuition

Annual Tuition	Yes	No
Less than $8,000	61.54%	38.46%
$8,000 to $18,000	48.28%	51.72%
More than $18,000	30.77%	69.23%

Table 17.4.1: Does your division outsource the maintenance of item records and inventory to any extent?

	Yes	No
Entire Sample	4.94%	95.06%

Table 17.4.2: Does your division outsource the maintenance of item records and inventory to any extent? Broken out by Type of College

Type of College	Yes	No
Community College	20.00%	80.00%
4-Year Degree Granting College	0.00%	100.00%
MA or PHD Granting College	4.35%	95.65%
Research University	13.33%	86.67%

Table 17.4.3: Does your division outsource the maintenance of item records and inventory to any extent? Broken out by Public or Private Status

Public or Private Status	Yes	No
Public	7.69%	92.31%
Private	0.00%	100.00%

Table 17.4.4: Does your division outsource the maintenance of item records and inventory to any extent? Broken out by Total Student Enrollment

Total Student Enrollment	Yes	No
Less than 10,000	3.23%	96.77%
10,000 to 20,000	0.00%	100.00%
More than 20,000	17.65%	82.35%

Does the Cataloging Division Outsource the Following Function?

Table 17.4.5: Item records and inventory Broken out by Annual Tuition

Annual Tuition	Yes	No
Less than $8,000	11.54%	88.46%
$8,000 to $18,000	3.45%	96.55%
More than $18,000	0.00%	100.00%

Does the Cataloging Division Outsource the Following Function?

Table 17.5.1: Physical processing, barcoding

	Yes	No
Entire Sample	20.99%	79.01%

Table 17.5.2: Physical processing, barcoding Broken out by Type of College

Type of College	Yes	No
Community College	0.00%	100.00%
4-Year Degree Granting College	7.89%	92.11%
MA or PHD Granting College	30.43%	69.57%
Research University	46.67%	53.33%

Table 17.5.3: Physical processing, barcoding Broken out by Public or Private Status

Public or Private Status	Yes	No
Public	28.85%	71.15%
Private	6.90%	93.10%

Table 17.5.4: Physical processing, barcoding Broken out by Total Student Enrollment

Total Student Enrollment	Yes	No
Less than 10,000	3.23%	96.77%
10,000 to 20,000	18.18%	81.82%
More than 20,000	58.82%	41.18%

Table 17.5.5: Physical processing, barcoding Broken out by Annual Tuition

Annual Tuition	Yes	No
Less than $8,000	23.08%	76.92%
$8,000 to $18,000	27.59%	72.41%
More than $18,000	11.54%	88.46%

Does the Cataloging Division Outsource the Following Function?

Table 17.6.1: Table of contents notes added

	Yes	No
Entire Sample	12.35%	87.65%

Table 17.6.2: Table of contents notes added Broken out by Type of College

Type of College	Yes	No
Community College	0.00%	100.00%
4-Year Degree Granting College	2.63%	97.37%
MA or PHD Granting College	13.04%	86.96%
Research University	40.00%	60.00%

Table 17.6.3: Table of contents notes added Broken out by Public or Private Status

Public or Private Status	Yes	No
Public	15.38%	84.62%
Private	6.90%	93.10%

Table 17.6.4: Table of contents notes added Broken out by Total Student Enrollment

Total Student Enrollment	Yes	No
Less than 10,000	0.00%	100.00%
10,000 to 20,000	18.18%	81.82%
More than 20,000	23.53%	76.47%

Table 17.6.5: Table of contents notes added Broken out by Annual Tuition

Annual Tuition	Yes	No
Less than $8,000	15.38%	84.62%
$8,000 to $18,000	6.90%	93.10%
More than $18,000	15.38%	84.62%

Does the Cataloging Division Outsource the Following Function?

Table 17.7.1: Book reviews added

	Yes	No
Entire Sample	11.11%	88.89%

Table 17.7.2: Book reviews added Broken out by Type of College

Type of College	Yes	No
Community College	0.00%	100.00%
4-Year Degree Granting College	10.53%	89.47%
MA or PHD Granting College	4.35%	95.65%
Research University	26.67%	73.33%

Table 17.7.3: Book reviews added Broken out by Public or Private Status

Public or Private Status	Yes	No
Public	5.77%	94.23%
Private	20.69%	79.31%

161

Table 17.7.4: Book reviews added Broken out by Total Student Enrollment

Total Student Enrollment	Yes	No
Less than 10,000	16.13%	83.87%
10,000 to 20,000	6.06%	93.94%
More than 20,000	11.76%	88.24%

Table 17.7.5: Book reviews added Broken out by Annual Tuition

Annual Tuition	Yes	No
Less than $8,000	0.00%	100.00%
$8,000 to $18,000	6.90%	93.10%
More than $18,000	26.92%	73.08%

Does the Cataloging Division Outsource the Following Function?
Table 17.8.1: Book jackets added

	No Response	Yes	No
Entire Sample	0.00%	16.05%	83.95%

Table 17.8.2: Book jackets added Broken out by Type of College

Type of College	Yes	No
Community College	0.00%	100.00%
4-Year Degree Granting College	13.16%	86.84%
MA or PHD Granting College	17.39%	82.61%
Research University	26.67%	73.33%

Table 17.8.3: Book jackets added Broken out by Public or Private Status

Public or Private Status	Yes	No
Public	11.54%	88.46%
Private	24.14%	75.86%

Table 17.8.4: Book jackets added Broken out by Total Student Enrollment

Total Student Enrollment	Yes	No
Less than 10,000	16.13%	83.87%
10,000 to 20,000	15.15%	84.85%
More than 20,000	17.65%	82.35%

Table 17.8.5: Book jackets added Broken out by Annual Tuition

Annual Tuition	Yes	No
Less than $8,000	7.69%	92.31%

| $8,000 to $18,000 | 17.24% | 82.76% |
| More than $18,000 | 23.08% | 76.92% |

Table 18: What types of library resources are outsourced? Please select all that apply

Table 18.1.1: Continuing resources (print)

	Yes	No
Entire Sample	8.64%	91.36%

Does the Cataloging Division Outsource the Following Cataloging Functions?

Table 18.1.2: Continuing resources (print) Broken out by Type of College

Type of College	Yes	No
Community College	0.00%	100.00%
4-Year Degree Granting College	13.16%	86.84%
MA or PHD Granting College	4.35%	95.65%
Research University	6.67%	93.33%

Table 18.1.3: Continuing resources (print) Broken out by Public or Private Status

Public or Private Status	Yes	No
Public	9.62%	90.38%
Private	6.90%	93.10%

Table 18.1.4: Continuing resources (print) Broken out by Total Student Enrollment

Total Student Enrollment	Yes	No
Less than 10,000	3.23%	96.77%
10,000 to 20,000	3.03%	96.97%
More than 20,000	29.41%	70.59%

Table 18.1.5: Continuing resources (print) Broken out by Annual Tuition

Annual Tuition	Yes	No
Less than $8,000	7.69%	92.31%
$8,000 to $18,000	13.79%	86.21%
More than $18,000	3.85%	96.15%

Does the Cataloging Division Outsource the Following Cataloging Functions?

Table 18.2.1: E-journals

	Yes	No
Entire Sample	28.40%	71.60%

Table 18.2.2: E-journals Broken out by Type of College

Type of College	Yes	No
Community College	0.00%	100.00%
4-Year Degree Granting College	28.95%	71.05%
MA or PHD Granting College	30.43%	69.57%
Research University	33.33%	66.67%

Table 18.2.3: E-journals Broken out by Public or Private Status

Public or Private Status	Yes	No
Public	34.62%	65.38%
Private	17.24%	82.76%

Table 18.2.4: E-journals Broken out by Total Student Enrollment

Total Student Enrollment	Yes	No
Less than 10,000	19.35%	80.65%
10,000 to 20,000	30.30%	69.70%
More than 20,000	41.18%	58.82%

Table 18.2.5: E-journals Broken out by Annual Tuition

Annual Tuition	Yes	No
Less than $8,000	26.92%	73.08%
$8,000 to $18,000	37.93%	62.07%
More than $18,000	19.23%	80.77%

Does the Cataloging Division Outsource the Following Cataloging Functions?

Table 18.3.1: E-books

	Yes	No
Entire Sample	40.74%	59.26%

Table 18.3.2: E-books Broken out by Type of College

Type of College	Yes	No
Community College	20.00%	80.00%
4-Year Degree Granting College	31.58%	68.42%
MA or PHD Granting College	52.17%	47.83%
Research University	53.33%	46.67%

Table 18.3.3: E-books Broken out by Public or Private Status

Public or Private Status	Yes	No

Public	50.00%	50.00%
Private	24.14%	75.86%

Table 18.3.4: E-books Broken out by Total Student Enrollment

Total Student Enrollment	Yes	No
Less than 10,000	22.58%	77.42%
10,000 to 20,000	45.45%	54.55%
More than 20,000	64.71%	35.29%

Table 18.3.5: E-books Broken out by Annual Tuition

Annual Tuition	Yes	No
Less than $8,000	53.85%	46.15%
$8.000 to $18,000	41.38%	58.62%
More than $18,000	26.92%	73.08%

Does the Cataloging Division Outsource the Following Cataloging Functions?

Table 18.4.1: AV formats

	Yes	No
Entire Sample	4.94%	95.06%

Table 18.4.2: AV formats Broken out by Type of College

Type of College	Yes	No
Community College	0.00%	100.00%
4-Year Degree Granting College	2.63%	97.37%
MA or PHD Granting College	4.35%	95.65%
Research University	13.33%	86.67%

Table 18.4.3: AV formats Broken out by Public or Private Status

Public or Private Status	Yes	No
Public	7.69%	92.31%
Private	0.00%	100.00%

Table 18.4.4: AV formats Broken out by Total Student Enrollment

Total Student Enrollment	Yes	No
Less than 10,000	0.00%	100.00%
10,000 to 20,000	0.00%	100.00%
More than 20,000	23.53%	76.47%

Table 18.4.5: AV formats Broken out by Annual Tuition

Annual Tuition	Yes	No
Less than $8,000	7.69%	92.31%
$8,000 to $18,000	6.90%	93.10%
More than $18,000	0.00%	100.00%

Does the Cataloging Division Outsource the Following Cataloging Functions?

Table 18.5.1: Foreign language resources for which the cataloging agency has no expertise

	Yes	No
Entire Sample	8.64%	91.36%

Table 18.5.2: Foreign language resources for which the cataloging agency has no expertise Broken out by Type of College

Type of College	Yes	No
Community College	0.00%	100.00%
4-Year Degree Granting College	5.26%	94.74%
MA or PHD Granting College	8.70%	91.30%
Research University	20.00%	80.00%

Table 18.5.3: Foreign language resources for which the cataloging agency has no expertise Broken out by Public or Private Status

Public or Private Status	Yes	No
Public	13.46%	86.54%
Private	0.00%	100.00%

Table 18.5.4: Foreign language resources for which the cataloging agency has no expertise Broken out by Total Student Enrollment

Total Student Enrollment	Yes	No
Less than 10,000	0.00%	100.00%
10,000 to 20,000	6.06%	93.94%
More than 20,000	29.41%	70.59%

Table 18.5.5: Foreign language resources for which the cataloging agency has no expertise Broken out by Annual Tuition

Annual Tuition	Yes	No
Less than $8,000	7.69%	92.31%
$8,000 to $18,000	17.24%	82.76%
More than $18,000	0.00%	100.00%

Does the Cataloging Division Outsource the Following Cataloging Functions?

Table 18.6.1: Other digital formats

	Yes	No
Entire Sample	3.70%	96.30%

Table 18.6.2: Other digital formats Broken out by Type of College

Type of College	Yes	No
Community College	0.00%	100.00%
4-Year Degree Granting College	2.63%	97.37%
MA or PHD Granting College	4.35%	95.65%
Research University	6.67%	93.33%

Table 18.6.3: Other digital formats Broken out by Public or Private Status

Public or Private Status	Yes	No
Public	5.77%	94.23%
Private	0.00%	100.00%

Table 18.6.4: Other digital formats Broken out by Total Student Enrollment

Total Student Enrollment	Yes	No
Less than 10,000	0.00%	100.00%
10,000 to 20,000	0.00%	100.00%
More than 20,000	17.65%	82.35%

Table 18.6.5: Other digital formats Broken out by Annual Tuition

Annual Tuition	Yes	No
Less than $8,000	3.85%	96.15%
$8,000 to $18,000	6.90%	93.10%
More than $18,000	0.00%	100.00%

Table 18.7.1: Materials in cataloging backlogs

	Yes	No
Entire Sample	6.17%	98.83%

Table 18.7.2: Materials in cataloging backlogs Broken out by Type of College

Type of College	Yes	No
Community College	0.00%	100.00%
4-Year Degree Granting College	0.00%	100.00%
MA or PHD Granting College	8.70%	91.30%
Research University	20.00%	80.00%

Table 18.7.3: Materials in cataloging backlogs Broken out by Public or Private Status

Public or Private Status	Yes	No
Public	7.69%	92.31%
Private	3.45%	96.55%

Table 18.7.4: Materials in cataloging backlogs Broken out by Total Student Enrollment

Total Student Enrollment	Yes	No
Less than 10,000	0.00%	100.00%
10,000 to 20,000	3.03%	96.97%
More than 20,000	23.53%	76.47%

Table 18.7.5: Materials in cataloging backlogs Broken out by Annual Tuition

Annual Tuition	Yes	No
Less than $8,000	7.69%	92.31%
$8,000 to $18,000	6.90%	93.10%
More than $18,000	3.85%	96.15%

Does the Cataloging Division Outsource the Following Cataloging Functions?

Table 18.8.1: All materials are outsourced

	Yes	No
Entire Sample	2.47%	97.53%

Table 18.8.2: All materials are outsourced Broken out by Type of College

Type of College	Yes	No
Community College	20.00%	80.00%
4-Year Degree Granting College	2.63%	97.37%
MA or PHD Granting College	0.00%	100.00%
Research University	0.00%	100.00%

Table 18.8.3: All materials are outsourced Broken out by Public or Private Status

Public or Private Status	Yes	No
Public	3.85%	96.15%
Private	0.00%	100.00%

Table 18.8.4: All materials are outsourced Broken out by Total Student Enrollment

Total Student Enrollment	Yes	No
Less than 10,000	3.23%	96.77%
10,000 to 20,000	3.03%	96.97%
More than 20,000	0.00%	100.00%

Table 18.8.5: All materials are outsourced Broken out by Annual Tuition

Annual Tuition	Yes	No
Less than $8,000	7.69%	92.31%
$8,000 to $18,000	0.00%	100.00%
More than $18,000	0.00%	100.00%

Table 18.9.1: Not applicable: no outsourcing done

	Yes	No
Entire Sample	35.80%	64.20%

Table 18.9.2: Not applicable: no outsourcing done Broken out by Type of College

Type of College	Yes	No
Community College	20.00%	80.00%
4-Year Degree Granting College	39.47%	60.53%
MA or PHD Granting College	47.83%	52.17%
Research University	13.33%	86.67%

Table 18.9.3: Not applicable: no outsourcing done Broken out by Public or Private Status

Public or Private Status	Yes	No
Public	23.08%	76.92%
Private	58.62%	41.38%

Table 18.9.4: Not applicable: no outsourcing done Broken out by Total Student Enrollment

Total Student Enrollment	Yes	No
Less than 10,000	58.06%	41.94%
10,000 to 20,000	30.30%	69.70%
More than 20,000	5.88%	94.12%

Table 18.9.5: Not applicable: no outsourcing done Broken out by Annual Tuition

Annual Tuition	Yes	No
Less than $8,000	23.08%	76.92%
$8,000 to $18,000	27.59%	72.41%
More than $18,000	57.69%	42.31%

If you have outsourced library resources, please briefly explain why you outsourced certain types of library resources.

1. Deleting holdings from OCLC because of time.
2. Using a consortium since we don't have need for a full-time cataloger.
3. Serials Solutions, Ebrary, LTI for authorities
4. We contract for MARC records for electronic journals available both by direct subscription and through aggregator databases. We do this because there is no way would could keep up with that volume of material in-house.
5. Approval plan - prefer to outsource than hire, train and support the development of appropriately motivated and qualified staff; Foreign language - the resistance of existing staff to learn and develop skills in bibliographic description of romanised languages is so great that all new donations or large purchases in languages other than english are outsourced or else the materials would languish in a backlog for years.
6. Free quality bibliographic records
7. We outsource cataloging for approval books using PromptCat and get them shelf-ready. This is over 80% of our collection. I was not involved in decision as to why since this was made a long time ago. We get records delivered to us for many e-book vendors but not all. We still catalog manually for some. We outsourced most of them because we don't have enough staff or time to catalog all individual ebook titles. We recently implemented a patron-driven acquisitions service for the same reasons and to make e-books discoverable right away and let patrons drive our purchase decisions to save costs aby basing them on actual use rather than a "just in case" model.
8. We outsource ebooks in order to provide additional access in a timely manner

9. We get records for government documents from MARCIVE because we couldn't keep up with the amount of work in house. We also get records for the DDA titles since we have no other way of knowing what titles are included.

10. We had a backlog we wanted to get processed

11. Outsourcing is based on economic reasons, quality, expediency and convenience

12. We started a shelf-ready program for new books. We get many ebook bibliographic records from vendors.

13. We buy ebook and ejournal packages that often have tens of thousands of records. It would be impossible to deal with that amount of cataloging with the staff remaining.

14. We tried ordering shelf ready materials from our vendor, but there were too many exceptions/errors. We found that we could do it cheaper ourselves.

15. The consortia offers this service to load the recent authority records & updates from Library of Congress. We made arrangements with Ebsco for a cheaper price to get their bibliographic records for E-resources (ejournals, ebooks) because we have a low budget for this type of work

16. We outsourced these areas to meet the high demand (by patrons, public services librarians, and administration) for speedy turnaround time of materials acquired and available to our patrons.

17. We outsource Authority control so that we can manage our authority data and keep it as clean and up-to-date as possible. We use OCLC cataloging partners to help supply bib records.

18. There were too many records to create to catch up with our current staffing

19. Print monographs: because we purchase too many monographs for our staff to process them. E-journals cataloging: easier to manage access and discovery. We are actively investigating outsourcing of authority control, AV materials cataloging, and TOCs added to records. Government documents: easier to manage access and discovery. E-books: easier to manage when records are batchloaded.

20. We try to have the machines do the work that is simple and easy and to have the people focused on what is difficult and interesting.

21. We are part of a consortia and we get it done through them.

22. We outsource ebook marc records because they come with the order. It's one less thing I don't have to do.

23. We don't have sufficient staff to catalog large packages of ebooks and ejournals; we lack expertise in non-Roman languages (e.g., Thai, Hebrew, Arabic); we lack expertise in cataloging music scores and sound recordings.

24. Current approval plan records: as 2 paraprofessional catalogers were transferred to the general academic library   Ca. 200 foreign language books, offprints, "in" analytics, etc. that have been here for a number of years and which may be used in a future project: the one person who could do the cataloging has limited foreign language skills and would take a long time to do it

25. The library has a policy to outsource. Given the increasing costs of shipping and outsourced-cataloguing, it doesn't make much sense. Now that the older cataloguers are retiring and the newer ones are starting at the bottom of the pay scale, it would be much less expensive and faster to hire a few more staff (even if they were just temporary) and catalogue things locally.

26. To save time and money.

27. OCLC

28. Authority work was outsourced because of the time it took to complete it properly.

29. We outsource our government documents only, due to attrition in the department.

30. We did not have the staff to do this work ourselves.

31. The only time we have outsourced was a set of 100 Arabic titles that no one had the language skills for.

32. ebook batch loads; we are just now experimenting with monographs (popular books)

33. Cataloging in languages other than English.

34. It is more cost-effective to subscribe to major databases and ebook packages that

selecting and cataloging one at a time.

35. We do not have the time or resources to catalog all the materials we purchase/subscribe to.

36. We use OCLC Cataloging Partners to get records for new materials faster. The books come shelf ready and 80% of them are ready to go to the shelves when they arrive. We use vendor records for e-serials and large-scale ebook purchases to get the records into the catalog quickly. We use OCLC Knowledge Base to link our records in WorldCat Local.

37. We load into the catalog thousands of ebooks, streaming videos and audio - too many to catalog manually

38. We purchase bib records for electronic resource material and books from YBP. This saves times for Acquisitions staff. Cataloging staff spend time with these purchased records for the usual reasons (making sure it is what record says it is, the links work, adding local data, holdings information, labeling, etc.)

39. We have tried small-scale outsourcing projects in the past, such as with city maps of places in our state and surrounding states with OCLC. Generally the only time we have outsourced is for a specific foreign-language need or format-based need. We have not outsourced our work for at least ten years.

40. Consortial purchases or vendor packages

41. Frees up staff for other duties.

42. Because we didn't have local expertise to do the work

43. We use a "shelf ready" provider for most of our print resources, which includes cataloging. For the most part cataloging consists of grabbing the best record in OCLC. We also send approximately 100 books per month to a cataloging service. For e-resources, we hire the same company to provide approximately 100 records per month of ebooks that our institution has licensed. WE take advantage of whatever batchload options are available through OCLC and other partner libraries.

44. Materials requiring original cataloging; ebook cataloging

45. Wasn't an option. To move into the realm of ebooks with any breadth it would be impossible to move at the speed needed without the vendor providing the data.

46. We have limitations in foreign languages

47. More cost effective, workload was impossible to manage with current staff resources

48. I guess I'm not real clear on what you mean by "Outsourced." We purchase our e-journals, and they are managed in an A-Z list (Ebsco). Is this what you mean? We download bibliographic records from OCLC. Does that mean we 'outsource' our bibliographic records? I guess I'm not aware of what level of outsource can be there. Are you talking about Vendor batch records?? We rarely add original records.

49. Get items on shelf faster

50. About 10 years ago (at a different institution) I outsourced unique items from our backlog, which turned out to be a disaster. I think outsourcing works best for mass-produced, popular items.

51. E-journals and ebooks not so much outsourced as vendor records modified and loaded to save considerable time.

52. We are too small to keep current with authority work without outsourcing so we subscribe to some services from Marcive. We also use Marcive to enhance records with additional data such as table of contents that we don't have the time or staff to accomplish ourselves.

53. Cheaper

What are the criteria you use, if any, to analyze and determine the best sources of high quality records for outsourced materials?

1. Cost is a big factor.
2. "What has been done" for close to 20 years but I think that this needs to be reviewed and that we could obtain better quality service for our money.
3. Choice of vendor was driven mostly by cost.
4. PCC / BIBCO / CONSER standard records; Language of cataloguing; Use of AACR; Reputation of library and its senior cataloguers; Reference to cataloging output (and the standards therein) by certain libraries;
5. completeness of the records with classification number assigned and LC subject headings
6. Completeness of records Accuracy of records Authority control nice, but not required URLs that reliably work Presence of subject headings   Call number nice, but not essential Coding accuracy nice, but if not, we can batch fix locally
7. Check vendor records vs. OCLC records
8. Cost, reliability and support services
9. I make sure the most important access data is accurate: title, author, edition, and date and that the processing is done correctly in consistently with what we do in-house.
10. Catalog librarian reviews the records to check for any errors. I run them through MARC Report to assist with that.
11. We want records that have LC call numbers, 856 fields with the direct links to the resource; prefer OCLC bib records
12. We review the MARC records and set up profiles with individual vendors as to the type of MARC records we will accept.
13. Look at subject headings (are there any?). Look for DLC, pcc, Level I or K (OCLC) indicators Existence or 090 or 050 xx call numbers Do ebook records contain 776 fields. What do the 856 fields look like? The 007 and 006 fields?
14. Do the records follow established cataloging standards? Do the records have Library of Congress subject headings?
15. We rarely have a choice. Either the vendor offers them or not. They seldom will improve quality for us. We have to do that.
16. That there is a complete record with subject headings.
17. I don't know enough to have any. If it gives the patron information and can be read, then that's good enough.
18. We look at cost, completeness of records, whether records have appropriate subjects, ability to provide cataloging in our timeframe.
19. Checking the received items for errors AND comparing them to the profile
20. We look to see if all of the core elements are present, are they free of spelling errors, to they appear to conform to the standards, do they contain the access points our users generally require.
21. Records adhere to standards.
22. Cataloged by DLC or a PCC library.
23. I do not know the criteria used for government documents, as it is of long standing. For other materials, we will consider fullness of access points and price.
24. We considered standards for full level cataloging as defined by OCLC Level I records.
25. Completeness; lack of errors; you have to accept crap just because of the volume
26. Examination of sample records provided at the time of contract bid. Continued monitoring once the contract is signed.
27. For ebooks, we go with the vendor that provides the most customization for our records, since we cannot afford customized load tables for our ebook records.
28. We use Worldcat Cataloging Partners and set the system to check the encoding level of records.
29. Accuracy and correctness of coding

30. We use a test database to check records before loading into the catalog. We have worked with vendors to improve records.
31. Type of record (permanent, subscription with title level access); accurate title; accurate edition; author; title-level URL; MARC formatting which can be used in our ILS; (recommended) Call numbers; LC subject headings; Cataloging records meeting current standards and MARC standards;
32. Depends on academic program needs
33. Adequate information in records, compliant with current standards, few or no typographical type errors, turnaround time,
34. Encoding level of the MARC record. Number of holdings attached in OCLC.
35. My manager likes them ...
36. Information from suppliers, demos at conferences, word of mouth, testing onsite
37. If you are talking about what criteria we use for acquiring records from OCLC, we use Elvl criteria to choose the best. If we would be using records provided by a vendor, I think we use price and take what we can get if it's part of a large set.
38. Only accept full-level records
39. Basically, human review. Some vendors have records that are so bad we do not load them into our catalog.
40. We take what we get

Table 19: What quality control methods do you use, if any, to assure vendor supplied records are accurate and complete? Please select all that apply.

Table 19.1.1: Use MarcEdit or other MARC editor to preview records and globally edit to local standards prior to loading

	Yes	No
Entire Sample	54.32%	45.68%

Table 19.1.2: Use MarcEdit or other MARC editor to preview records and globally edit to local standards prior to loading Broken out by Type of College

Type of College	Yes	No
Community College	0.00%	100.00%
4-Year Degree Granting College	47.37%	52.63%
MA or PHD Granting College	69.57%	30.43%
Research University	66.67%	33.33%

Table 19.1.3: Use MarcEdit or other MARC editor to preview records and globally edit to local standards prior to loading Broken out by Public or Private Status

Public or Private Status	Yes	No
Public	57.69%	42.31%
Private	48.28%	51.72%

Table 19.1.4: Use MarcEdit or other MARC editor to preview records and globally edit to local standards prior to loading Broken out by Total Student Enrollment

Total Student Enrollment	Yes	No
Less than 10,000	38.71%	61.29%
10,000 to 20,000	60.61%	39.39%
More than 20,000	70.59%	29.41%

Table 19.1.5: Use MarcEdit or other MARC editor to preview records and globally edit to local standards prior to loading Broken out by Annual Tuition

Annual Tuition	Yes	No
Less than $8,000	69.23%	30.77%
$8,000 to $18,000	41.38%	58.62%
More than $18,000	53.85%	46.15%

Do you use the following quality control measure?

Table 19.2.1: Use local integrated system to review loaded records and globally edit to local standards

	Yes	No
Entire Sample	32.10%	67.90%

Table 19.2.2: Use local integrated system to review loaded records and globally edit to local standards Broken out by Type of College

Type of College	Yes	No
Community College	20.00%	80.00%
4-Year Degree Granting College	23.68%	76.32%
MA or PHD Granting College	34.78%	65.22%
Research University	53.33%	46.67%

Table 19.2.3: Use local integrated system to review loaded records and globally edit to local standards Broken out by Public or Private Status

Public or Private Status	Yes	No
Public	30.77%	69.23%
Private	34.48%	65.52%

Table 19.2.4: Use local integrated system to review loaded records and globally edit to local standards Broken out by Total Student Enrollment

Total Student Enrollment	Yes	No
Less than 10,000	29.03%	70.97%
10,000 to 20,000	18.18%	81.82%
More than 20,000	64.71%	35.29%

Table 19.2.5: Use local integrated system to review loaded records and globally edit to local standards Broken out by Annual Tuition

Annual Tuition	Yes	No
Less than $8,000	11.54%	88.46%
$8,000 to $18,000	48.28%	51.72%
More than $18,000	34.62%	65.38%

Do you use the following quality control measure?

Table 19.3.1: Review all vendor records whenever possible and spot check vendor records when complete review is not possible

	Yes	No
Entire Sample	38.27%	61.73%

Table 19.3.2: Review all vendor records whenever possible and spot check vendor records when complete review is not possible Broken out by Type of College

Type of College	Yes	No
Community College	0.00%	100.00%
4-Year Degree Granting College	34.21%	65.79%
MA or PHD Granting College	43.48%	56.52%
Research University	53.33%	46.67%

Table 19.3.3: Review all vendor records whenever possible and spot check vendor records when complete review is not possible Broken out by Public or Private Status

Public or Private Status	Yes	No
Public	40.38%	59.62%
Private	34.48%	65.52%

Table 19.3.4: Review all vendor records whenever possible and spot check vendor records when complete review is not possible Broken out by Total Student Enrollment

Total Student Enrollment	Yes	No
Less than 10,000	32.26%	67.74%
10,000 to 20,000	36.36%	63.64%
More than 20,000	52.94%	47.06%

Table 19.3.5: Review all vendor records whenever possible and spot check vendor records when complete review is not possible Broken out by Annual Tuition

Annual Tuition	Yes	No
Less than $8,000	34.62%	65.38%
$8,000 to $18,000	34.48%	65.52%
More than $18,000	46.15%	53.85%

Do you use the following quality control measure?

Table 19.4.1: Always spot check all vendor records

	Yes	No
Entire Sample	14.81%	85.91%

Table 19.4.2: Always spot check all vendor records Broken out by Type of College

Type of College	Yes	No
Community College	0.00%	100.00%
4-Year Degree Granting College	13.16%	86.84%
MA or PHD Granting College	8.70%	91.30%
Research University	33.33%	66.67%

Table 19.4.3: Always spot check all vendor records Broken out by Public or Private Status

Public or Private Status	Yes	No
Public	13.46%	86.54%
Private	17.24%	82.76%

Table 19.4.4: Always spot check all vendor records Broken out by Total Student Enrollment

Total Student Enrollment	Yes	No

Less than 10,000	12.90%	87.10%
10,000 to 20,000	18.18%	81.82%
More than 20,000	11.76%	88.24%

Table 19.4.5: Always spot check all vendor records Broken out by Annual Tuition

Annual Tuition	Yes	No
Less than $8,000	7.69%	92.31%
$8,000 to $18,000	13.79%	86.21%
More than $18,000	23.08%	76.92%

Do you use the following quality control measure?
Table 19.5.1: No or minimal review performed

	Yes	No
Entire Sample	8.64%	91.36%

Table 19.5.2: No or minimal review performed Broken out by Type of College

Type of College	Yes	No
Community College	20.00%	80.00%
4-Year Degree Granting College	7.89%	92.11%
MA or PHD Granting College	4.35%	95.65%
Research University	13.33%	86.67%

Table 19.5.3: No or minimal review performed Broken out by Public or Private Status

Public or Private Status	Yes	No
Public	9.62%	90.38%
Private	6.90%	93.10%

Table 19.5.4: No or minimal review performed Broken out by Total Student Enrollment

Total Student Enrollment	Yes	No
Less than 10,000	6.45%	93.55%
10,000 to 20,000	12.12%	87.88%
More than 20,000	5.88%	94.12%

Table 19.5.5: No or minimal review performed Broken out by Annual Tuition

Annual Tuition	Yes	No
Less than $8,000	11.54%	88.46%
$8,000 to $18,000	10.34%	89.66%

More than $18,000	3.85%	96.15%

CHAPTER 8: STATE OF CATALOGING EDUCATION IN LIBRARY SCHOOLS

What are your opinions and thoughts regarding cataloging education in present and future ALA-accredited library and information schools?

1. Should be balanced with some theory or something more than the practical and skill side of cataloging. This helps student prepare to be thoughtful and mindful catalogers.
2. It is still a must to teach this. I balked at taking a cataloging course having already worked as a copy cataloger for almost 10 years but it was very beneficial.
3. Education should be teaching new technologies as they emerge. Should require internships. Cataloging should be required for all students. History of cataloging to give context.
4. I don't have much direct contact with this lately, but what I seem to hear is that cataloging/metadata education is not sufficiently emphasized in many library schools.
5. MUST require how information is organized and classified.
6. Need a strong theoretical basis and be user-focused. Practical application is important but tie it to broader discovery environment so we can see why it is important to apply rules and concepts and their continuing relevance.
7. The current cataloging and metadata education is very poor. We are seeing many non librarians in faculty positions
8. Since cataloging is no longer a required course in many programs, people aren't being exposed to the concepts used in cataloging. This is unfortunate.
9. Schools should require a basic cataloging class since most library school students have no idea what goes on in technical services.
10. Library schools do not adequately prepare entry level cataloguers for the job. More emphasis should be placed the increasing the number of cataloguing courses offered, provide courses in specialized formats and integrate a greater degree of practicum in the curriculum
11. I think understanding cataloging and the MARC record are essential to helping any librarian be able to search effectively. The basic structure and information in a bibliographic record should be required learning by every librarian.
12. Seems not enough classes to support new graduates entering cataloging profession
13. If cataloging is to remain a vital part of librarianship, cataloging must continue to be taught in ALA-accredited library and information schools.
14. Every library student needs to take a cataloging course.
15. It really needs to improve. I realize that some schools have good cataloging education, but mine was brief and inadequate. there need to be more consistency in such education.
16. At a loss to say what will help. It would be great to have LIS schools partner with libraries for practical internships in all areas of cataloging. This will give newly minted catalogers professional experience, prior to working in an institution.
17. We have not hired a formally trained cataloger in over 10 years. We have hired paraprofessionals and have trained them as needed.
18. More courses need to be offered and all courses need to be hands on and practical.
19. A necessity to understand access to information.
20. I thinking that there is little emphasis spent on it's importance and how it can aid those outside of cataloging in searching.
21. I think that cataloging education has fallen by the wayside in many library schools. In many schools, it is no longer required for students to take at least one cataloging course. It is often "rebranded" as "organization of library collections" or some such, which leads to the dilution of the topic. So brand new librarians who are not interested in cataloging do not understand catalog data and why it is there. That means that catalogers must provide much more information to their colleagues. I do think that the emphasis on practical internships is a good one for catalogers. I would not hire a

cataloging librarian without some practical experience, whether it was an internship during library school or paraprofessional experience. The last time I trained a new cataloging librarian, many of the competencies listed in question 44 did not even exist, or were just emerging.

22. The focus is no longer on how to perform our work within libraries. Unless a student has had extensive internship or practical experience within libraries we must train from ground zero. We have tried to tell them this but they won't listen.

23. It is severely lacking because library schools have thought that cataloging was/is going away. It seems that every librarian should know how to catalog a book, even a reference librarian because it will allow them to understand why some searches work and others don't.

24. Still teach the old as well as the new standards and reinforce general knowledge.

25. I have none.

26. I think ALA accredited schools shouldn't devalue cataloging. It seems they like to stress educated new professionals on non-MARC metadata rather than MARC cataloging.

27. Cataloging theory and practice should be a required subject for LIS students, because all librarians should have an understanding of how catalog records are created. Unfortunately, current education is spotty and focuses largely on theory; few students have a real understanding of HOW to catalog anything.

28. Every student should take at least one cataloging class which should include at least one copy and one original cataloging project AND should then show what those cataloged records look like in the ILS and in a One Search catalog (this will show GIGO!)

29. I think that it is better in some schools than other. I think that cataloguers need to be trained as well-rounded metadata librarians who can catalogue or create metadata for any type of resource, in any metadata container and also create their own schema where necessary. I think that over all there just isn't even training.

30. Very limited. As a fairly new professional, I can attest to having learned 90% of what I know in internship and on the job.

31. Cataloging education is still needed and of course should lead changes in cataloging.

32. While cataloging has always been on-the-job training, cataloging education today seems to be even less complete. We have not hired a new librarian cataloger (except the Head of Cataloging) in over ten years.

33. Theory as well as practice should be taught.

34. I think the instruction that is there is good, unfortunately, it isn't always available. I also think cataloging should be considered a core service and be required at all ALA-accredited institutions.

35. Necessary!

36. A big sparse.

37. Students need to understand that in order to provide service to the public, you must understand what goes into a cataloging record, therefore more cataloging instruction is important. Our reference librarians (including the director) have no idea why it is important to have a professional cataloger and copy-catalogers to provide them the information they require.

38. My degree gave me a good foundation in cataloging theory, but I didn't really learn cataloging until I "did" it in my various jobs.

39. More emphasis needs to be given to the possibilities for metadata. More opportunities for internships need to be available.

40. We need to do a better job of defending cataloging as essential job that should be done by MLIS degreed librarians.

41. More programming skills, XML, would be helpful

42. I have not hired any recent graduates in cataloging, so I don't know how well library schools are preparing students in cataloging.

43. It's dysfunctional. It should *always* include an apprenticeship in the field.

44. Need more preparation on choosing systems, selecting schema, understanding impact of data input and indexing on retrieval

45. A lot of library schools are either no longer teaching cataloging or teaching just a basic introduction which is a mistake. I think the issue here is we need to be repackaged to modern terminology. the term cataloging carries as much baggage as the term librarian, neither of which applies to the jobs we do today. We have been doing metadata and catalog maintenance for centuries, hence we seem to be suffering from a perception issue. Our university will still continue to hire professionally trained catalogers, no matter what we may call them. It's important that librarians and staff have had cataloging training so that they are employable. As I said before, we have a lot of power and we control various databases which require interlinking controlled data to work. This cannot happen with untrained individuals, whether they have gotten a library degree or not.

46. Sorely lacking, doesn't prepare people for actual cataloging work

47. I think education for traditional, MARC-based cataloging is woefully inadequate and has been for some time. I'm aware that most library schools offer no more than one cataloging class beyond the basic "organization of information" course that all must take and some places offer none. And, the emphasis has also strongly shifted towards metadata creation and learning schemas, as it should.

48. Cataloging is the information infrastructure and is essential to quality public services

49. They all need to scramble to keep up. Cataloging has been de-emphasized, but it needs to be taught so that all understand it, not just catalogers.

50. It does not seem to be as important as it once was and should be a required course.

51. More emphasis should be placed on cataloging and on general computer programming and scripting skills

52. It's not something I've thought about much.

53. I have not kept up with what library schools are doing with cataloging. The last time I checked they were starting to not require a cataloging course for their graduates.

54. I'm very disappointed in ALA in every aspect; they do nothing of value

55. We had one take a class this past year and it was MARC and had very little review of RDA... this will need to change but it doesn't help the libraries or librarians who were not on "this" side of the transition

56. Needs to have more metadata and RDA prep

57. Seems to be moving toward metadata training instead, and this is appropriate

58. Cataloging is an essential skill for every librarian and should be required for an MLS. If a reference librarian doesn't understand how subject headings and linking entries are created, they won't be able to use the catalog effectively to assist patrons.

59. It's diminishing. I had one course, and it covered basic concepts. The best education will be to work as a copy-cataloger and mentor under another professional cataloger. It takes years to learn, not a semester. I wasn't impressed with my education in general, so I don't have much hope for cataloging education.

60. New catalogers will always require on-the-job training. Internships are useful for determining whether LIS-program students have aptitude for cataloging

61. very few students seem to take traditional cataloging courses; workers are better trained in library technician programs

62. I had good training (20 years ago) but it sounds like new grads don't learn much cataloging. That's a shame.

63. I wonder if cataloging is really being emphasized as much as it should.

64. Catalogers must be familiar with current developments in computer technology, both hardware and software, and learn the comparative advantages and disadvantages of traditional library cataloging versus keyword searching of full text resources.

65. Important

Table 20: Please categorize the preparedness of your recent library hires in the following cataloging and metadata competencies, philosophies, principles and practices. Select all categories that apply.

Table 20.1.1 Classification Systems

	No Response	Not at all prepared	Minimally prepared	Prepared	Well prepared
Entire Sample	24.69%	6.17%	33.33%	27.16%	8.64%

Table 20.1.2: Classification Systems Broken out by Type of College

Type of College	No Response	Not at all prepared	Minimally prepared	Prepared	Well prepared
Community College	40.00%	20.00%	0.00%	0.00%	40.00%
4-Year Degree Granting College	26.32%	5.26%	26.32%	34.21%	7.89%
MA or PHD Granting College	26.09%	0.00%	47.83%	17.39%	8.70%
Research University	13.33%	13.33%	40.00%	33.33%	0.00%

Table 20.1.3: Classification Systems Broken out by Public or Private Status

Public or Private Status	No Response	Not at all prepared	Minimally prepared	Prepared	Well prepared
Public	17.31%	9.62%	36.54%	25.00%	11.54%
Private	37.93%	0.00%	27.59%	31.03%	3.45%

Table 20.1.4: Classification Systems Broken out by Total Student Enrollment

Total Student Enrollment	No Response	Not at all prepared	Minimally prepared	Prepared	Well prepared
Less than 10,000	35.48%	0.00%	22.58%	32.26%	9.68%
10,000 to 20,000	27.27%	6.06%	33.33%	21.21%	12.12%
More than 20,000	0.00%	17.65%	52.94%	29.41%	0.00%

Table 20.1.5: Classification Systems Broken out by Annual Tuition

Annual Tuition	No Response	Not at all prepared	Minimally prepared	Prepared	Well prepared
Less than $8,000	15.38%	11.54%	30.77%	26.92%	15.38%
$8,000 to $18,000	27.59%	6.90%	31.03%	27.59%	6.90%
More than $18,000	30.77%	0.00%	38.46%	26.92%	3.85%

Preparedness of Recent Library Hires in this Area or Skill

Table 20.2.1: Subject /Genre Thesauri Systems

	No Response	Not at all prepared	Minimally prepared	Prepared	Well prepared
Entire Sample	25.93%	9.88%	33.33%	23.46%	7.41%

Table 20.2.2: Subject /Genre Thesauri Systems Broken out by Type of College

Type of College	No Response	Not at all prepared	Minimally prepared	Prepared	Well prepared
Community College	40.00%	20.00%	0.00%	20.00%	20.00%
4-Year Degree Granting College	28.95%	10.53%	26.32%	26.32%	7.89%
MA or PHD Granting College	26.09%	4.35%	43.48%	17.39%	8.70%
Research University	13.33%	13.33%	46.67%	26.67%	0.00%

Table 20.2.3: Subject /Genre Thesauri Systems Broken out by Public or Private Status

Public or Private Status	No Response	Not at all prepared	Minimally prepared	Prepared	Well prepared
Public	19.23%	13.46%	36.54%	21.15%	9.62%
Private	37.93%	3.45%	27.59%	27.59%	3.45%

Table 20.2.4: Subject /Genre Thesauri Systems Broken out by Total Student Enrollment

Total Student Enrollment	No Response	Not at all prepared	Minimally prepared	Prepared	Well prepared
Less than 10,000	38.71%	3.23%	29.03%	19.35%	9.68%
10,000 to 20,000	27.27%	12.12%	21.21%	30.30%	9.09%
More than 20,000	0.00%	17.65%	64.71%	17.65%	0.00%

Table 20.2.5: Subject /Genre Thesauri Systems Broken out by Annual Tuition

Annual Tuition	No Response	Not at all prepared	Minimally prepared	Prepared	Well prepared
Less than $8,000	19.23%	7.69%	38.46%	19.23%	15.38%
$8,000 to $18,000	27.59%	17.24%	24.14%	27.59%	3.45%
More than $18,000	30.77%	3.85%	38.46%	23.08%	3.85%

Table 20.3.1: Classification and Subject /Genre Analysis Principles, Rules and Tools

	No Response	Not at all prepared	Minimally prepared	Prepared	Well prepared
Entire Sample	25.93%	9.88%	32.10%	24.69%	7.41%

Table 20.3.2: Classification and Subject /Genre Analysis Principles, Rules and Tools Broken out by Type of College

Type of College	No Response	Not at all prepared	Minimally prepared	Prepared	Well prepared
Community College	40.00%	20.00%	0.00%	0.00%	40.00%
4-Year Degree Granting College	26.32%	7.89%	28.95%	31.58%	5.26%
MA or PHD Granting College	26.09%	4.35%	43.48%	21.74%	4.35%
Research University	20.00%	20.00%	33.33%	20.00%	6.67%

Table 20.3.3: Classification and Subject /Genre Analysis Principles, Rules and Tools Broken out by Public or Private Status

Public or Private Status	No Response	Not at all prepared	Minimally prepared	Prepared	Well prepared
Public	17.31%	13.46%	34.62%	25.00%	9.62%
Private	41.38%	3.45%	27.59%	24.14%	3.45%

Table 20.3.4: Classification and Subject /Genre Analysis Principles, Rules and Tools Broken out by Total Student Enrollment

Total Student Enrollment	No Response	Not at all prepared	Minimally prepared	Prepared	Well prepared
Less than 10,000	35.48%	6.45%	25.81%	22.58%	9.68%
10,000 to 20,000	30.30%	9.09%	27.27%	27.27%	6.06%
More than 20,000	0.00%	17.65%	52.94%	23.53%	5.88%

Table 20.3.5: Classification and Subject /Genre Analysis Principles, Rules and Tools Broken out by Annual Tuition

Annual Tuition	No Response	Not at all prepared	Minimally prepared	Prepared	Well prepared
Less than $8,000	15.38%	15.38%	30.77%	23.08%	15.38%
$8,000 to $18,000	27.59%	10.34%	31.03%	27.59%	3.45%
More than $18,000	34.62%	3.85%	34.62%	23.08%	3.85%

Preparedness of Recent Library Hires in this Area or Skill
Table 20.4.1: Java and PERL Script Applications

	No Response	Not at all prepared	Minimally prepared	Prepared	Well prepared
Entire Sample	34.57%	46.91%	13.58%	3.70%	1.23%

Table 20.4.2: Java and PERL Script Applications Broken out by Type of College

Type of College	No Response	Not at all prepared	Minimally prepared	Prepared	Well prepared
Community College	40.00%	40.00%	0.00%	0.00%	20.00%
4-Year Degree Granting College	39.47%	42.11%	15.79%	2.63%	0.00%
MA or PHD Granting College	30.43%	47.83%	17.39%	4.35%	0.00%
Research University	26.67%	60.00%	6.67%	6.67%	0.00%

Preparedness of Recent Library Hires in this Area or Skill

Table 20.4.3: Java and PERL Script Applications Broken out by Public or Private Status

Public or Private Status	No Response	Not at all prepared	Minimally prepared	Prepared	Well prepared
Public	25.00%	53.85%	13.46%	5.77%	1.92%
Private	51.72%	34.48%	13.79%	0.00%	0.00%

Table 20.4.4: Java and PERL Script Applications Broken out by Total Student Enrollment

Total Student Enrollment	No Response	Not at all prepared	Minimally prepared	Prepared	Well prepared
Less than 10,000	48.39%	29.03%	16.13%	3.23%	3.23%
10,000 to 20,000	30.30%	51.52%	12.12%	6.06%	0.00%
More than 20,000	17.65%	70.59%	11.76%	0.00%	0.00%

Table 20.4.5: Java and PERL Script Applications Broken out by Annual Tuition

Annual Tuition	No Response	Not at all prepared	Minimally prepared	Prepared	Well prepared
Less than $8,000	19.23%	57.69%	11.54%	7.69%	3.85%
$8,000 to $18,000	41.38%	41.38%	13.79%	3.45%	0.00%
More than $18,000	42.31%	42.31%	15.38%	0.00%	0.00%

Preparedness of Recent Library Hires in this Area or Skill

Table 20.5.1: Cataloging Rules and Tools (including Descriptive Cataloging)

	No Response	Not at all prepared	Minimally prepared	Prepared	Well prepared
Entire Sample	27.16%	8.64%	28.40%	28.40%	7.41%

Table 20.5.2: Cataloging Rules and Tools (including Descriptive Cataloging) Broken out by Type of College

Type of College	No Response	Not at all prepared	Minimally prepared	Prepared	Well prepared
Community College	40.00%	20.00%	0.00%	0.00%	40.00%
4-Year Degree Granting College	28.95%	5.26%	23.68%	36.84%	5.26%
MA or PHD Granting College	26.09%	13.04%	39.13%	21.74%	0.00%
Research University	20.00%	6.67%	33.33%	26.67%	13.33%

Table 20.5.3: Cataloging Rules and Tools (including Descriptive Cataloging) Broken out by Public or Private Status

Public or Private Status	No Response	Not at all prepared	Minimally prepared	Prepared	Well prepared
Public	19.23%	13.46%	30.77%	28.85%	7.69%
Private	41.38%	0.00%	24.14%	27.59%	6.90%

Table 20.5.4: Cataloging Rules and Tools (including Descriptive Cataloging) Broken out by Total Student Enrollment

Total Student Enrollment	No Response	Not at all prepared	Minimally prepared	Prepared	Well prepared
Less than 10,000	38.71%	6.45%	19.35%	25.81%	9.68%
10,000 to 20,000	27.27%	9.09%	27.27%	33.33%	3.03%
More than 20,000	5.88%	11.76%	47.06%	23.53%	11.76%

Table 20.5.5: Cataloging Rules and Tools (including Descriptive Cataloging) Broken out by Annual Tuition

Annual Tuition	No Response	Not at all prepared	Minimally prepared	Prepared	Well prepared
Less than $8,000	15.38%	7.69%	34.62%	34.62%	7.69%
$8,000 to $18,000	31.03%	13.79%	20.69%	27.59%	6.90%
More than $18,000	34.62%	3.85%	30.77%	23.08%	7.69%

Preparedness of Recent Library Hires in this Area or Skill

Table 20.6.1: Information Technology and Social Behavior in the Organizational Context

	No Response	Not at all prepared	Minimally prepared	Prepared	Well prepared
Entire Sample	33.33%	16.05%	28.40%	20.99%	1.23%

Table 20.6.2: Information Technology and Social Behavior in the Organizational Context Broken out by Type of College

Type of College	No Response	Not at all prepared	Minimally prepared	Prepared	Well prepared
Community College	40.00%	20.00%	20.00%	0.00%	20.00%
4-Year Degree Granting College	34.21%	15.79%	26.32%	23.68%	0.00%
MA or PHD Granting College	34.78%	13.04%	26.09%	26.09%	0.00%
Research University	26.67%	20.00%	40.00%	13.33%	0.00%

Table 20.6.3: Information Technology and Social Behavior in the Organizational Context Broken out by Public or Private Status

Public or Private Status	No Response	Not at all prepared	Minimally prepared	Prepared	Well prepared
Public	26.92%	19.23%	32.69%	19.23%	1.92%
Private	44.83%	10.34%	20.69%	24.14%	0.00%

Table 20.6.4: Information Technology and Social Behavior in the Organizational Context Broken out by Total Student Enrollment

Total Student Enrollment	No Response	Not at all prepared	Minimally prepared	Prepared	Well prepared
Less than 10,000	41.94%	12.90%	12.90%	29.03%	3.23%
10,000 to 20,000	33.33%	12.12%	39.39%	15.15%	0.00%
More than 20,000	17.65%	29.41%	35.29%	17.65%	0.00%

Table 20.6.5: Information Technology and Social Behavior in the Organizational Context Broken out by Annual Tuition

Annual Tuition	No Response	Not at all prepared	Minimally prepared	Prepared	Well prepared
Less than $8,000	23.08%	23.08%	26.92%	23.08%	3.85%
$8,000 to $18,000	37.93%	10.34%	34.48%	17.24%	0.00%
More than $18,000	38.46%	15.38%	23.08%	23.08%	0.00%

Preparedness of Recent Library Hires in this Area or Skill

Table 20.7.1: Metadata standards for Digital Resources (Dublin Core, MODS, VRA, Open Archives Initiative, etc.)

	No Response	Not at all prepared	Minimally prepared	Prepared	Well prepared
Entire Sample	27.16%	30.86%	25.93%	13.58%	2.47%

Table 20.7.2: Metadata standards for Digital Resources (Dublin Core, MODS, VRA, Open Archives Initiative, etc.) Broken out by Type of College

Type of College	No Response	Not at all prepared	Minimally prepared	Prepared	Well prepared
Community College	40.00%	40.00%	0.00%	0.00%	20.00%
4-Year Degree Granting College	31.58%	34.21%	18.42%	15.79%	0.00%
MA or PHD Granting College	26.09%	21.74%	43.48%	8.70%	0.00%
Research University	13.33%	33.33%	26.67%	20.00%	6.67%

Table 20.7.3: Metadata standards for Digital Resources (Dublin Core, MODS, VRA, Open Archives Initiative, etc.) Broken out by Public or Private Status

Public or Private Status	No Response	Not at all prepared	Minimally prepared	Prepared	Well prepared
Public	19.23%	38.46%	25.00%	13.46%	3.85%
Private	41.38%	17.24%	27.59%	13.79%	0.00%

Table 20.7.4: Metadata standards for Digital Resources (Dublin Core, MODS, VRA, Open Archives Initiative, etc.) Broken out by Total Student Enrollment

Total Student Enrollment	No Response	Not at all prepared	Minimally prepared	Prepared	Well prepared
Less than 10,000	38.71%	19.35%	29.03%	9.68%	3.23%
10,000 to 20,000	30.30%	36.36%	21.21%	12.12%	0.00%
More than 20,000	0.00%	41.18%	29.41%	23.53%	5.88%

Table 20.7.5: Metadata standards for Digital Resources (Dublin Core, MODS, VRA, Open Archives Initiative, etc.) Broken out by Annual Tuition

Annual Tuition	No Response	Not at all prepared	Minimally prepared	Prepared	Well prepared
Less than $8,000	15.38%	42.31%	26.92%	11.54%	3.85%
$8,000 to $18,000	31.03%	31.03%	20.69%	13.79%	3.45%
More than $18,000	34.62%	19.23%	30.77%	15.38%	0.00%

Preparedness of Recent Library Hires in this Area or Skill

Table 20.8.1: Abstracting and Indexing

	No Response	Not at all prepared	Minimally prepared	Prepared	Well prepared
Entire Sample	32.10%	23.46%	33.33%	9.88%	1.23%

Table 20.8.2: Abstracting and Indexing Broken out by Type of College

Type of College	No Response	Not at all prepared	Minimally prepared	Prepared	Well prepared
Community College	40.00%	20.00%	0.00%	20.00%	20.00%
4-Year Degree Granting College	34.21%	18.42%	31.58%	15.79%	0.00%
MA or PHD Granting College	30.43%	21.74%	43.48%	4.35%	0.00%
Research University	26.67%	40.00%	33.33%	0.00%	0.00%

Table 20.8.3 :Abstracting and Indexing Broken out by Public or Private Status

Public or Private Status	No Response	Not at all prepared	Minimally prepared	Prepared	Well prepared
Public	25.00%	30.77%	36.54%	5.77%	1.92%
Private	44.83%	10.34%	27.59%	17.24%	0.00%

Table 20.8.4: Abstracting and Indexing Broken out by Total Student Enrollment

Total Student Enrollment	No Response	Not at all prepared	Minimally prepared	Prepared	Well prepared
Less than 10,000	41.94%	16.13%	29.03%	9.68%	3.23%
10,000 to 20,000	30.30%	21.21%	36.36%	12.12%	0.00%
More than 20,000	17.65%	41.18%	35.29%	5.88%	0.00%

Table 20.8.5: Abstracting and Indexing Broken out by Annual Tuition

Annual Tuition	No Response	Not at all prepared	Minimally prepared	Prepared	Well prepared
Less than $8,000	19.23%	26.92%	42.31%	7.69%	3.85%
$8,000 to $18,000	37.93%	27.59%	27.59%	6.90%	0.00%
More than $18,000	38.46%	15.38%	30.77%	15.38%	0.00%

Preparedness of Recent Library Hires in this Area or Skill

Table 20.9.1: Electronic delivery of Services

	No Response	Not at all prepared	Minimally prepared	Prepared	Well prepared
Entire Sample	34.57%	16.05%	27.16%	19.75%	2.47%

Table 20.9.2: Electronic delivery of Services Broken out by Type of College

Type of College	No Response	Not at all prepared	Minimally prepared	Prepared	Well prepared
Community College	40.00%	0.00%	40.00%	0.00%	20.00%
4-Year Degree Granting College	39.47%	10.53%	15.79%	31.58%	2.63%
MA or PHD Granting College	30.43%	17.39%	34.78%	17.39%	0.00%
Research University	26.67%	33.33%	40.00%	0.00%	0.00%

Table 20.9.3: Electronic delivery of Services Broken out by Public or Private Status

Public or Private Status	No Response	Not at all prepared	Minimally prepared	Prepared	Well prepared
Public	26.92%	23.08%	32.69%	13.46%	3.85%
Private	48.28%	3.45%	17.24%	31.03%	0.00%

Table 20.9.4: Electronic delivery of Services Broken out by Total Student Enrollment

Total Student Enrollment	No Response	Not at all prepared	Minimally prepared	Prepared	Well prepared
Less than 10,000	45.16%	6.45%	16.13%	29.03%	3.23%
10,000 to 20,000	36.36%	9.09%	36.36%	15.15%	3.03%
More than 20,000	11.76%	47.06%	29.41%	11.76%	0.00%

Table 20.9.5: Electronic delivery of Services Broken out by Annual Tuition

Annual Tuition	No Response	Not at all prepared	Minimally prepared	Prepared	Well prepared
Less than $8,000	23.08%	15.38%	42.31%	11.54%	7.69%
$8,000 to $18,000	41.38%	20.69%	17.24%	20.69%	0.00%
More than $18,000	38.46%	11.54%	23.08%	26.92%	0.00%

Preparedness of Recent Library Hires in this Area or Skill

Table 20.10.1: Technical Services in Libraries

	No Response	Not at all prepared	Minimally prepared	Prepared	Well prepared
Entire Sample	27.16%	8.64%	34.57%	23.46%	6.17%

Table 20.10.2: Technical Services in Libraries Broken out by Type of College

Type of College	No Response	Not at all prepared	Minimally prepared	Prepared	Well prepared
Community College	40.00%	0.00%	20.00%	0.00%	40.00%
4-Year Degree Granting College	28.95%	2.63%	23.68%	39.47%	5.26%
MA or PHD Granting College	26.09%	17.39%	34.78%	17.39%	4.35%
Research University	20.00%	13.33%	66.67%	0.00%	0.00%

Table 20.10.3: Technical Services in Libraries Broken out by Public or Private Status

Public or Private Status	No Response	Not at all prepared	Minimally prepared	Prepared	Well prepared
Public	19.23%	13.46%	42.31%	17.31%	7.69%
Private	41.38%	0.00%	20.69%	34.48%	3.45%

Table 20.10.4: Technical Services in Libraries Broken out by Total Student Enrollment

Total Student Enrollment	No Response	Not at all prepared	Minimally prepared	Prepared	Well prepared
Less than 10,000	38.71%	3.23%	25.81%	25.81%	6.45%
10,000 to 20,000	27.27%	6.06%	30.30%	27.27%	9.09%
More than 20,000	5.88%	23.53%	58.82%	11.76%	0.00%

Table 20.10.5: Technical Services in Libraries Broken out by Annual Tuition

Annual Tuition	No Response	Not at all prepared	Minimally prepared	Prepared	Well prepared
Less than $8,000	15.38%	7.69%	50.00%	15.38%	11.54%
$8,000 to $18,000	31.03%	13.79%	24.14%	27.59%	3.45%
More than $18,000	34.62%	3.85%	30.77%	26.92%	3.85%

Table 20.11.1: Web and Local Network System Administration and Management

	No Response	Not at all prepared	Minimally prepared	Prepared	Well prepared
Entire Sample	35.80%	27.16%	27.16%	7.41%	2.47%

Table 20.11.2: Web and Local Network System Administration and Management Broken out by Type of College

Type of College	No Response	Not at all prepared	Minimally prepared	Prepared	Well prepared
Community College	60.00%	20.00%	0.00%	0.00%	20.00%
4-Year Degree Granting College	42.11%	18.42%	26.32%	10.53%	2.63%
MA or PHD Granting College	30.43%	26.09%	39.13%	4.35%	0.00%
Research University	20.00%	53.33%	20.00%	6.67%	0.00%

Table 20.11.3: Web and Local Network System Administration and Management Broken out by Public or Private Status

Public or Private Status	No Response	Not at all prepared	Minimally prepared	Prepared	Well prepared
Public	28.85%	30.77%	34.62%	3.85%	1.92%
Private	48.28%	20.69%	13.79%	13.79%	3.45%

Table 20.11.4: Web and Local Network System Administration and Management Broken out by Total Student Enrollment

Total Student Enrollment	No Response	Not at all prepared	Minimally prepared	Prepared	Well prepared
Less than 10,000	45.16%	16.13%	25.81%	9.68%	3.23%
10,000 to 20,000	36.36%	30.30%	27.27%	3.03%	3.03%
More than 20,000	17.65%	41.18%	29.41%	11.76%	0.00%

Table 20.11.5: Web and Local Network System Administration and Management Broken out by Annual Tuition

Annual Tuition	No Response	Not at all prepared	Minimally prepared	Prepared	Well prepared
Less than $8,000	23.08%	26.92%	46.15%	0.00%	3.85%
$8,000 to $18,000	44.83%	24.14%	17.24%	10.34%	3.45%
More than $18,000	38.46%	30.77%	19.23%	11.54%	0.00%

Preparedness of Recent Library Hires in this Area or Skill

197

Table 20.12.1: Cataloging Formats: Books

	No Response	Not at all prepared	Minimally prepared	Prepared	Well prepared
Entire Sample	27.16%	7.41%	23.46%	28.40%	13.58%

Table 20.12.2: Cataloging Formats: Books Broken out by Type of College

Type of College	No Response	Not at all prepared	Minimally prepared	Prepared	Well prepared
Community College	40.00%	20.00%	0.00%	0.00%	40.00%
4-Year Degree Granting College	28.95%	5.26%	13.16%	36.84%	15.79%
MA or PHD Granting College	26.09%	8.70%	39.13%	26.09%	0.00%
Research University	20.00%	6.67%	33.33%	20.00%	20.00%

Table 20.12.3: Cataloging Formats: Books Broken out by Public or Private Status

Public or Private Status	No Response	Not at all prepared	Minimally prepared	Prepared	Well prepared
Public	19.23%	9.62%	25.00%	32.69%	13.46%
Private	41.38%	3.45%	20.69%	20.69%	13.79%

Table 20.12.4: Cataloging Formats: Books Broken out by Total Student Enrollment

Total Student Enrollment	No Response	Not at all prepared	Minimally prepared	Prepared	Well prepared
Less than 10,000	38.71%	6.45%	9.68%	32.26%	12.90%
10,000 to 20,000	27.27%	6.06%	27.27%	27.27%	12.12%
More than 20,000	5.88%	11.76%	41.18%	23.53%	17.65%

Table 20.12.5: Cataloging Formats: Books Broken out by Annual Tuition

Annual Tuition	No Response	Not at all prepared	Minimally prepared	Prepared	Well prepared
Less than $8,000	15.38%	7.69%	23.08%	42.31%	11.54%
$8,000 to $18,000	31.03%	13.79%	17.24%	27.59%	10.34%
More than $18,000	34.62%	0.00%	30.77%	15.38%	19.23%

Table 20.13.1: Cataloging Formats: Non Books, Digital Resources

	No Response	Not at all prepared	Minimally prepared	Prepared	Well prepared
Entire Sample	28.40%	17.28%	32.10%	16.05%	6.17%

Table 20.13.2: Cataloging Formats: Non Books, Digital Resources Broken out by Type of College

Type of College	No Response	Not at all prepared	Minimally prepared	Prepared	Well prepared
Community College	40.00%	20.00%	0.00%	0.00%	40.00%
4-Year Degree Granting College	31.58%	15.79%	26.32%	18.42%	7.89%
MA or PHD Granting College	26.09%	26.09%	39.13%	8.70%	0.00%
Research University	20.00%	6.67%	46.67%	26.67%	0.00%

Table 20.13.3: Cataloging Formats: Non Books, Digital Resources Broken out by Public or Private Status

Public or Private Status	No Response	Not at all prepared	Minimally prepared	Prepared	Well prepared
Public	19.23%	23.08%	36.54%	17.31%	3.85%
Private	44.83%	6.90%	24.14%	13.79%	10.34%

Table 20.13.4: Cataloging Formats: Non Books, Digital Resources Broken out by Total Student Enrollment

Total Student	No Response	Not at all	Minimally	Prepared	Well

Enrollment		prepared	prepared		prepared
Less than 10,000	41.94%	9.68%	22.58%	16.13%	9.68%
10,000 to 20,000	27.27%	15.15%	39.39%	12.12%	6.06%
More than 20,000	5.88%	35.29%	35.29%	23.53%	0.00%

Table 20.13.5: Cataloging Formats: Non Books, Digital Resources Broken out by Annual Tuition

Annual Tuition	No Response	Not at all prepared	Minimally prepared	Prepared	Well prepared
Less than $8,000	15.38%	19.23%	42.31%	19.23%	3.85%
$8,000 to $18,000	31.03%	24.14%	24.14%	17.24%	3.45%
More than $18,000	38.46%	7.69%	30.77%	11.54%	11.54%

Preparedness of Recent Library Hires in this Area or Skill

Table 20.14.1: Cataloging Formats: Continuing and Integrating Resources

	No Response	Not at all prepared	Minimally prepared	Prepared	Well prepared
Entire Sample	29.63%	18.52%	34.57%	11.11%	6.17%

Table 20.14.2: Cataloging Formats: Continuing and Integrating Resources Broken out by Type of College

Type of College	No Response	Not at all prepared	Minimally prepared	Prepared	Well prepared
Community College	40.00%	20.00%	0.00%	0.00%	40.00%
4-Year Degree Granting College	31.58%	18.42%	23.68%	18.42%	7.89%
MA or PHD Granting College	30.43%	26.09%	34.78%	8.70%	0.00%
Research University	20.00%	6.67%	73.33%	0.00%	0.00%

Table 20.14.3: Cataloging Formats: Continuing and Integrating Resources Broken out by Public or Private Status

Public or Private Status	No Response	Not at all prepared	Minimally prepared	Prepared	Well prepared
Public	21.15%	25.00%	38.46%	11.54%	3.85%
Private	44.83%	6.90%	27.59%	10.34%	10.34%

Table 20.14.4: Cataloging Formats: Continuing and Integrating Resources Broken out by Total Student Enrollment

Total Student Enrollment	No Response	Not at all prepared	Minimally prepared	Prepared	Well prepared
Less than 10,000	41.94%	12.90%	25.81%	9.68%	9.68%
10,000 to 20,000	27.27%	18.18%	33.33%	15.15%	6.06%
More than 20,000	11.76%	29.41%	52.94%	5.88%	0.00%

Table 20.14.5: Cataloging Formats: Continuing and Integrating Resources Broken out by Annual Tuition

Annual Tuition	No Response	Not at all prepared	Minimally prepared	Prepared	Well prepared
Less than $8,000	15.38%	19.23%	46.15%	15.38%	3.85%
$8,000 to $18,000	34.48%	20.69%	27.59%	10.34%	6.90%
More than $18,000	38.46%	15.38%	30.77%	7.69%	7.69%

Table 20.15.1: Cataloging Special Materials: Law

	No Response	Not at all prepared	Minimally prepared	Prepared	Well prepared
Entire Sample	33.33%	39.51%	20.99%	3.70%	2.47%

Table 20.15.2: Cataloging Special Materials: Law Broken out by Type of College

Type of College	No Response	Not at all prepared	Minimally prepared	Prepared	Well prepared
Community College	40.00%	20.00%	0.00%	20.00%	20.00%
4-Year Degree Granting College	39.47%	28.95%	23.68%	5.26%	2.63%
MA or PHD Granting College	30.43%	47.83%	21.74%	0.00%	0.00%
Research University	20.00%	60.00%	20.00%	0.00%	0.00%

Table 20.15.3: Cataloging Special Materials: Law Broken out by Public or Private Status

Public or Private Status	No Response	Not at all prepared	Minimally prepared	Prepared	Well prepared
Public	25.00%	48.08%	23.08%	1.92%	1.92%
Private	48.28%	24.14%	17.24%	6.90%	3.45%

Table 20.15.4: Cataloging Special Materials: Law Broken out by Total Student Enrollment

Total Student Enrollment	No Response	Not at all prepared	Minimally prepared	Prepared	Well prepared
Less than 10,000	45.16%	25.81%	22.58%	3.23%	3.23%
10,000 to 20,000	33.33%	36.36%	21.21%	6.06%	3.03%
More than 20,000	11.76%	70.59%	17.65%	0.00%	0.00%

Table 20.15.5: Cataloging Special Materials: Law Broken out by Annual Tuition

Annual Tuition	No Response	Not at all prepared	Minimally prepared	Prepared	Well prepared
Less than $8,000	15.38%	50.00%	30.77%	0.00%	3.85%
$8,000 to $18,000	44.83%	31.03%	17.24%	3.45%	3.45%
More than $18,000	38.46%	38.46%	15.38%	7.69%	0.00%

Table 20.16.1: Cataloging Special Materials: Music

	No Response	Not at all prepared	Minimally prepared	Prepared	Well prepared
Entire Sample	29.63%	38.27%	23.46%	4.94%	3.70%

Table 20.16.2: Cataloging Special Materials: Music Broken out by Type of College

Type of College	No Response	Not at all prepared	Minimally prepared	Prepared	Well prepared
Community College	40.00%	20.00%	0.00%	20.00%	20.00%
4-Year Degree Granting College	31.58%	26.32%	28.95%	7.89%	5.26%
MA or PHD Granting College	30.43%	47.83%	21.74%	0.00%	0.00%
Research University	20.00%	60.00%	20.00%	0.00%	0.00%

Table 20.16.3: Cataloging Special Materials: Music Broken out by Public or Private Status

Public or Private Status	No Response	Not at all prepared	Minimally prepared	Prepared	Well prepared
Public	21.15%	50.00%	25.00%	1.92%	1.92%
Private	44.83%	17.24%	20.69%	10.34%	6.90%

Table 20.16.4: Cataloging Special Materials: Music Broken out by Total Student Enrollment

Total Student Enrollment	No Response	Not at all prepared	Minimally prepared	Prepared	Well prepared
Less than 10,000	41.94%	19.35%	25.81%	6.45%	6.45%
10,000 to 20,000	27.27%	36.36%	27.27%	6.06%	3.03%
More than 20,000	11.76%	76.47%	11.76%	0.00%	0.00%

Table 20.16.5: Cataloging Special Materials: Music Broken out by Annual Tuition

Annual Tuition	No Response	Not at all prepared	Minimally prepared	Prepared	Well prepared
Less than $8,000	15.38%	53.85%	26.92%	0.00%	3.85%
$8,000 to $18,000	34.48%	31.03%	27.59%	3.45%	3.45%
More than $18,000	38.46%	30.77%	15.38%	11.54%	3.85%

Preparedness of Recent Library Hires in this Area or Skill

Table 20.17.1: Cataloging Special Materials: Archives and Rare Materials

	No Response	Not at all prepared	Minimally prepared	Prepared	Well prepared
Entire Sample	32.10%	32.10%	27.16%	3.70%	4.94%

Table 20.17.2 Cataloging Special Materials: Archives and Rare Materials Broken out by Type of College

Type of College	No Response	Not at all prepared	Minimally prepared	Prepared	Well prepared
Community College	40.00%	20.00%	0.00%	0.00%	40.00%
4-Year Degree Granting College	36.84%	26.32%	23.68%	7.89%	5.26%
MA or PHD Granting College	30.43%	43.48%	26.09%	0.00%	0.00%
Research University	20.00%	33.33%	46.67%	0.00%	0.00%

Table 20.17.3: Cataloging Special Materials: Archives and Rare Materials Broken out by Public or Private Status

Public or Private Status	No Response	Not at all prepared	Minimally prepared	Prepared	Well prepared
Public	23.08%	40.38%	28.85%	1.92%	5.77%
Private	48.28%	17.24%	24.14%	6.90%	3.45%

Table 20.17.4: Cataloging Special Materials: Archives and Rare Materials Broken out by Total Student Enrollment

Total Student Enrollment	No Response	Not at all prepared	Minimally prepared	Prepared	Well prepared
Less than 10,000	45.16%	19.35%	29.03%	3.23%	3.23%
10,000 to 20,000	30.30%	27.27%	27.27%	6.06%	9.09%
More than 20,000	11.76%	64.71%	23.53%	0.00%	0.00%

Table 20.17.5: Cataloging Special Materials: Archives and Rare Materials Broken out by Annual Tuition

Annual Tuition	No Response	Not at all prepared	Minimally prepared	Prepared	Well prepared
Less than $8,000	15.38%	42.31%	34.62%	0.00%	7.69%
$8,000 to $18,000	41.38%	24.14%	24.14%	3.45%	6.90%
More than $18,000	38.46%	30.77%	23.08%	7.69%	0.00%

Preparedness of Recent Library Hires in this Area or Skill
Table 20.18.1: XML and/or XSLT

	No Response	Not at all prepared	Minimally prepared	Prepared	Well prepared
Entire Sample	28.40%	37.04%	17.28%	13.58%	3.70%

Table 20.18.2: XML and/or XSLT Broken out by Type of College

Type of College	No Response	Not at all prepared	Minimally prepared	Prepared	Well prepared
Community College	40.00%	40.00%	0.00%	0.00%	20.00%
4-Year Degree Granting College	34.21%	28.95%	13.16%	21.05%	2.63%
MA or PHD Granting College	26.09%	47.83%	17.39%	8.70%	0.00%
Research University	13.33%	40.00%	33.33%	6.67%	6.67%

Table 20.18.3: XML and/or XSLT Broken out by Public or Private Status

Public or Private Status	No Response	Not at all prepared	Minimally prepared	Prepared	Well prepared
Public	19.23%	51.92%	13.46%	11.54%	3.85%
Private	44.83%	10.34%	24.14%	17.24%	3.45%

Table 20.18.4: XML and/or XSLT Broken out by Total Student Enrollment

Total Student Enrollment	No Response	Not at all prepared	Minimally prepared	Prepared	Well prepared
Less than 10,000	41.94%	25.81%	19.35%	9.68%	3.23%
10,000 to 20,000	30.30%	39.39%	15.15%	12.12%	3.03%
More than 20,000	0.00%	52.94%	17.65%	23.53%	5.88%

Table 20.18.5: XML and/or XSLT Broken out by Annual Tuition

Annual Tuition	No Response	Not at all prepared	Minimally prepared	Prepared	Well prepared
Less than $8,000	15.38%	57.69%	19.23%	3.85%	3.85%
$8,000 to $18,000	34.48%	34.48%	6.90%	17.24%	6.90%
More than $18,000	34.62%	19.23%	26.92%	19.23%	0.00%

Preparedness of Recent Library Hires in this Area or Skill
Table 20.19.1: Economics and Metrics of Information

	No Response	Not at all prepared	Minimally prepared	Prepared	Well prepared
Entire Sample	34.57%	38.27%	20.99%	3.70%	2.47%

Table 20.19.2: Economics and Metrics of Information Broken out by Type of College

Type of College	No Response	Not at all prepared	Minimally prepared	Prepared	Well prepared
Community College	40.00%	40.00%	0.00%	0.00%	20.00%
4-Year Degree Granting College	39.47%	26.32%	23.68%	7.89%	2.63%
MA or PHD Granting College	30.43%	43.48%	26.09%	0.00%	0.00%
Research University	26.67%	60.00%	13.33%	0.00%	0.00%

Table 20.19.3: Economics and Metrics of Information Broken out by Public or Private Status

Public or Private Status	No Response	Not at all prepared	Minimally prepared	Prepared	Well prepared
Public	26.92%	46.15%	23.08%	1.92%	1.92%
Private	48.28%	24.14%	17.24%	6.90%	3.45%

Table 20.19.4: Economics and Metrics of Information Broken out by Total Student Enrollment

Total Student Enrollment	No Response	Not at all prepared	Minimally prepared	Prepared	Well prepared
Less than 10,000	45.16%	29.03%	22.58%	0.00%	3.23%
10,000 to 20,000	33.33%	39.39%	18.18%	6.06%	3.03%
More than 20,000	17.65%	52.94%	23.53%	5.88%	0.00%

Table 20.19.5: Economics and Metrics of Information Broken out by Annual Tuition

Annual Tuition	No Response	Not at all prepared	Minimally prepared	Prepared	Well prepared
Less than $8,000	19.23%	46.15%	26.92%	3.85%	3.85%
$8,000 to $18,000	44.83%	31.03%	20.69%	0.00%	3.45%
More than $18,000	38.46%	38.46%	15.38%	7.69%	0.00%

Preparedness of Recent Library Hires in this Area or Skill

Table 20.20.1: Discovery Tools and Applications

	No Response	Not at all prepared	Minimally prepared	Prepared	Well prepared
Entire Sample	30.86%	17.28%	30.86%	18.52%	2.47%

Table 20.20.2: Discovery Tools and Applications Broken out by Type of College

Type of College	No Response	Not at all prepared	Minimally prepared	Prepared	Well prepared
Community College	40.00%	0.00%	40.00%	0.00%	20.00%
4-Year Degree Granting College	36.84%	15.79%	21.05%	26.32%	0.00%
MA or PHD Granting College	26.09%	21.74%	30.43%	17.39%	4.35%
Research University	20.00%	20.00%	53.33%	6.67%	0.00%

Table 20.20.3: Discovery Tools and Applications Broken out by Public or Private Status

Public or Private Status	No Response	Not at all prepared	Minimally prepared	Prepared	Well prepared
Public	21.15%	23.08%	34.62%	17.31%	3.85%
Private	48.28%	6.90%	24.14%	20.69%	0.00%

Table 20.20.4: Discovery Tools and Applications Broken out by Total Student Enrollment

Total Student	No Response	Not at all	Minimally	Prepared	Well

Enrollment		prepared	prepared		prepared
Less than 10,000	45.16%	19.35%	12.90%	19.35%	3.23%
10,000 to 20,000	30.30%	12.12%	39.39%	15.15%	3.03%
More than 20,000	5.88%	23.53%	47.06%	23.53%	0.00%

Table 20.20.5: Discovery Tools and Applications Broken out by Annual Tuition

Annual Tuition	No Response	Not at all prepared	Minimally prepared	Prepared	Well prepared
Less than $8,000	15.38%	23.08%	38.46%	15.38%	7.69%
$8,000 to $18,000	37.93%	13.79%	27.59%	20.69%	0.00%
More than $18,000	38.46%	15.38%	26.92%	19.23%	0.00%

Preparedness of Recent Library Hires in this Area or Skill

Table 20.21.1: Authority control

	No Response	Not at all prepared	Minimally prepared	Prepared	Well prepared
Entire Sample	28.40%	22.22%	33.33%	12.35%	3.70%

Table 20.21.2: Authority control Broken out by Type of College

Type of College	No Response	Not at all prepared	Minimally prepared	Prepared	Well prepared
Community College	40.00%	20.00%	0.00%	0.00%	40.00%
4-Year Degree Granting College	31.58%	15.79%	31.58%	21.05%	0.00%
MA or PHD Granting College	30.43%	30.43%	34.78%	4.35%	0.00%
Research University	13.33%	26.67%	46.67%	6.67%	6.67%

Table 20.21.3: Authority control Broken out by Public or Private Status

Public or Private Status	No Response	Not at all prepared	Minimally prepared	Prepared	Well prepared
Public	19.23%	26.92%	36.54%	11.54%	5.77%
Private	44.83%	13.79%	27.59%	13.79%	0.00%

Table 20.21.4: Authority control Broken out by Total Student Enrollment

Total Student Enrollment	No Response	Not at all prepared	Minimally prepared	Prepared	Well prepared
Less than 10,000	41.94%	19.35%	25.81%	9.68%	3.23%
10,000 to 20,000	27.27%	12.12%	39.39%	18.18%	3.03%
More than 20,000	5.88%	47.06%	35.29%	5.88%	5.88%

Table 20.21.5: Authority control Broken out by Annual Tuition

Annual Tuition	No Response	Not at all prepared	Minimally prepared	Prepared	Well prepared
Less than $8,000	15.38%	19.23%	50.00%	7.69%	7.69%
$8,000 to $18,000	31.03%	27.59%	27.59%	10.34%	3.45%
More than $18,000	38.46%	19.23%	23.08%	19.23%	0.00%

Preparedness of Recent Library Hires in this Area or Skill

Table 20.22.1: Web Usability, User Research, and Human Interface Design

	No Response	Not at all prepared	Minimally prepared	Prepared	Well prepared
Entire Sample	33.33%	18.52%	28.40%	16.05%	3.70%

210

Table 20.22.2: Web Usability, User Research, and Human Interface Design Broken out by Type of College

Type of College	No Response	Not at all prepared	Minimally prepared	Prepared	Well prepared
Community College	40.00%	40.00%	0.00%	0.00%	20.00%
4-Year Degree Granting College	36.84%	13.16%	21.05%	26.32%	2.63%
MA or PHD Granting College	30.43%	13.04%	43.48%	13.04%	0.00%
Research University	26.67%	33.33%	33.33%	0.00%	6.67%

Table 20.22.3: Web Usability, User Research, and Human Interface Design Broken out by Public or Private Status

Public or Private Status	No Response	Not at all prepared	Minimally prepared	Prepared	Well prepared
Public	25.00%	21.15%	36.54%	13.46%	3.85%
Private	48.28%	13.79%	13.79%	20.69%	3.45%

Table 20.22.4: Web Usability, User Research, and Human Interface Design Broken out by Total Student Enrollment

Total Student Enrollment	No Response	Not at all prepared	Minimally prepared	Prepared	Well prepared
Less than 10,000	45.16%	6.45%	22.58%	19.35%	6.45%
10,000 to 20,000	30.30%	24.24%	30.30%	15.15%	0.00%
More than 20,000	17.65%	29.41%	35.29%	11.76%	5.88%

Table 20.22.5: Web Usability, User Research, and Human Interface Design Broken out by Annual Tuition

Annual Tuition	No Response	Not at all prepared	Minimally prepared	Prepared	Well prepared
Less than $8,000	19.23%	23.08%	38.46%	11.54%	7.69%
$8,000 to $18,000	41.38%	10.34%	31.03%	17.24%	0.00%
More than $18,000	38.46%	23.08%	15.38%	19.23%	3.85%

Table 20.23.1: International MARC Bibliographic, Authority and Holdings Standards

	No Response	Not at all prepared	Minimally prepared	Prepared	Well prepared
Entire Sample	28.40%	19.75%	30.86%	14.81%	6.17%

Table 20.23.2: International MARC Bibliographic, Authority and Holdings Standards Broken out by Type of College

Type of College	No Response	Not at all prepared	Minimally prepared	Prepared	Well prepared
Community College	40.00%	20.00%	0.00%	0.00%	40.00%
4-Year Degree Granting College	31.58%	15.79%	26.32%	21.05%	5.26%
MA or PHD Granting College	26.09%	34.78%	34.78%	4.35%	0.00%
Research University	20.00%	6.67%	46.67%	20.00%	6.67%

Table 20.23.3: International MARC Bibliographic, Authority and Holdings Standards Broken out by Public or Private Status

Public or Private Status	No Response	Not at all prepared	Minimally prepared	Prepared	Well prepared
Public	19.23%	23.08%	36.54%	13.46%	7.69%
Private	44.83%	13.79%	20.69%	17.24%	3.45%

Table 20.23.4: International MARC Bibliographic, Authority and Holdings Standards Broken out by Total Student Enrollment

Total Student Enrollment	No Response	Not at all prepared	Minimally prepared	Prepared	Well prepared
Less than 10,000	41.94%	16.13%	25.81%	9.68%	6.45%
10,000 to 20,000	27.27%	24.24%	30.30%	12.12%	6.06%
More than 20,000	5.88%	17.65%	41.18%	29.41%	5.88%

Table 20.23.5: International MARC Bibliographic, Authority and Holdings Standards Broken out by Annual Tuition

Annual Tuition	No Response	Not at all prepared	Minimally prepared	Prepared	Well prepared
Less than $8,000	15.38%	15.38%	53.85%	3.85%	11.54%
$8,000 to $18,000	31.03%	20.69%	17.24%	27.59%	3.45%
More than $18,000	38.46%	23.08%	23.08%	11.54%	3.85%

Preparedness of Recent Library Hires in this Area or Skill

Table 20.24.1: Data modeling, warehousing, mining

	No Response	Not at all prepared	Minimally prepared	Prepared	Well prepared
Entire Sample	34.57%	40.74%	16.05%	6.17%	2.47%

Table 20.24.2: Data modeling, warehousing, mining Broken out by Type of College

Type of College	No Response	Not at all prepared	Minimally prepared	Prepared	Well prepared
Community College	40.00%	40.00%	0.00%	0.00%	20.00%
4-Year Degree Granting College	39.47%	31.58%	18.42%	7.89%	2.63%
MA or PHD Granting College	30.43%	47.83%	17.39%	4.35%	0.00%
Research University	26.67%	53.33%	13.33%	6.67%	0.00%

Table 20.24.3: Data modeling, warehousing, mining Broken out by Public or Private Status

Public or Private Status	No Response	Not at all prepared	Minimally prepared	Prepared	Well prepared
Public	26.92%	50.00%	15.38%	5.77%	1.92%
Private	48.28%	24.14%	17.24%	6.90%	3.45%

Table 20.24.4: Data modeling, warehousing, mining Broken out by Total Student Enrollment

Total Student Enrollment	No Response	Not at all prepared	Minimally prepared	Prepared	Well prepared
Less than 10,000	45.16%	19.35%	25.81%	6.45%	3.23%
10,000 to 20,000	33.33%	54.55%	9.09%	0.00%	3.03%
More than 20,000	17.65%	52.94%	11.76%	17.65%	0.00%

Table 20.24.5: Data modeling, warehousing, mining Broken out by Annual Tuition

Annual Tuition	No Response	Not at all prepared	Minimally prepared	Prepared	Well prepared
Less than $8,000	19.23%	53.85%	23.08%	0.00%	3.85%
$8,000 to $18,000	44.83%	31.03%	10.34%	10.34%	3.45%
More than $18,000	38.46%	38.46%	15.38%	7.69%	0.00%

Preparedness of Recent Library Hires in this Area or Skill

Table 20.25.1: Information Systems Analysis

	No Response	Not at all prepared	Minimally prepared	Prepared	Well prepared
Entire Sample	35.80%	39.51%	14.81%	7.41%	2.47%

Table 20.25.2: Information Systems Analysis Broken out by Type of College

Type of College	No Response	Not at all prepared	Minimally prepared	Prepared	Well prepared
Community College	40.00%	20.00%	20.00%	0.00%	20.00%
4-Year Degree Granting College	39.47%	31.58%	15.79%	10.53%	2.63%
MA or PHD Granting College	30.43%	43.48%	21.74%	4.35%	0.00%
Research University	33.33%	60.00%	0.00%	6.67%	0.00%

Table 20.25.3: Information Systems Analysis Broken out by Public or Private Status

Public or Private Status	No Response	Not at all prepared	Minimally prepared	Prepared	Well prepared
Public	28.85%	46.15%	15.38%	7.69%	1.92%
Private	48.28%	27.59%	13.79%	6.90%	3.45%

Table 20.25.4: Information Systems Analysis Broken out by Total Student Enrollment

Total Student Enrollment	No Response	Not at all prepared	Minimally prepared	Prepared	Well prepared
Less than 10,000	45.16%	22.58%	25.81%	3.23%	3.23%
10,000 to 20,000	33.33%	48.48%	9.09%	6.06%	3.03%
More than 20,000	23.53%	52.94%	5.88%	17.65%	0.00%

Table 20.25.5: Information Systems Analysis Broken out by Annual Tuition

Annual Tuition	No Response	Not at all prepared	Minimally prepared	Prepared	Well prepared
Less than $8,000	23.08%	46.15%	23.08%	3.85%	3.85%
$8,000 to $18,000	44.83%	31.03%	10.34%	10.34%	3.45%
More than $18,000	38.46%	42.31%	11.54%	7.69%	0.00%

Preparedness of Recent Library Hires in this Area or Skill

Table 20.26.1: Programming Languages and Applications

	No Response	Not at all prepared	Minimally prepared	Prepared	Well prepared
Entire Sample	33.33%	45.68%	13.58%	4.94%	2.47%

Table 20.26.2 Programming Languages and Applications Broken out by Type of College

Type of College	No Response	Not at all prepared	Minimally prepared	Prepared	Well prepared
Community College	40.00%	40.00%	0.00%	0.00%	20.00%
4-Year Degree Granting College	36.84%	42.11%	7.89%	10.53%	2.63%
MA or PHD Granting College	30.43%	43.48%	26.09%	0.00%	0.00%
Research University	26.67%	60.00%	13.33%	0.00%	0.00%

Table 20.26.3: Programming Languages and Applications Broken out by Public or Private Status

Public or Private Status	No Response	Not at all prepared	Minimally prepared	Prepared	Well prepared
Public	25.00%	51.92%	17.31%	3.85%	1.92%
Private	48.28%	34.48%	6.90%	6.90%	3.45%

Table 20.26.4: Programming Languages and Applications Broken out by Total Student Enrollment

Total Student Enrollment	No Response	Not at all prepared	Minimally prepared	Prepared	Well prepared
Less than 10,000	45.16%	29.03%	19.35%	3.23%	3.23%
10,000 to 20,000	30.30%	54.55%	9.09%	3.03%	3.03%
More than 20,000	17.65%	58.82%	11.76%	11.76%	0.00%

Table 20.26.5: Programming Languages and Applications Broken out by Annual Tuition

Annual Tuition	No Response	Not at all prepared	Minimally prepared	Prepared	Well prepared
Less than $8,000	19.23%	57.69%	15.38%	3.85%	3.85%
$8,000 to $18,000	41.38%	37.93%	13.79%	3.45%	3.45%
More than $18,000	38.46%	42.31%	11.54%	7.69%	0.00%

Preparedness of Recent Library Hires in this Area or Skill

Table 20.27.1: Relational database design

	No Response	Not at all prepared	Minimally prepared	Prepared	Well prepared
Entire Sample	33.33%	40.74%	19.75%	2.47%	3.70%

Table 20.27.2: Relational database design Broken out by Type of College

Type of College	No Response	Not at all prepared	Minimally prepared	Prepared	Well prepared
Community College	40.00%	40.00%	0.00%	0.00%	20.00%
4-Year Degree Granting College	36.84%	34.21%	18.42%	5.26%	5.26%
MA or PHD Granting College	30.43%	47.83%	21.74%	0.00%	0.00%
Research University	26.67%	46.67%	26.67%	0.00%	0.00%

Table 20.27.3: Relational database design Broken out by Public or Private Status

Public or Private Status	No Response	Not at all prepared	Minimally prepared	Prepared	Well prepared
Public	25.00%	48.08%	23.08%	1.92%	1.92%
Private	48.28%	27.59%	13.79%	3.45%	6.90%

Table 20.27.4: Relational database design Broken out by Total Student Enrollment

Total Student Enrollment	No Response	Not at all prepared	Minimally prepared	Prepared	Well prepared
Less than 10,000	45.16%	29.03%	16.13%	3.23%	6.45%
10,000 to 20,000	30.30%	39.39%	27.27%	0.00%	3.03%
More than 20,000	17.65%	64.71%	11.76%	5.88%	0.00%

Table 20.27.5: Relational database design Broken out by Annual Tuition

Annual Tuition	No Response	Not at all prepared	Minimally prepared	Prepared	Well prepared
Less than $8,000	19.23%	46.15%	30.77%	0.00%	3.85%
$8,000 to $18,000	41.38%	37.93%	13.79%	3.45%	3.45%
More than $18,000	38.46%	38.46%	15.38%	3.85%	3.85%

Preparedness of Recent Library Hires in this Area or Skill

Table 20.28.1: OCLC Systems and Services

	No Response	Not at all prepared	Minimally prepared	Prepared	Well prepared
Entire Sample	29.63%	18.52%	23.46%	22.22%	6.17%

Table 20.28.2: OCLC Systems and Services Broken out by Type of College

Type of College	No Response	Not at all prepared	Minimally prepared	Prepared	Well prepared
Community College	40.00%	20.00%	0.00%	0.00%	40.00%
4-Year Degree Granting College	34.21%	13.16%	23.68%	26.32%	2.63%
MA or PHD Granting College	26.09%	21.74%	26.09%	21.74%	4.35%
Research University	20.00%	26.67%	26.67%	20.00%	6.67%

Table 20.28.3: OCLC Systems and Services Broken out by Public or Private Status

Public or Private Status	No Response	Not at all prepared	Minimally prepared	Prepared	Well prepared
Public	19.23%	19.23%	25.00%	26.92%	9.62%
Private	48.28%	17.24%	20.69%	13.79%	0.00%

Table 20.28.4: OCLC Systems and Services Broken out by Total Student Enrollment

Total Student Enrollment	No Response	Not at all prepared	Minimally prepared	Prepared	Well prepared
Less than 10,000	45.16%	12.90%	16.13%	22.58%	3.23%
10,000 to 20,000	27.27%	15.15%	27.27%	21.21%	9.09%
More than 20,000	5.88%	35.29%	29.41%	23.53%	5.88%

Table 20.28.5: OCLC Systems and Services Broken out by Annual Tuition

Annual Tuition	No Response	Not at all prepared	Minimally prepared	Prepared	Well prepared
Less than $8,000	15.38%	19.23%	15.38%	38.46%	11.54%
$8,000 to $18,000	31.03%	17.24%	34.48%	13.79%	3.45%
More than $18,000	42.31%	19.23%	19.23%	15.38%	3.85%

Table 20.29.1: Digital Libraries and Collections

	No Response	Not at all prepared	Minimally prepared	Prepared	Well prepared
Entire Sample	32.10%	18.52%	24.69%	23.46%	1.23%

Table 20.29.2: Digital Libraries and Collections Broken out by Type of College

Type of College	No Response	Not at all prepared	Minimally prepared	Prepared	Well prepared
Community College	40.00%	20.00%	0.00%	20.00%	20.00%
4-Year Degree Granting College	34.21%	15.79%	18.42%	31.58%	0.00%
MA or PHD Granting College	26.09%	21.74%	39.13%	13.04%	0.00%
Research University	33.33%	20.00%	26.67%	20.00%	0.00%

Preparedness of Recent Library Hires in this Area or Skill

Table 20.29.3: Digital Libraries and Collections Broken out by Public or Private Status

Public or Private Status	No Response	Not at all prepared	Minimally prepared	Prepared	Well prepared
Public	25.00%	23.08%	26.92%	23.08%	1.92%
Private	44.83%	10.34%	20.69%	24.14%	0.00%

Table 20.29.4: Digital Libraries and Collections Broken out by Total Student Enrollment

Total Student Enrollment	No Response	Not at all prepared	Minimally prepared	Prepared	Well prepared
Less than 10,000	41.94%	16.13%	19.35%	19.35%	3.23%
10,000 to 20,000	30.30%	9.09%	33.33%	27.27%	0.00%
More than 20,000	17.65%	41.18%	17.65%	23.53%	0.00%

Table 20.29.5: Digital Libraries and Collections Broken out by Annual Tuition

Annual Tuition	No Response	Not at all prepared	Minimally prepared	Prepared	Well prepared
Less than $8,000	23.08%	26.92%	30.77%	15.38%	3.85%
$8,000 to $18,000	34.48%	10.34%	20.69%	34.48%	0.00%
More than $18,000	38.46%	19.23%	23.08%	19.23%	0.00%

Preparedness of Recent Library Hires in this Area or Skill

Table 20.30.1: Practicum: Experiential Learning

	No Response	Not at all prepared	Minimally prepared	Prepared	Well prepared
Entire Sample	32.10%	17.28%	34.57%	9.88%	6.17%

Table 20.30.2: Practicum: Experiential Learning Broken out by Type of College

Type of College	No Response	Not at all prepared	Minimally prepared	Prepared	Well prepared
Community College	40.00%	0.00%	40.00%	0.00%	20.00%
4-Year Degree Granting College	36.84%	15.79%	21.05%	15.79%	10.53%
MA or PHD Granting College	26.09%	17.39%	47.83%	8.70%	0.00%
Research University	26.67%	26.67%	46.67%	0.00%	0.00%

Table 20.30.3: Practicum: Experiential Learning Broken out by Public or Private Status

Public or Private Status	No Response	Not at all prepared	Minimally prepared	Prepared	Well prepared
Public	23.08%	23.08%	38.46%	11.54%	3.85%
Private	48.28%	6.90%	27.59%	6.90%	10.34%

Table 20.30.4: Practicum: Experiential Learning Broken out by Total Student Enrollment

Total Student Enrollment	No Response	Not at all prepared	Minimally prepared	Prepared	Well prepared
Less than 10,000	45.16%	12.90%	19.35%	9.68%	12.90%
10,000 to 20,000	30.30%	18.18%	36.36%	12.12%	3.03%
More than 20,000	11.76%	23.53%	58.82%	5.88%	0.00%

Table 20.30.5: Practicum: Experiential Learning Broken out by Annual Tuition

Annual Tuition	No Response	Not at all prepared	Minimally prepared	Prepared	Well prepared
Less than $8,000	19.23%	23.08%	42.31%	7.69%	7.69%
$8,000 to $18,000	37.93%	17.24%	27.59%	13.79%	3.45%
More than $18,000	38.46%	11.54%	34.62%	7.69%	7.69%

Preparedness of Recent Library Hires in this Area or Skill

221

Table 20.31.1: Information Storage, Retrieval, Architecture

	No Response	Not at all prepared	Minimally prepared	Prepared	Well prepared
Entire Sample	35.80%	20.99%	33.33%	7.41%	2.47%

Table 20.31.2: Information Storage, Retrieval, Architecture Broken out by Type of College

Type of College	No Response	Not at all prepared	Minimally prepared	Prepared	Well prepared
Community College	60.00%	20.00%	0.00%	0.00%	20.00%
4-Year Degree Granting College	39.47%	21.05%	23.68%	13.16%	2.63%
MA or PHD Granting College	30.43%	17.39%	47.83%	4.35%	0.00%
Research University	26.67%	26.67%	46.67%	0.00%	0.00%

Table 20.31.3: Information Storage, Retrieval, Architecture Broken out by Public or Private Status

Public or Private Status	No Response	Not at all prepared	Minimally prepared	Prepared	Well prepared
Public	28.85%	26.92%	38.46%	3.85%	1.92%
Private	48.28%	10.34%	24.14%	13.79%	3.45%

Table 20.31.4: Information Storage, Retrieval, Architecture Broken out by Total Student Enrollment

Total Student Enrollment	No Response	Not at all prepared	Minimally prepared	Prepared	Well prepared
Less than 10,000	45.16%	12.90%	25.81%	12.90%	3.23%
10,000 to 20,000	36.36%	21.21%	36.36%	3.03%	3.03%
More than 20,000	17.65%	35.29%	41.18%	5.88%	0.00%

Preparedness of Recent Library Hires in this Area or Skill

Table 20.31.5: Information Storage, Retrieval, Architecture Broken out by Annual Tuition

Annual Tuition	No Response	Not at all prepared	Minimally prepared	Prepared	Well prepared
Less than $8,000	19.23%	30.77%	42.31%	3.85%	3.85%
$8,000 to $18,000	48.28%	13.79%	31.03%	3.45%	3.45%
More than $18,000	38.46%	19.23%	26.92%	15.38%	0.00%

Preparedness of Recent Library Hires in this Area or Skill

Table 20.32.1: Social Networking and Information

	No Response	Not at all prepared	Minimally prepared	Prepared	Well prepared
Entire Sample	33.33%	8.64%	19.75%	27.16%	11.11%

Table 20.32.2: Social Networking and Information Broken out by Type of College

Type of College	No Response	Not at all prepared	Minimally prepared	Prepared	Well prepared
Community College	40.00%	0.00%	20.00%	0.00%	40.00%
4-Year Degree Granting College	34.21%	7.89%	13.16%	36.84%	7.89%
MA or PHD Granting College	30.43%	4.35%	26.09%	26.09%	13.04%
Research University	33.33%	20.00%	26.67%	13.33%	6.67%

Table 20.32.3: Social Networking and Information Broken out by Public or Private Status

Public or Private Status	No Response	Not at all prepared	Minimally prepared	Prepared	Well prepared
Public	26.92%	9.62%	21.15%	28.85%	13.46%
Private	44.83%	6.90%	17.24%	24.14%	6.90%

Table 20.32.4: Social Networking and Information Broken out by Total Student Enrollment

Total Student Enrollment	No Response	Not at all prepared	Minimally prepared	Prepared	Well prepared
Less than 10,000	41.94%	0.00%	16.13%	32.26%	9.68%
10,000 to 20,000	30.30%	12.12%	24.24%	21.21%	12.12%
More than 20,000	23.53%	17.65%	17.65%	29.41%	11.76%

Table 20.32.5: Social Networking and Information Broken out by Annual Tuition

Annual Tuition	No Response	Not at all prepared	Minimally prepared	Prepared	Well prepared
Less than $8,000	23.08%	3.85%	38.46%	23.08%	11.54%
$8,000 to $18,000	37.93%	10.34%	3.45%	37.93%	10.34%
More than $18,000	38.46%	11.54%	19.23%	19.23%	11.54%

Preparedness of Recent Library Hires in this Area or Skill

Table 20.33.1: Electronic Publishing and Scholarly Communication

	No Response	Not at all prepared	Minimally prepared	Prepared	Well prepared
Entire Sample	32.10%	16.05%	33.33%	17.28%	1.23%

Table 20.33.2: Electronic Publishing and Scholarly Communication Broken out by Type of College

Type of College	No Response	Not at all prepared	Minimally prepared	Prepared	Well prepared
Community College	40.00%	0.00%	40.00%	0.00%	20.00%
4-Year Degree Granting College	34.21%	10.53%	28.95%	26.32%	0.00%
MA or PHD Granting College	26.09%	21.74%	34.78%	17.39%	0.00%
Research University	33.33%	26.67%	40.00%	0.00%	0.00%

Table 20.33.3: Electronic Publishing and Scholarly Communication Broken out by Public or Private Status

Public or Private Status	No Response	Not at all prepared	Minimally prepared	Prepared	Well prepared
Public	25.00%	19.23%	40.38%	13.46%	1.92%
Private	44.83%	10.34%	20.69%	24.14%	0.00%

Table 20.33.4: Electronic Publishing and Scholarly Communication Broken out by Total Student Enrollment

Total Student Enrollment	No Response	Not at all prepared	Minimally prepared	Prepared	Well prepared
Less than 10,000	41.94%	12.90%	22.58%	19.35%	3.23%
10,000 to 20,000	30.30%	15.15%	39.39%	15.15%	0.00%
More than 20,000	17.65%	23.53%	41.18%	17.65%	0.00%

Table 20.33.5: Electronic Publishing and Scholarly Communication Broken out by Annual Tuition

Annual Tuition	No Response	Not at all prepared	Minimally prepared	Prepared	Well prepared
Less than $8,000	23.08%	19.23%	46.15%	7.69%	3.85%
$8,000 to $18,000	34.48%	10.34%	31.03%	24.14%	0.00%
More than $18,000	38.46%	19.23%	23.08%	19.23%	0.00%

Preparedness of Recent Library Hires in this Area or Skill

Table 20.34.1: Principles of Historical and Contemporary Bibliographic Control

	No Response	Not at all prepared	Minimally prepared	Prepared	Well prepared
Entire Sample	32.10%	22.22%	27.16%	14.81%	3.70%

Table 20.34.2: Principles of Historical and Contemporary Bibliographic Control Broken out by Type of College

Type of College	No Response	Not at all prepared	Minimally prepared	Prepared	Well prepared
Community College	40.00%	20.00%	0.00%	0.00%	40.00%
4-Year Degree Granting College	34.21%	18.42%	21.05%	23.68%	2.63%
MA or PHD Granting College	30.43%	26.09%	39.13%	4.35%	0.00%
Research University	26.67%	26.67%	33.33%	13.33%	0.00%

Table 20.34.3: Principles of Historical and Contemporary Bibliographic Control Broken out by Public or Private Status

Public or Private Status	No Response	Not at all prepared	Minimally prepared	Prepared	Well prepared
Public	23.08%	26.92%	28.85%	15.38%	5.77%
Private	48.28%	13.79%	24.14%	13.79%	0.00%

Table 20.34.4: Principles of Historical and Contemporary Bibliographic Control Broken out by Total Student Enrollment

Total Student Enrollment	No Response	Not at all prepared	Minimally prepared	Prepared	Well prepared
Less than 10,000	45.16%	16.13%	25.81%	9.68%	3.23%
10,000 to 20,000	27.27%	24.24%	24.24%	18.18%	6.06%
More than 20,000	17.65%	29.41%	35.29%	17.65%	0.00%

Table 20.34.5: Principles of Historical and Contemporary Bibliographic Control Broken out by Annual Tuition

Annual Tuition	No Response	Not at all prepared	Minimally prepared	Prepared	Well prepared
Less than $8,000	19.23%	23.08%	34.62%	15.38%	7.69%
$8,000 to $18,000	37.93%	24.14%	17.24%	17.24%	3.45%
More than $18,000	38.46%	19.23%	30.77%	11.54%	0.00%

19190119R00122

Made in the USA
Charleston, SC
10 May 2013